CONFESSIONS OF AN AMERICAN SIKH

LOCKED UP IN INDIA, CORRUPT COPS & MY ESCAPE FROM A "NEW AGE" TANTRIC YOGA CULT

CONFESSIONS OF AN AMERICAN SIKH

LOCKED UP IN INDIA, CORRUPT COPS & MY ESCAPE FROM A "NEW AGE" TANTRIC YOGA CULT

GURSANT SINGH

Cataloging-in-Publication Data

Singh, Gursant
Confessions of an American Sikh/Gursant Singh

p. cm.

ISBN-13: 978-1481172752
ISBN-10: 1481172751

Confessions of an American Sikh

Cover design: Jeff Fielder

Published in the United States of America

1 3 5 7 9 10 8 6 4 2

Foreword

As a young Sikh boy growing up in England with Punjabi parents in the early seventies, I was intrigued to learn that we would be visited by Gora (Caucasian) Sikhs from America on Sunday. I hadn't met any converts before and was eager to see them, especially these 'white' ones, and ask what motivated them to become Sikhs. The group arrived in a minibus with their mentor, Yogi Harbhajan Singh, but not till very late; that barely left time for a quick hello and a cup of tea before their scheduled appearance at the local Gurdwara. Yogiji was given the stage but said nothing other than, "John Singh will tell you his story." Sadly, little of it made much sense to a nine year old. Soon afterwards, the Yogi and his group departed.

Having just completed my undergraduate degree at Cambridge, I spent the summer of 1984 on an American adventure working at Cornell University. There I met a couple of 3HO Sikhs, whom I joined a few times for a Sunday morning service at their house. The placement of a photograph of Yogi Bhajan by the Guru Granth Sahib seemed inappropriate to me but, other than that, I enjoyed their commitment, company and hospitality.

Four years later, having gained a doctorate at Cambridge, I moved to New Mexico to work at the Los Alamos National Laboratory. I was pleasantly surprised to find a sizeable community of Sikhs living in the nearby town of Española, and learnt that it was home to Yogi Harbhajan Singh when he wasn't at his Los Angeles headquarters. I was naturally drawn to attend the Sunday services and to participate in the congregational singing. The discipline and dedication of the Española Sikhs was humbling, and I made several good friends there whom I still remember with fondness.

Following an internet search for 'ex-3HO'in late 2003, I came across a couple of forums run by former members. Many had spent years doing Yogi Bhajan's bidding, no matter how questionable, but felt abused and angry when they eventually saw through his deception.

In this book, Gursant Singh tells his story. We learn about his early life and subsequent association with Yogi Bhajan through flashbacks in the central narrative, an intriguing tale of conspiracy, corruption, bureaucracy, greed, outrageous suggestions and moments of heart breaking sadness, disappointment and reflection. Gursant is refreshingly candid, telling everything warts and all, and his writing style is engaging and easy to read.

Dr. Devinderjit Singh

St. Catherine's College

Oxford, England 23rd August, 2012

introduction

On Sunday, August 5th, 2012, a lone gunman walked into a Sikh Gurdwara in Oak Creek, Wisconsin and began deliberately shooting at a group of people who were there for worship. These people were all Sikhs and, in the aftermath, six of them lay dead and two were seriously wounded as well as a police officer who had been ambushed by the gunman while offering aid to one of the wounded.

The Gurdwara president, Satwant Singh Kaleka, attacked the gunman with a ceremonial sword, trying to disable him. Even after being shot Satwant Singh returned to the attack and was shot again. He eventually died of his wounds. His courageous efforts had given others a chance to get out of the main *diwan* (prayer room) and saved many lives.

For many in the world—and especially in the United States—this was the first they had heard about the fifth most practiced religion in the world. There are about twenty seven million Sikhs in the world with the majority (83% or about twenty two and a half million) living in India. In the last fifty years the Sikh Diaspora has grown tremendously with migration, not only to English speaking countries (USA, Canada, UK, New Zealand and Australia) where Sikhs have consistently sought to settle, but also to European countries such as France, Germany and Italy, the latter being where Sikhs are now the backbone of the Parmesan cheese industry.

Why is there so little known about Sikhs that—especially in the

US- they are often mistaken for the Taliban? There are a number of reasons for this. Sikhs tend to be insular and inward looking in their communities, with quite large portions of their populace unable to speak more than a few words of English. In addition, the older generation tends to want to do things the way they were done back in Punjab and are reticent to reach out to the larger community or even to people of other faiths.

The results have been isolation, misunderstanding, hostility and now, tragedy.

I adopted the Sikh path—*Sikhi*—over thirty years ago. As you will read, my initial attraction was to yoga, taught by a spiritual teacher—Yogi Bhajan—who was also a Sikh. He was a charismatic man and I fell heavily under his influence, where I remained for many years.

Tragically, his motives and clandestine actions belied the words he spoke and the lessons he taught. There came a point in my life where I had to decide whether to remain loyal to him and follow his version of *Sikhi*, or follow my conscience and what I learned in India from many dedicated *Gursikhs* (devout followers of Sikhi) about the true path of Guru Nanak, the founder of the Sikh way of life.

It was during my time in the Amritsar Central Jail that I thought of writing this book. As soon as I had Internet access, I began to research what it might take to create a written record of my experiences. In effect, this book was created as it happened and certainly before I knew how it would finish.

My hope was that I could help others to learn from my experiences; not only those in India, but also those within the 3HO spiritual organization to which I devoted thirty years of my life. India can be fun, entertaining and spiritually inspiring; at the same time it can be harsh and unforgiving, especially if you fall foul of the law as I did.

The spiritual path of the seeker can provide endless inspiration and satisfaction. But, like India, it can bring you face to face with your deepest fears and weaknesses. It is my fervent hope that others will learn from my mistakes and perhaps deepen their own spiritual experience by reading about what I had to go through. Thus this book is the story of my spiritual coming of age; my loss of innocence, if you will.

I wish to offer my deepest gratitude to Akal Purkh, Waheguru, the Creator and Sustainer of the incredible universe in which we live.

Let me also give thanks to Guru Nanak Sahib and his nine illustrious human successors. It is the grace of Guru Nanak that brought me to his teachings and it was his kindness that enabled me to find the true path of Sikhi.

Finally I humbly offer obeisance to Siri Guru Granth Sahib, the word of God and living Guru for all Sikhs.

—*Gursant Singh*

chapter 1

One minute I'm sitting in the Amritsar police station, sharing my vacation photos with the officers, cracking jokes, drinking sparkling water, and all this great stuff. The next minute, the bastards are tossing me in a cell!

"Guru *Sant* Singh, I know you are innocent, but my superior insists," says S.H.O. Mohander Singh when he gets off the phone. Even though he's clearly the main man around here, he says there's nothing he can do. He has to take orders from his boss. Mohander Singh takes me outside, into the gloaming, where the bleating of Amritsar's traffic is winding down for the night and the sun disappears ingloriously behind a veil of smog. We walk around to the side of the building, through a gap in a crumbling concrete wall, and into the police yard.

It's the week of Lohri, an Indian holiday to celebrate the growth of the winter crop and the passing of Winter Solstice. Since its theme is the worship of fire, everyone burns a bonfire out of scrap wood, trash, cow-dung, whatever they've got. People just start fires wherever they want to—in the street, on the sidewalk, in an alley. Nobody cares what you do. The air is thick with smoke. I wince with my first lungful, but Mohander Singh takes it in like incense.

The enclosure is a junkyard, nothing more. Wrecked tuk-tuks come here to die. Weeds are growing up around a bunch of rusted scrap metal and some busted old bicycle rickshaws. An overturned fruit cart, still covered with smashed bananas and papayas, must be a recent edition. It's shrouded in flies as fat and loud as bees. We come to a grate in the sidewall of the cop shop. It's barred with iron and stands wide and high as my dad's old garage door in Claremont. Through the bars, florescent light tubes illuminate an eight-by-ten cell. Mohander Singh sticks a key in a padlock, and the grate swings wide.

"You should go in," he says with a tired smile.

Ushering me through the Punjab's various forms of legal limbo has been his full time job for two days now, and the strain is finally starting to show.

I don't exactly want to go in, but what the hell. What am I going to do? Try and run? I briefly consider it. With my gleaming white mug, white turban, white knee-length, Indian-style shirt—called a *kurta*, long grey beard, and American hiking boots, I'd be damn easy to spot. I go on in.

I turn, smile back at Mohander Singh, and joke, "It's not the Taj, but it'll have to do."

"You should be serious, Guru *Sant* Singh," he says. "This is Indian jail. It's not a joke."

He slams the gate, rams the lock through its hasp and with a polite "good night," vanishes into the haze.

The air in Amritsar is always hazy and smoky except during the monsoon season when daily rainstorms give temporary respite to the lungs of its million or so inhabitants. Tonight, the fires from the Lohri festival have thickened the smoke and pollution that constantly enfolds this city. Amritsar, on India's Northwest border and a mere twenty miles from Pakistan, is the most holy city of the Sikhs and the center of Sikh spirituality and politics. Founded in 1574 by the fourth Sikh guru, Guru Ram Das, Amritsar is a bustling center of Punjabi culture and commerce. What sets this city apart from all others is the place of pilgrimage at its heart, its spiritual center: the Harimandir Sahib, better known in the West as the Golden Temple.

The temple itself sits like a radiant, shining jewel in the middle of a manmade *sarovar* (man-made pool), about 150 yards square, located within a complex of buildings and parks at the center of the city. The pool is known as the *Amrit Sarovar*--pool of nectar. It was from here that the city took its name.

Arriving in Amritsar is much the same as arriving in any other Indian city. Whether by train, plane, bus or automobile, you soon find yourself caught up in narrow streets, traffic jams, too many people, endless noise and pollution.

Around the temple it's a different world. The marble paving under your bare feet—and for as far as the eye can see—is spotlessly clean and shiny. The hundreds of pilgrims walking around the *sarovar* move with an air of devotion and spiritual fervor. The aura of peace and tranquility is palpable. The amplified voices of the singers inside the temple bounce off the surrounding buildings and divine music—*Gurbani Kirtan*--fills your ears. In the middle of the *sarovar*—as if floating on water—sits the Golden Temple itself, the sun's reflection glistening on its gold covered domes.

This was my third visit to Amritsar. As a devout Sikh, I always have a very special place in my heart for the spiritual radiance and peace of the Golden Temple. In spite of my dread for the filth, pollution and constant noise of the rest of the city, I always feel a surge of excitement as I set foot in Amritsar, knowing that this land was so blessed by the touch of the feet of our beloved Gurus. My earthly reason for being there was to take advantage of bargain basement prices for the dental work I so badly needed. I certainly never expected to see the inside of a jail cell in the Amritsar Police Station.

I assess my new surroundings. Blood and feces decorate the cell's concrete walls and a rusty drain takes the prisoners' urine away. Dadaji is already in there, and he is crying like a baby. His elegantly tailored clothes are creased and rumpled; his measured, calculated speech replaced by an emotion laden torrent of apology and regret.

"I'm so sorry! I'm so sorry Guru *Sant* Singh! This is so bad for my family! Oh God, I'll have to sell the bureau and move away!"

This isn't the Dadaji I've known all month—the successful business man and self-proclaimed "wise father." I mean, mucus is clogging up his neatly trimmed mustache and running down his face. Poor guy. He didn't receive the royal treatment, like me. Back in the interrogation room, I suspect the cops really put him through the wringer although he says that he paid a lot of money to the police just to keep them from roughing us up. I just think the whole thing is some giant surreal joke. How many Americans can say they've been in an Indian prison? This is cool as hell!

I can't figure out why Dadaji is panicking. He should surrender to the will of God, like me. But he doesn't know how. There's nothing I can do for the guy, so I just leave him there, rocking on the floor among the roaches and mouse crap. Three other men share the cell with us—sleeping off beatings, by the look of it.

Mohander Singh didn't tell me how long I would be here or even what the charges were. To tell the truth, I don't think any of the officers even know. Over the past couple days I have formed the distinct impression that they have been making up the protocol for my arrest as they went along. Well, let them have their fun. I deserve to spend a night or two in jail, anyway. Not for anything I've done in the Punjab, but just generally.

As the evening wears on, I try to get in a deeply penitent mood, but I can't. It is all too funny.

"Fraud," moans Dadaji. "It's fraud!"

"What's fraud?"

"The charges, Guru *Sant* Singh! Fraud! Oh God! I'm ruined! This is all my fault! All my fault!" he whines.

Technically, he's right. It *is* his fault. He was greedy, I guess, and now I'm being made out as some kind of bad guy. An ugly American. A user. Is that what I am? I hope not. I just wanted to be one of them, that's all. A real Punjabi; a real Sikh. That's why I signed up with Dadaji's marriage bureau—an Indian matchmaking service. I thought I might meet a nice girl and settle down, but things took a wrong turn somewhere.

This fraud charge is going to ruin his reputation, business, marriage, everything. Technically, yeah, it was his carelessness that set us both up for a fall. Technically. But the way I see it is totally different.

The fact that I have never seen the inside of a jail cell before is a raw miracle, for which I thank my spiritual lifestyle. I've been living this way for thirty years. Studying the Sikh Path, connecting with God, and gaining incredible power over people, money, and everything. The only power I seem to be lacking is power over my own ego.

Even so, to live as a Sikh has its limits. Maintaining my spiritual energy takes about three hours every day, practising meditation during the sacred hours before sunrise. This is powerful stuff, but it can be dangerous, you know. Someone can abuse the power. I've abused it, for sure. No doubt about it. This is exactly what I'm saying. Today, my karma finally bit me in the ass, and Dadaji went down with the ship.

The way I see it, he is a casualty of my disaster, my whole life's karma, not the other way around. But there is no point trying to explain it to him. He wouldn't understand.

"Guru *Sant* Singh, you are lucky to be having no family," he moans.

"I have family."

"No. India family. No family in India."

"Why's that?"

"Police, they make them pay and throw also them in jail if they do not pay. Brother, father, even mother maybe. Thank God my sisters are being married many years past. This is . . . they can, they could, they should . . . never marry after. They will, I mean they would. . . how do you say?"

He tilts his head and makes a gesture, like he's hanging himself with a rope.

"Commit suicide?" I reply.

"That is it, only."

The three other men in the cell lay there like dishrags, unmoving, but pretty soon I notice all six eyes darting curiously from Dadaji to me and back again.

"What do you think they're in here for?" I ask Dadaji.

"That is not my concern," he says. But I can't leave it alone.

"Seriously," I reply. "Why don't you ask them? Ask them what they're in for."

Dadaji looks at them, then back at me. "They are nobody," he says. "Don't concern yourself with those men."

"They're not nobody! They're people. Look at them. They look like hell. C'mon, I want to know what they did. Maybe they're falsely accused, like us. Why not? There's nothing else to do. Let's talk to them."

I have so much energy it is ridiculous. I am having an adventure and Dadaji is having the worst night of his life. But I'm right. There *is* nothing else to do. So, in Hindi, he asks them what's their story. One guy answers briefly.

"They're thieves," says Dadaji and leaves it at that.

"Yeah?" I say, "What did they steal?"

"What did you steal?" I ask the men in English, knowing they won't understand.

Though continuing to lie perfectly still, they all smile broadly, as if we were old college buddies being reunited. I am not surprised. Here, practically everyone likes me automatically. It's because I'm a white Sikh. Most Punjabis have never seen or even imagined one before. And with me, I have this long beard—evidence of my 30-year dedication to Sikhi, which is how the Punjabis refer to the Sikh Path. Indians really respect that, even non-practicing Sikhs. They know it means I'm a spiritual warrior. I mean the cops, the women, their parents, even my Indian dentist—everybody respects that. Everyone here wants to talk to me and get pictures taken with me.

One of the thieves says something to Dadaji, who replies. Then the thief just starts talking. He talks and talks and talks, and I have to keep asking Dadaji to tell him to stop so I can get a translation. The other thieves start talking too, and now we can't shut them up. Here is what, according to Dadaji, they say:

These guys are career criminals. "Snatchers," they call themselves. They stole eight lakh rupees—about $20,000. I don't know who from or how, but what they did was they went on a spree: five-star hotels, booze, heroin, hashish. Anything that looked good, they bought it and consumed it. They traveled all around India, on the lam. They bragged of rubbing elbows with tourists in Goa. That means white people like me. Seemingly the biggest thrill of their whole debauchery was staying where the white people stay and eating where the white people eat. And here they even managed to get thrown in prison with me, a white person! Lucky them!

They still have not moved from where they lie, so I ask Dadaji to find out if they were beaten.

They answer and Dadaji translates, "No, they are not beaten. They are stretched. One two three four policemen grab legs and arms and they are pulling."

Basically an old-fashioned "draw and quarter," but without the horses.

The Punjab Police have a reputation for severe- brutality. There is no Police Review Board in Amritsar and activities such as stuffing bodily cavities with hot chilies or pulling someone's legs apart until they form a 180 degree angle (known locally as *cheera)* do happen; everyone knows this.

Then Dadaji explains it further, off-handedly, like this is all common knowledge. He tells me some thieves get beaten and others get the stretching treatment. It depends. The beatings are for common criminals, when the victims aren't going to bother pressing charges.

"The victim he comes to policeman, is paying nice tip. He says, 'Give him some way to remember me,' you know," says Dadaji. So the cops do a little *cheera*. But Dadaji says if nobody makes it worth their while, the cops will sometimes just yell at the thief, tell him he is a worthless bum, and let him go.

I had seen one of the policemen do this, the day before, while I was waiting around in the station house. Officer Harminder Singh, a tall Sikh with an uncut beard, gave some pickpockets lengthy fatherly lectures, then let them go. He acted very stern, the criminals acted very contrite. Maybe it was theater but, as far as I could see, it was the end of the matter.

Dadaji explains that when someone is actually pressing charges, then the criminals get *cheera*. Since it only damages the victim inside, it doesn't leave marks or blood. Assuming the criminal can't afford bail, a cursory doctor's exam puts him in the pink of health so he can be transferred to Amritsar Central Prison the very next day and await his hearing. No one's the wiser.

Off-handedly, Dadaji adds, "In the prison, he is maybe waiting many years for a trial."

He further explains that the snatchers' problem is that by the time they got caught, they had spent all the money. There wasn't anything for the victim to recover, which really pissed him off. So, of course, the victim tipped the cops to get them good.

"Who could blame him?" says one of the thieves, amiably. A little blood comes up when he laughs it off.

Then I learn the thieves are all married. I think that's great. In India, even career criminals live with their in-laws! I tell Dadaji to ask them if they think their wives will leave them over this.

Dadaji laughs and says something in Hindi. Then they laugh, too.

"Of course not! Why would they?" says Dadaji.

I like it.

Outside the bars, dirty puppies scurry around in the twilight. The fluorescent tubes in the ceiling stay on all night and attract moths, mosquitoes, rats, feral cats, you name it. The creatures wander through the bars at will, checking out their new neighbors. Somehow Dadaji falls asleep, but I don't envy him. A rat with whiskers the length of my hand climbs right up on him and looks ready to eat his eyes out. I kick it away.

I don't even try to sleep. I chant. I tune everything out by chanting the *Waheguru* mantra for hours. I'm still learning: how to submit to a greater power, how to be obedient, how to live in the spirit instead of the body.

chapter 2

Here in my cell, it turns out the cramped quarters, unknown future, and smell of urine, feces, garbage, and smoldering plastic comprise a perfect recipe for the deepest meditation of my life.

I don't see God.

What I see is Dadaji and I getting arrested a couple of days ago. I see the first night we spent locked in some sort of station-office cum nap room, upstairs. Then I see the next day, when we were ushered through the confusing business of getting arraigned and posting bail. Then I see myself getting dropped off in this cell like so much lost baggage. I see every scene play out again, in slow motion.

Finally, I realize I've got a problem. Not jail. Jail isn't a problem in and of itself. The problem is that I am totally alone.

If my teacher Yogi Bhajan were alive, he would have me out of jail by sunup with a single phone call, but he isn't. Since his death and my divorce, I haven't had a friend in the world. Everyone I care about, or used to care about, is gone. Back in the States I have nothing and nobody is waiting for me to return.

Maybe this is why I feel so unconcerned and unafraid. I mean, look! Here I am stuck in a foreign jail, in a third world country, on trumped-up charges, thousands of miles from home. Outside of the cops and Dadaji, no one knows I'm here and I doubt anyone cares. I should be terrified but I'm not; in fact, I'm slightly amused by it all, it's all so surreal.

Next thing I know, I open my eyes and it's morning. Birds are singing, the sun is up, and the cats and rats and centipedes have all gone back to their lairs. Someone opens the grate and several officers grab me and Dadaji roughly. They drag us out of the jail cell and around front of the station house. Yesterday, these guys were serving me chai. Go figure. I'm all set to explain the concept of unnecessary roughness and try to get everyone to talk sense, but then I see the mob.

Folding tables and chairs have been arranged on the pavement. The place is lousy with television crews and reporters, all out for blood. Someone shoves a ski mask over Dadaji's head, and the flashbulbs go off like an A-bomb.

Then I see a policeman; not one of the guys I met yesterday, but someone new. He is in uniform, but without the requisite olive-colored turban. This means he is not a Sikh. Probably a Hindu. I smell trouble. He is standing on a hastily-constructed dais and answering questions from the press. He seems to know me. He points at me. I later learn this is S.S.P. Vijay Pratap, Mohander Singh's commanding officer—the one who ordered my arrest. His hair is slicked back with grease and he is looking made-for-TV.

"Officer, of what are these men accused?" asks one of the many newsmen. He wields a bulbous microphone like a scimitar.

"These two men have been caught red-handed, conspiring in a marriage fraud racket. Perhaps the worst in a decade! Perhaps the worst that Amritsar has seen to date."

"What are their crimes?"

"You could say, 'sweet dreams' were posted as misconceptions by this man Guru *Sant* Singh Khalsa and his partner.

The other man is known only as Dadaji. See him there? He is an unlicensed and unregulated marriage broker. These ideas of marriage were pushed toward these girls. Marriage to a westerner. An American! This American man. . ."

"Has anyone come forward . . .?"

"Let me finish. These notions of marriage to a white American Sikh man were alleged, and money was taken from each of the aspiring girls . . ."

"How much money?"

"Fifty thousand rupees apiece."

"Is it proven?"

"Yes. An FIR (First Information Report) was filed and the case is in a state of being proven. A *challan* (formal charge) will be filed against these men very soon. The girls have come forward. These brave girls have come forward as witnesses, and the prosecution will prove these allegations most assuredly."

"How did the arrest take place?"

"Okay, the arrest took place as seen on television, on the six o'clock news Wednesday night, as ordered by myself. These conspirators have been uncovered as part of a lengthy investigation at the highest levels of command, led by myself, Vijay Pratap, S.S.P. of Amritsar. These men will be brought to justice! I promise the people of Amritsar and all the unmarried girls that have fallen prey to these conspirators, and I promise their fathers, especially, that I will put these men through the justice process."

I turn to Dadaji and ask, "You're unlicensed? Did he say you're unlicensed?"

"Only a little bit, Guru *Sant* Singh," he answers, but he is not looking at me. He is looking through the eye holes of his ski mask at his wife, who is crouched against a wall, holding two children tightly and covering her face with the tail end of her sari. Later I discover that Dadaji himself requested the ski mask as he didn't want the TV viewers--or anyone else who might happen to see him--to recognize him. It's a big shame in India to be arrested even though everyone knows the Punjab police are corrupt as hell.

"Dadaji? Did he say you charged the women fifty thousand rupees? You didn't charge them fifty thousand, did you? Did you?"

He doesn't answer. His eyes are on his wife, but when she finally looks up, he looks down. She must have come to plead his innocence, but never got a chance. V.J. Pratap had us both in the bag already. Still, it is nice that she came. She didn't just turn around and denounce him, like one of these modern American women. She is here in his darkest hour. He hasn't even been faithful to her, but Indian women aren't so concerned with the sex bit. It's the security they are after. This is a strange time to envy the man, but I do. Security wasn't enough for my wife.

After Pratap's little speech, the camera jockeys film every bit of the subsequent handcuffing drama. The cops even chain Dadaji and I together like wild elephants. It is utterly absurd. Scary too, with the chains and all, but I'm laughing anyway. Who could take these people seriously? The newsmen are absolutely wetting themselves with the excitement of catching Dadaji and I, supposedly hardened criminals.

I am not embarrassed, just annoyed. This whole dog and pony show is based on lies. How can any of these officers call themselves Sikhs? That is what I want to ask. I want to shout it in their faces—how can you call yourself a Sikh? How can you!—But I don't.

Being a Sikh means a lot to me; it's my whole life. When I started with Yogiji it was his yoga that attracted me. My early yoga experiences gave me strength, power, and confidence. A real endorphin rush. Gradually, as I learned about Sikhi I felt something very deep and powerful stir inside me.

The Sikh way of life, *Sikhi*, was founded by Guru Nanak, a great saint and teacher born in 1469 in a village in the Punjab, now in Pakistan, not really all that far from Amritsar. His followers became known as Sikhs (students) and formed a spiritual community that refuted the age-old Hindu tradition of caste, holding all people to be equal, including women. These were radical ideas for the time and did not sit well with the minor Hindu kings and Brahmin priests that held the largely Hindu population in temporal and religious servitude. Under constant threat of persecution from the Islamic Mughal rulers of India, as well as attacks from the Hindu kings, the Sikhs morphed into a warrior sect, always ready to defend not only their own community, but also downtrodden Hindus, against the cruelties of the Mughal and Hindu rulers. In fact, the Sikhs were fighting off Islamic Mughal invaders centuries before US Navy Seals killed Osama Bin Laden in Pakistan within 150 miles of Amritsar.

Everything I had every read about Sikhs spoke of their commitment to truth, to righteousness, to justice. How could these Punjabi Police call themselves Sikhs when they were colluding in the arrest and arraignment of innocent men?

The cops shove us in a police car and drive off. I am informed that we are on our way to Amritsar Central Prison.

I protest, "This is ridiculous! I posted bail! Dadaji, tell them we posted bail!"

Dadaji tells them, but the cops reply that the bail takes a while to process. In the meantime, we will be kept in the clink. I can't imagine how they "process" bail, but now that I know how Indians "post" bail, I know it is probably inconceivable to the western imagination. We spent all day yesterday dealing with it and still we are going to jail! It figures. The whole experience started with a lawyer and ended with a farmer. . .

Our first night under arrest, no one on the entire Punjabi Police force knew what to do with us. Me being a foreigner threw the cops into a whirl of confusion. It was as if they had caught a couple of baboons stealing a sack of rice and were equally considering releasing them into the wild, making them into pets, or executing them in the town square.

Mohander Singh freely admitted to me that he didn't want to screw up my arrest and get into trouble, so he planned to keep Dadaji and me over night, then, in the morning, ask a certain judge what to do. So, instead of the jail, the cops locked us in some sort of policeman's off-duty room. There were cots on the floor and a poster on the wall of Lord Shiva with the Ganges flowing through his head. I wasn't worried. I figured in the morning Dadaji would get a fine, I would get my laptop and traveler's checks back, and someone would offer me an official apology. I planned to accept it graciously.

I even befriended one of the policemen who seemed a cut above the rest. Officer Harminder Singh was a pretty well educated guy by Punjabi standards, having studied criminology at college. He was courteous and friendly, loaning me 500 rupees when I was waiting to get my traveler's checks back from the police impound. His father, a policeman too, was killed in action during the 80's when his company tried to arrest militant Sikhs.

The next morning, Harminder Singh and some other officers took us to see the judge. I guess they could have just called the guy on the phone, but I think they wanted to prove I was real. Dadaji bribed them not to haul us out into the street in handcuffs, but he couldn't afford all they wanted, so Dadaji got the cuffs with a coat draped over his hands. They just let me go around free.

Since the cop shop didn't have a police car to spare, all five of us crowded into one of Amritsar's ubiquitous, three-wheeled, yellow, auto rickshaws—India's answer to the taxicab—like some family going for a weekend outing. Hunched over and squeezed into the open-air tin can, three of us could sit, cheek-to-cheek, while the other three stood, or rather crouched, their crotches and armpits in our faces. All around us, city busses dumped high-sulfur diesel fumes directly into the vehicle, as we chugged along.

It was Sunday, and that's all the weekend Indians get. The judge was at home in his housecoat and slippers. He came to the door all smiles, saying, "Oh ho! What have we here?"

I explained the misunderstanding.

"Well, son," he said, "There is nothing I can do for you. You are in the Indian legal system, now!"

Then he told the cops to make sure Dadaji and I got "advocates," meaning attorneys, right away.

Dadaji had an advocate already, so he gave the cops directions and we all piled into another auto rickshaw and headed downtown. In the auto, Dadaji insisted he would pay all my legal fees. He didn't want me to suffer for his own foolishness. But when we got there and the advocate said it would cost 33,000 rupees to post my bail, about a thousand bucks, Dadaji went mute as marble.

"Oh, come on," I said to the advocate, a man named Rajeev. "If I were Indian, you'd charge me one tenth of that!"

"That is my fee," he replied.

A real sleazebag. What do you expect? Slicked-back hair. A gaudy, polyester suit. Indian, American, European, Asian . . . it doesn't matter where they are from. I know his kind. Hell, I am his kind. No way was I going to hand him all that cash.

"I'd rather represent myself!" I hollered.

"Don't be a fool!" he hollered right back. "They'll keep you in jail forever. You'll never get out!"

"So what? I don't care! Let them!"

I walked out the door and slammed it.

Out in the hall, I consulted with Officer Harminder Singh, whom I had, by then, come to trust. He said Rajeev was right. At the very least, I had to have the bastard post bail for me, or else I really would rot in jail. So I went back into the office and worked out a deal with the guy. He would post my bail, and I would pay him 8,000 rupees once I got my traveler's checks returned from the cops. I would have a few hundred dollars left over to live on, if that. He agreed and made a phone call.

Pretty soon, Dadaji and I were standing in front of a judge, alongside a disheveled old farmer and his wife. The old man's straggly beard fell to his waist, uncombed, and he looked overworked. She looked underworked.

The farmer told the judge he had a parcel of land to put up for my bail, and the judge said okay. That was that.

"Don't worry," said Rajeev later. "There isn't really any land, and they weren't using their real names."

"Is this going to get me in trouble?" I asked. "I don't want any trouble!"

"It's nothing. It's the way it's always done. All the judges know."

So, you see, now that the "bail" is "posted" I only have to wait for it to be "processed" according to the appropriate "procedures." No problem.

chapter 3

As it turns out, Amritsar Central Prison isn't half bad. They grow all their own vegetables! It's not so much like a prison. More like an ashram for the naughty.

Dadaji has a distant relative who works at the prison, so he conspires to get us special treatment, and we get it! Although we have to sleep locked in our cells at night, we are able to wander around the compound all day. Big weedy fields, a majestic Sikh temple (called a *Gurdwara*), a beautiful Hindu temple (called a *Mandir*), and acres of gardens. Except for sleeping on the cold cement floors, I kind of liked it.

For me, prison is like a spiritual retreat. The police allowed me to bring two "holy books" to the jail with me. One is a *Nitnem Gutka*, a book of daily prayers written by the Sikh Gurus. The other is the *Bhagavad Gita*, the classic Hindu text on spiritual surrender and duty. I read these books whenever I can which is often, since I have a whole lot of time on my hands. When I grow tired of reading I practice yoga and meditate.

The whole experience is beginning to feel like a spiritual epiphany. For the first time in my life I understand the concept taught in the *Gita*:

"The God within us is the only reality. This body is only an illusion."

Maybe I'll reach enlightenment right here in prison. I certainly feel myself right on the cusp.

Dadaji thinks I'm crazy. "How can you be meditating like this? It is prison. It is prison, Guru *Sant* Singh!"

I just smile, submitting to God's will. "Justice will prevail, Dadaji, I'm sure of it."

"How you are being so sure of it, this justice? This is India, Guru *Sant* Singh! This is prison!"

"Yes, India! As long as I stay spiritually pure, I'm sure God will have mercy on me."

Dadaji looks at me with a combination of pity and scorn, but what can you do? He is a Hindu. He worships stone idols.

This whole prison experience is exactly like something Yogi Bhajan might have thought up: the organic gardens, the barred cells, the concrete floors, the "special treatment" for certain people. Except, of course, Yogiji would have probably had us all eating nothing but boiled undershirts for forty days.

At the Eugene, Oregon ashram—and even more so once I moved to L.A.—I stuck to Bhajan's program like glue. I was up at 3:00 a.m., taking a cold shower and screaming, "Waheguru, Waheguru, Waheguru!" It's something like "Praise the Guru who takes me from the darkness to the light." It is also just fun to shout stuff in a cold shower.

Then, of course, came the three and a half hours of morning sadhana, starting when the angle of the sun was a perfect sixty degrees. The chanting is so cleansing and so good for you, too. These chants are sacred sounds, and what they do is clean your brain completely. I used them, as instructed, to rebuild my personal identity, pituitary gland, and intuition. The chanting was what gave us our spiritual power. To some degree, this power enabled us to control things—maybe not world events--we were working up to that.

We would chant "Long Ek Ong Kar" every morning. This was the main mantra Yogiji had given us. But that wasn't the only chant we had. Yogiji taught us hundreds of them. There were so many chants, so many diets, exercises, stretches, ancient alchemical remedies, deep breathing techniques—you couldn't possibly do them all. They gave you power over yourself, over others, over the universe. They made you submissive and strong, all at once. Intuitive and direct, all at once. They prolonged life, raised consciousness, perfected the body, and gave you a better boner. It was a proven, five-thousand-year-old path to ultimate power; at least that's what Yogiji told us.

Sure, people called us brainwashed. And yeah, our brains were washed. Washed clean in the blood of all the Sikh warriors and the ten Gurus since the fifteenth century. Washed in the sounds of their names and the name of God and all the highest vibratory frequencies of the world.

"Give me a good brain wash," we would say. "Better than a cold shower!"

Since he is Hindu, Dadaji takes me into the Mandir every day and we get fed there. It is good organic food, right out of the garden. I mean, can you beat that? You can bathe in the courtyard, too, if you call a bucket poured over the head "bathing." I smell like a garbage-eating leper, so I do it. I strip down to my shorts and start splashing around. As I squat there shivering, wishing for soap, one of the inmates comes up and takes my clothes! He is a big guy—scarred, muscle-bound, and mean looking. A bushy black beard sticks out of his face like a plant reaching for the sun.

He dunks my clothes in a bucket, twists them into ropes, and whirls them around his head. Muscles ripple across his barrel chest as he swings my clothes. He whips the floor with them. His ferocity is appalling. Then he dunks them and spanks them and punches them and whips them some more as if giving me a preview of the beating I'm about to receive. He whirls them around his head again and again, fixing me with a malevolent glare. I stand aside quaking, terrified, hands over my balls. I can't fight the man. No way. I wonder if I am expected to. I look around at the others, but no one reacts to the scene at all.

When he is finished, he spreads the clothes out gently across a dry piece of pavement and walks away.

I put them on again. Now I'm wet, but clean. I ask Dadaji what that was all about.

He asks around, discretely.

"That man is a murderer," Dadaji finally tells me. "Oh, he is one accidental murderer. You know, very sad case. He only meant to give him a good beating, but then he is killing him, this man."

"Oh, manslaughter."

"What?"

"Never mind."

"Anyway, Guru *Sant* Singh, he is Hindu. He is looking for good deeds to build back his karma."

He's washing clothes as *seva*! I feel like someone has triggered a light bulb in my brain. *Seva* is real big in India, especially amongst the Sikhs. It means selfless service and is considered one of the best ways to clear bad karma and achieve spiritual greatness. The Golden Temple runs on *seva*. While the number of paid employees is probably in the hundreds the number of people doing *seva* there at any time of the day or night can run into thousands.

Each of the main entrances of the temple complex has a place for pilgrims to surrender their shoes and each of these is manned—day and night—by *sevadars* (volunteers). The *parikarma (*marble causeway) around the *sarovar* is constantly being washed by teams with buckets and long swathes of cloth, again all volunteers. The Guru Ram Das Langar—an enormous free kitchen that feeds between 50,000 to 90,000 every day—is almost totally run by *sevadars*.

Now it makes sense to me why this man hangs out at the temple all day and washes peoples' clothes by beating them against the pavement, whether the people want it or not. I look around and eventually notice there are a lot of guys doing it. My man has moved on to whipping someone else's kurta, and some of the other washers are prowling around with nothing to do. It is getting a little tense, what with the competition for available clothes, so I split. Dadaji comes outside with me.

"Washing is women's work," says Dadaji after a while. "You know that? Nobody wants to wash. Only those men wash."

I get it. Washing demands a special level of humility that only deeply penitent men can muster. The clothes washers are all assassins, wife killers, throat-slashers. Lesser criminals stick to weeding gardens. As for me, I'll stick to my *Nitnem* and the *Bhagavad Gita*.

chapter 4

Throughout the course of the week, Dadaji's family brings water, food, and blankets. But still, these people don't have much. They bring you a blanket, someone at home is doing without. They always ask me what I need, but I don't need a lot. I have my yoga to do, that's all. But there is another side to it, too—I don't want to be in their debt.

I can see it now: some blankets, a couple of new *kurtas*, a few home-cooked meals, and pretty soon they are presenting me with some toothless old cousin that needs a husband. They will have done so much for me by then, I won't dare turn her down. I know how these people work.

I do ask for a packet of fresh underwear, which is about the world's most incredible gift right now; my fondest desire. Dadaji's people bring me that. I can tell they want to bring me more. They want to pull me into their world, their family, their little universe. These Indian families are so intense. I suddenly get a disturbing mental picture of lots of worms in a can. Oozing over each other—slithering, tangling themselves up, so involved in each other's lives. So intertwined. Inseparable.

I still want an Indian wife, but I could do without the in-laws, cousins, nieces, nephews and nosey great aunts. The more I see of Dadaji's family, the more I realize this. But I need the in-laws too.

When Yogiji first came to the West he would say "I do not want to have disciples; I came to train teachers." Even though we acted like disciples—and he seemed quite happy when we did and chastised us when we didn't—this was his creed throughout the years. He would tell us that we would all be "ten times greater teachers than him!" and would drop hints about how he would pass his leadership on to the most deserving amongst us.

This led to a state of mind that could be called "SGS" (spiritual grandeur syndrome) amongst many of Yogiji's male (and some of the female) students. A victim of SGS would always be subconsciously planning to be ready to take over the leadership from Yogiji after he passed away. He would imagine himself as teacher to millions and receiving the same kind of pampering and attention as Yogiji, perhaps even more so.

I was no exception. Yogiji was all too well aware of this in myself and everyone else and often went out of his way to feed our fantasies and encourage our egomaniac speculation.

Yes you guessed it; "You'll be ten times greater than me!" were Yogiji's words to me once in a private meeting.

Even before I met Yogiji I had a touch of SGS. I remember standing in front of the mirror after watching the movie "Patton" in 1970 and thinking to myself how God had destined me for greatness like General George Patton. Idolizing military commanders like Patton--rather than spiritual leaders--made sense when I was 13 years old and second in command at the Harding Military Academy in Glendora.

After joining Yogiji's group and wanting to do what I felt he wanted, these delusions of grandeur began to escalate.

Harbhajan Singh Puri—Yogi Bhajan for short—had been a customs officer at Palam International Airport in Delhi. He was big and burly--six feet four and over two hundred pounds—and carried himself with the bearing of a king or eastern potentate. Without a doubt he was the most intimidating man I have ever met in my life. Not in the same way as a Mafia don—although he could act that way if needs be—but with an energy that seemed to surround and overwhelm everyone with whom he came in contact. It was all but impossible to say "no" to him when he commanded, cajoled, wheedled or flat out screamed at you. He could do all of these with equal effectiveness.

Not surprisingly Yogiji had dominated the organization and no one else was allowed to achieve great ability, fame or success as a spiritual teacher.

Now Yogiji was dead. It seemed to me that there was an obvious need for another charismatic, knowledgeable, powerful spiritual teacher with an Indian wife; someone like…like…well, like me.

Now, as I look back, it's hard for me to believe how much I bought into Yogi Bhajan's shtick. I truly felt that the organization needed new, strong leadership. And that maybe I was just the man to do it. I felt like I didn't just need a wife. I needed her whole family to rally around me. If I wanted to follow in Yogi Bhajan's footsteps--and I really did--I felt that I needed to start out with the whole package. By that I mean an Indian Sikh wife and a whole Punjabi family. That would have given me a real connection to the motherland. I would have had such an aura of authenticity; it would have been a huge advantage over all these American yoga teachers, with their fancy teaching certificates and whatnot.

Ever since Yogi Bhajan died, I had been contemplating how to grow into the role of a successful spiritual teacher. So I created a logical, multi-step plan. My new wife would, of course, be an essential part of it. When I got tossed in prison, I was so close to following through on step two; so close I could taste it. Step two was, of course, to manifest a Punjabi Sikh wife; the first step had been divorcing Sat Siri Kaur, my previous wife.

Our relationship had been deteriorating for some time and our mutual attraction had all but disappeared. In addition, I knew that I could not count on her to support my plan. She was not the kind of woman who would back me up no matter what. She was the type to always ask: *Why? Why? Are you sure? What about this? What about that?*

No, what I needed was an Indian wife, and preferably some kids by her, to get the project off the ground. But even without the project, I very much like the idea of marrying an Indian Sikh woman. She would already have plenty of training in how to be a good wife, so I wouldn't have to coach her at all. I felt sure she would be delighted to marry an American, with all the status that offers. I wasn't super rich, but I had money, and I knew I could always make more. Her family would be thrilled with that. Hey, there would be something for everyone; a win-win situation!

I believed that an Indian wife would stand by me no matter what. I knew she would be a good cook; that would be vital since I can't cook worth a damn. I was totally into fantasizing about what a great life we would have together. I mean, what more do you need? I could give her beautiful saris and jewelry, a house in the U.S., whatever she might want. But beyond that—and getting back to the plan—I was certain that marrying her would, quite frankly, do a great deal to advance my spiritual image.

Creating that image would be essential to building a following; that much I learned from Yogi Bhajan. Of course, being Indian, Yogiji had it easy. He had a legit Indian wife and a couple of legit kids. His whole family was Indian, and he knew all this ancient yoga. It was easy enough for him to come to the spiritual desert that was America in the sixties and start handing out water. Spiritual water for the thirsty. People went crazy for it.

As for me, my plan is on hold, to say the least. The truth is, I have given this whole plan up to God. If God wills me to marry an Indian lady and become a spiritual teacher, then so be it, and if he doesn't, I have to accept that. That is what I do every day with my yoga, chanting, and meditations. I try to surrender to the will of God.

When I am not doing my practice, I stick to Dadaji like glue. He gets me food at the Mandir, translates for me, his family brings me stuff—he's my prison babysitter. It is okay. I am humble enough to accept it. And, in fact, I am grateful. I can't really blame him for getting me tossed in jail when he is doing so much to help me out now.

The truth is, I don't even think it is his fault we are in here. I think we were both framed. Over this past week, he and I have had some long talks about what exactly he did do.

"Guru *Sant* Singh" he says, "I only charged the standard price! One standard price to join my marriage bureau! 1100 rupees! Same, same! "

When a girl becomes a member of his bureau, she and her family can meet all the other members they want—just like any American dating service. (Except there are no dates. The meetings are formal family affairs.) But, of course, based on the advertising campaign he started, all about me, these girls only wanted to meet yours truly: the big prize. He says he didn't bilk anyone. Didn't promise anything. Certainly never took 50,000 rupees from anyone.

"C'mon!" he tells me, "I'd take it if I could, Guru *Sant* Singh. I would! But who would be so stupid to pay me 50,000 rupees just to meet one man? No one is so stupid like this!"

I believe him, although I have a feeling he might be leaving out some details. It doesn't matter. The legal issues are Dadaji's concern. Getting right with God is mine. He says the police won't stop making life hell for me until they've bled me dry for every penny they can get in "tips." Then they will probably still keep me in jail so I can't rat them out to the American embassy.

I don't want to believe it. God would not do that to me. Yogi Bhajan wouldn't let Him.

"Guru *Sant* Singh, I too am like this. I am too successful. I am proud seeming. Wearing suits. Having parties. Enjoying life. Ha! They will take it all. They will take everything, I swear it. I must now sell my house, the bureau, everything! I will have to sell!"

It sounds bad, but we are in this together. In fact, I think we will be friends for life, Dadaji and I. Well, friends might not be the right word, but something.

But then, after a week in jail, he gets released. I don't.

Suddenly Dadaji is like a man I never met. He starts gathering up all the blankets and pillows his wife brought us.

I ask if he can leave some for me. I am going to be all alone now, on the concrete.

He doesn't want to!

"They'll take care of you great here! It's a great place!" he says, hoisting his stuff.

"Do you think your son could keep on bringing boiled water? Otherwise, I don't know what I'll drink . . ."

"Are you kidding?" he says. "Oh, there is nothing as good as the water they have here! This place is the best! They'll feed you great here!" he says to me. He goes on and on about it, as if we haven't just shared the same experience for two weeks. It isn't the food I am worried about, and he knows it.

That son of a bitch leaves me one blanket, reluctantly, and now I have to drink the prison water. Goodbye Dadaji, hello dysentery.

chapter 5

After Dadaji leaves, I get two new cell mates, both Sikhs: Dr. Sobha Singh and Amrik Singh, who seem to be good friends. As it turns out, they both speak perfect English. Apparently, Dr. Sobha Singh is an advocate as well as a doctor. He tells me his story:

"Oh, Guru *Sant* Singh," he says. "It all started because I was having a dalliance with a certain woman. A very certain special woman. She is not my wife. She is, in fact, another man's wife. I don't mind admitting it because she is so beautiful. You should see her. Oh, she is *so* beautiful."

His eyes wander to a blank spot on the wall, and he goes off into a reverie. I think cheating on your wife is despicable. I'm a one-woman-at-a-time man. To me, marriage is essential. I am kind of embarrassed by his admission and not sure I want to hear more.

Amrik Singh nudges Sobha Singh out of it, saying, "Tell him about the bullets, Sobha Singh."

"Oh yes, well, Guru *Sant* Singh, her husband found out about our affair. I don't know who told him. Maybe she even told him herself, I don't know. I don't want to know anymore! I really don't . . . What he did, the bastard, was he just got a gun. I don't know how he came across this gun. Who can get a gun just like that? He must have known some bad actors, I think. Who can get a gun? What sort of person? It is not possible. This is not America, you know, where everybody has a gun."

"Do you have a gun?" asks Amrik Singh of me, in the middle of all this.

"Yes," I reply. "I have several."

His eyes go wide and he looks at Sobha Singh, but Sobha's eyes are focused on infinity.

"And he took this gun," says Sobha Singh, "and he shot two bullets in his own wall. Bang! Bang! One lodged in the concrete, and one went right into his bloody Ganesha. Who shoots his own Ganesha, I ask you? Who? Then the little trickster called the police. The cops came, and he told them it was me that tried to kill him, and these two bullet holes were the proof! So then what happened was, the police drove over to my house and picked me up for attempted murder. Right in front of all my neighbors!"

"And coincidentally," says Amrik Singh, "I was at his house just then. I was only seeking help for a computer glitch. Sobha Singh is very good with computers."

"Yes, Amrik Singh and I were working on the computer just then."

"And the police pushed open the door. They stormed into the room like crazy people, and put us both in handcuffs!" says Amrik Singh.

"But Amrik Singh, why did they arrest you?" I ask.

"Just for being there," says Amrik Singh.

"And here we are, Guru *Sant* Singh. Here we are," says Sobha Singh.

"You must have been . . . awfully surprised!" is all I can think to say.

"Yes, of course we were surprised. We were very surprised indeed!"

"But tell me, Guru *Sant* Singh," asks Amrik Singh, "In America, you really have a gun? But why? What for? Pardon me for asking, but . . . are you a murderer?"

While Sobha Singh and Amrik Singh may not have much of

an appreciation for guns, I know they understand warfare. After all, they are Sikhs, and, traditionally, Sikhs have a great warrior tradition.

Sikhs were generally a peaceful bunch until the fifth Guru, Guru Arjun, was tortured to death with the acquiescence of the ruling Islamic Mughal emperor, Jahangir, in 1606. His son, Hargobind, then was ordained as the sixth Guru, at which time he expressed his determination to wear two swords, one for *Miri* (temporal power) and the other for *Piri* (spiritual power), thus giving the Sikhs the ability to defend themselves and others.

Under the inspiration of Guru Hargobind the Sikhs fought off numerous attacks by the Imperial forces, as well as the armies of minor Hindu Rajas whose domains bordered on that of the Guru. Both the Emperor and the Rajas felt threatened by the Guru's philosophy of equality, as well as his growing power and popularity.

In 1675, Guru Tegh Bahadur, ninth Guru and son of Guru Hargobind, was tortured and killed by Aurangzeb, the ruling emperor and grandson of Jahangir. What made the Guru's sacrifice unique was that he did it not for the Sikhs, but for the sake of the Hindus of Kashmir whom Aurangzeb was slaughtering by the thousands in an attempt to convert the whole of India to Islam. Guru Tegh Bahadur's son, the nine year old Gobind Rai, became the tenth Guru.

On hearing of his father`s martyrdom, the young Gobind Rai vowed to change sparrows into hawks, create such a creed of warrior whose very appearance would deny them anonymity in a crowd and whose indomitable spirit would inspire them to deeds of mercy, courage and righteousness.

Guru Gobind Rai created a society of *Sant-Sipahi* (warrior saints) to which he gave the name *Khalsa,* meaning "The Pure", and the distinctive identity of the turban, the sword and uncut hair. A Sikh who takes baptism into the *Khalsa* must wear the articles of faith known as the 5 Ks:

Kesh (unshorn hair)
Kara (iron bracelet)
Kirpan (ceremonial dagger)
Kanga (wooden comb)
Kachera (a type of underwear worn by medieval warriors in India)

At that time he designated that all male Sikhs should carry the last name of Singh, meaning Lion, thus Guru Gobind Rai became Guru Gobind Singh. Female Sikhs were all given the last name of Kaur, meaning Princess.

Mention the name Guru Gobind Singh to most Sikhs and you can feel their energy change. Their spines stiffen and a faraway look comes into their eyes. It's the look of a spiritual warrior.

If Sikhs hadn't taken up arms, India would be a Muslim land today and Hinduism would be a part of ancient history, nothing more.

A big part of the Sikh belief system is that it is right to fight for a cause and for those who can't or won't defend themselves. It is kind of like the cowboy code of honor. Sikhs are always at the ready to help someone in need with the Punjabi version of a "Much obliged, Ma'am." And if that help involves a little swordplay—or a shootout—it would not be the first time.

So I tell my story to Amrik Singh and Sobha Singh in a way they can understand. I don't say I was trained as a military commander, I say "warrior." They understand that.

As a kid I used to go out in mom's rose garden and pop off pigeons with a .22. Dad loved it. I could hit anything with that little rimshot rifle, so he bought me an M1 Garand. We would bounce way out into the woods in an old army jeep and shoot bottles and cans. It was the life! Boy Scout badges, NRA medals and target-shooting ribbons hung off the walls of my bedroom like dragon scales.

At 13, I made the California state rifle team. They flew me to Lake Erie for the national matches and billeted me in a WWII barracks with a bunch of obnoxious high schoolers. Out on the rifle range, I beat those redneck assholes and set a record for *perfect* all-day score. But back at the barracks, it was a different story.

I was the youngest, shy as hell, and did not want any part of their ignorant druggy banter. Those kids were into stealing, getting high, and raising hell; no discipline at all. They teased me constantly and couldn't give a shit that I held the junior record for open sights.

We ate our three squares in this stinky, echoing cafeteria, and one time a gang of them decided to taunt me.

"Look at Clark! Eating with a spoon!"

There I was, eating something with a spoon. What's the crime?

"He's not big enough to use a fork, are you Clark?"

"Poor little Clark. He can't handle a fork. Look at that spoon! Just look at it!"

They had a girl with them. She was cute as anything and mocking me like hell. I will never forget it.

Both in military school and at the shooting matches, there was always some group of idiots trying to make life hell for me. Sure, I felt pretty irritated by their taunts but it was not in my nature to react. I would channel my anger into my shooting and never let it show. Nobody could beat my record for perfect all-day score, and that was all that mattered to me. For all I know, it still stands today.

I eventually left military school and my war-hero dreams behind, but my shooting prowess paid off much later, in Los Angeles, when Yogi Bhajan hired me as one of his personal body guards. Yogi Bhajan, who we just called Yogiji, always had a white Mercedes driving in front of the car he was in with another one behind. The other guards and I would ride in those, looking all serious while wearing our knee-length, white, flowing kurtas, loose white pants, and white turbans. We were always carrying concealed 44 magnum caliber handguns, which were illegal, but only a misdemeanor in California.

Those were heady days. Yogiji and his top-level cronies went out to lunch every day in Beverly Hills. I'm talking La Scala. Places like that. White glove service. He would take the whole entourage, including all the body guards and, of course, his two right hand men— both of whom, Yogiji named Hari Jiwan Singh and Harijiwan Singh, no doubt because of their similar karmic destinies.

The movie stars and executive bigwigs that ate at La Scala got used to seeing us coming, like a sea of white, like a roiling cloud— our white turbans with the golden emblems pinned at the centers. We would cluster around some big table, eating the gourmet fare and making a big, lively scene, looking so pompous and rich. Yogiji would drop two or three grand, just on lunch. Just on lunch! Making a big show of it. That is the kind of lifestyle it was.

I don't tell all of this to Sobha Singh and Amrik Singh, though. I just tell them about my military training. My sharpshooting medals. Also, I mention that I actually tried out for the Olympic sharpshooting team five times.

They share a glance that means newfound respect for me, and just like that, we become friends. I am not a man who makes friends. So here, in prison of all places, in India of all places, especially after this recent business with Dadaji, I find it terrifically ironic that I now have two friends. My first two friends outside of the Happy Healthy Holy Organization. We call it "3HO."

chapter 6

A man rattles the bars of our cell. He has one of those wonky eyes that is always pointing the wrong direction. When I first met Wall Eye, I thought he was a prison guard. He wears a half-uniform that makes him look almost like a guard, but he is actually a lifer.

It is hard to tell the difference between the guards and the guys serving life sentences here, because they both have the run of the place, and they are both very mellow. The guards don't carry weapons, and they are pals with the prisoners. Seriously. They sit around and play checkers and talk about what corrupt bastards the Punjabi Police are. These guards know half the prisoners are here on false charges, so they just treat everyone like innocents. It feels like one big family—another reason why I can't take the whole thing seriously. The guards are too nice to really be guards, the prisoners too cooperative to be prisoners. Compared to what my stepson—Sat Siri's son K.P.--told me of prison in America, this place is more like being confined to an unkempt city park. The meekness of these people is heartwarming, really. I almost feel more welcome here in prison than I did back home at the ashram in New Mexico.

On my first day in prison, Wall Eye gave me an orientation tour, pointing out the Gurdwara, the Mandir, and the gardens. He explained the eating and sleeping schedules in great detail, like the place was a spa. So friendly!

Apparently, this is his job— giving tours to the rookies. Everyone serving a sentence here has a job. It is a self-supporting prison, I guess. You are either a cook or a field hand or a dishwasher or something—whatever you are good at. It is like a real community, where everyone is busy.

They also keep Wall Eye busy working in the prison office, and he knows everything that is going on behind the scenes. He is also a very devout Sikh and actually wears the kirpan, the Sikh's symbolic dagger. Here he is, a murderer in jail for life, and they let the guy carry a dagger! It is not sharp, but still. Sometimes I don't know what to make of it.

Wall Eye says, "Don't worry Guru *Sant* Singh. There has been a mix-up in the office, but you will be released soon."

"I'll say there's been a mix-up!"

"It is because your father's name is not the same as yours. Your papers were filed incorrectly. They were lost, but they have been found. Few days, just wait few days," he says. "Small, small time, Guru *Sant* Singh. Doooooooon't worry."

My father and mother were both devout Christians; and that's how I was brought up. We were in church every Sunday; of course. But there was also Wednesday night service, which we often attended, Bible classes and Vacation Bible Camp in the summer. I was into it! So many people say how they were forced to attend Sunday School or Bible classes and hated it. Not me; I looked forward to it and loved it.

I can still picture myself sitting there in Bible class. We had two spinster teachers—they were twins—and one of them, Heather Cooper, cherished me as her favorite student. She went on a trip to Israel—the Holy Land—and brought me back a little clay vase that she said was from ancient times and was similar to those which had contained the Dead Sea Scrolls. I treated that little vase as a treasure. She was always talking about Jesus and her love for Jesus affected me deeply. At that time of my life, I felt very close to Jesus.

My favorite quote from the Bible was when Jesus said: "My kingdom is not of this world." I knew I was merely visiting this world and should not regard it as a permanent home. Even at that young age I could see that money, sex, power; all these things gave temporary enjoyment but were impermanent.

I spent a lot of time on my own and did not easily form relationships; I felt like my only true friend was Jesus. I spent hours reading the Bible and looking at my notes from Bible class.

As I grew into adolescence my perspective changed. I started to see things in the church that were not always as they should have been. Our church's youth minister, one of the most vocal and enthusiastic in expressing his love for Jesus, suddenly ran away with one of the girls from his youth group, leaving behind his wife and children.

Another one of our ministers had a serious drinking problem. Although alcohol was affecting his ability to do his job, everyone pretended everything was fine. That is until his dysfunctionality became impossible to ignore.

My own father had begun drinking and smoking. He began to open his business on a Sunday; something he would previously never do.

It all seemed like so much hypocrisy to me and I began to drift away from the church, even though I still loved Jesus. Perhaps my disillusionment at that time became the source of one of my main character traits, one that has caused me no end of trouble over the years: my inability to stomach untruth, lies, disingenuousness and deceit in any form. Especially by those who hold positions of power and leadership over others.

At the same time I was having experiences that most Christians would say were "of the Devil." I was highly sensitive and experienced lucid dreaming and what some call "astral travel." I found that I would be aware that I was in a dream and could direct what was happening. I remember once walking around at my high school and wondering whether I was awake or asleep. Maybe I was trying to escape the Earth that I saw as temporary by going deeper into my dreams.

Occasionally, though, the dreams took on a dark edge. I felt like I was hovering out of my body and crushingly alone. The surety of my aloneness was the terrifying thing. It seemed as though nothing and no one could ever cure it, ever cancel it out. In one dream, I was paralyzed. Evil aliens were in my room, getting ready to take me away to their home planet. But the shadowy figures paused in their preparations. They began to debate whether or not they should bring my mother along as well. Some insisted she was too old, others suggested she would be difficult to carry. Then again, she had some very special bodily organ that must be harvested—a real unusual specimen. For hours, I struggled to wake up, but could not.

When you see people on those TV shows claiming they have had an alien abduction, that's how this dream felt.

Many times, I had exhilarating dreams of traveling to planets beyond our Solar system. Maybe I was just watching too many "Star Trek" episodes.

Once, as I was waking up in the morning, I even found my mouth involuntarily moving with the words "*Alpha*"- "*Vega*" as if I was receiving a supernatural psychic transmission from distant stars. I also heard beautiful, never heard before, classical music in my dreams. The dreams gave me a sense of connection to a supreme power over the entire universe. I believed I was tied into mystical forces beyond the ken of mere mortals.

These dreams resulted in what I can only call a sense of being exalted and special. I was always wondering why I was on this tiny earth and could not stop my mind from thinking "What is our bigger purpose in life?" From an early age I started dealing with it by running. After a few miles, my mind would go mercifully blank and gave me a sense of well-being for a short time. I got pretty good, too, as I became the best miler at Claremont High with a 4:28 mile. I even came in second in one race to Steve Scott at upland High who became one of the greatest mile runners in American history. I left high school and enrolled at Texas Christian University, but my long-distance running eventually led me to the University of Oregon, which had a great cross-country team famous for spawning Olympic athletes. But even the running did not make my anxiety go away. Medication, exhaustion, a new mattress—nothing worked.

When I arrived at the University of Oregon, I found myself at the center of the Self-Awareness movement in late-seventies America. The U of O campus had everything: Sodium Pentothal, polarity therapy, bioenergetics, primal scream, acupuncture, you name it. People would get together and try out all these new ideas, either with a teacher, a doctor or just on their own.

After military school and then Texas Christian, I was a conservative fish out of water in ultra-hippie Eugene. In retrospect I think I was missing the deep spiritual connection I had with God since I was a child. My rejection of the church had left a spiritual void of which I wasn't really aware. But, once I lapsed into acute depression and anxiety, I decided anything was worth a try.

I started taking all the consciousness-raising classes and doing all the encounter groups I could. I sent my dad all the bills, and he paid them, out of guilt, I suppose, for all those beatings. It was thousands of dollars and never ended. There was always more: meditation, tai chi, holistic psychology, EST, cleansing diets, transcendental energetics, juice fasts, homeopathy.

But I never felt any better.

Finally I took a kundalini yoga class with one Dr. Sat Kir*pal* Singh. Twenty people sitting on fat green mats in a stinky old gym. Sat Kir*pal* Singh was a big guy. Very fit, imposing, and confident. He sported a long, flowing beard and wore a white, knee-length Indian tunic; white, loose-fitting pants; and a high, tight, white turban. Magnificent!

His yoga gave me strength, power, and confidence. A real endorphin rush. He taught more classes too: aura reading, biokinesiology, health food, Ayurvedic medicine, Jyotish astrology, numerology, gem therapy. I wanted to be around Sat Kir*pal* Singh all the time, so I took every one of his classes. Eventually, he noticed.

He invited me to his home, his ashram: three white houses in the Eugene suburbs. He told me the group was called 3HO—the Happy, Healthy, Holy Organization, but the ashramites also called themselves Sikhs. They explained theirs was an Indian religion from the Punjab: more enlightened than Hinduism, more exotic than Christianity.

I wanted that.

Everyone dressed like Sat Kir*pal* Singh. Everything in the whole place was white: the walls, the tables, the chairs, the clothes, the people, the countertops. If it wasn't white, it was gilded. Gold plated stuff was a big theme, too.

Best of all, they were into God, money, guns, and, eventually, taking over the world.

I left my stuff in the dorm and moved in that very night. Called the University and told them to donate my crap to charity for all I cared.

chapter 7

By the time Wall Eye leaves me with his admonishment to wait patiently, I notice my cell mates have been whispering. They turn to me.

"Guru *Sant* Singh? We were just wondering—how did you ever meet that Dadaji fellow?"

"Dadaji? You know him?" I ask, suddenly aware that I must be the focal point of prison gossip. They share another one of those glances.

"Actually," says Sobha Singh, "he's infamous."

I had heard famous, not infamous. All we have is time, so I tell them everything.

I met Dadaji through Bunty. I met Bunty at the Golden Temple. That is how this whole thing started.

When my plane landed in Amritsar, the sun was just setting, and I headed right over to the Golden Temple. It was the first day of Bandi Chhor Divas; and I didn't want to miss anything. This is a Sikh holiday that celebrates the sixth Guru, Guru Hargobind's exit from prison where he had been imprisoned by Emperor Jahangir. The holiday falls at the same time as Diwali, a huge Hindu festival and few people bother to make the distinction between them.

This is a big holiday. And I mean big. I stashed my shoes at the shoe booth, where one of the sevadars took them and gave me a metal token with the number of the bin where he had placed them. Funnily enough, the ritual is exactly like what you go through at an American bowling alley. I walked over the marble entrance, through a trough of running water for cleansing the feet. Through a huge, white archway and I was inside the temple compound.

It's always a heart stopping moment for me when I see the Harimandir Sahib after a few years absence. No photo, video nor movie does it justice. Plated in 24-karat gold and lit up with floodlights, it gleams like a fallen sun. The temple reflects off the holy *sarovar* that surrounds it, creating the illusion of two shining, golden temples. What really affects you, though, is the spiritual glow that it emanates. This is radiant energy that cannot be captured by the camera's eye.

From 2:30 am until 9:30 pm sacred Gurbani Kirtan, the Divine Music of the Sikhs, is sung by professional singers, singing in relays. As overwhelming as is the sight of the Harimandir, so are the sounds of the singing. There are white painted buildings on all four sides of the *sarovar* and the music, amplified by a powerful sound system, resounds and reverberates around the huge courtyard created by the buildings. These are our prayers, our gospels, our poetry to God.

That night, fireworks exploded in the night sky. Holiday lights wrapped every pillar and post of the Golden Temple, and impenetrable masses of devotees circled the *parikarma*--the marble paved walkway around all four sides of the sacred pool. The funny thing is that—even though the devotees were jam packed shoulder to shoulder—there was such an air of calmness and benevolence that I didn't feel the least bit scared being in such a crush of humanity.

Everything glittered; everything was on fire, glowing, sparkling. People sang and chanted all over the place, reciting poetry. They splashed in the nectar pond where oil lamps floated around like stars in the sky. I got crushed up against a wall, but didn't care. I was just glad to be back.

That is when I met Bunty, an Indian man in a gold-flecked turban, who was crushed up against the wall right along with me. When I said "Holy crap!" he laughed, surprising me by responding in English. We engaged in a shouted conversation, surrounded by the sweet incense and cacophony of a true devotion we both felt deeply. I mentioned I had just arrived in India. He laughed and told me he owned a hotel right around the corner: Hotel Grace. Later that night, I moved in. I paid for one month, up front.

I was glad to finally find an ally in Amritsar. Even with all the devotion and spirituality it's easy to get lonely when you are the only white face around. Bunty was in his early 40's. His wife ran a local beauty salon. I eventually discovered Bunty was interested in having a little sex on the side with girls. He actually asked me to hook him up with a 19 year old Indian girl I met that worked next door to Dadaji. Really sleazy guy; but I was ready for some company.

Apart from my desire to reconnect with my spiritual heritage, my main reason for coming to India was to do one of these medical tourism things and get my teeth capped on the cheap. This idea of looking for a Punjabi Sikh bride was just floating around in my head, still in the "what if" stage.

The next day, Bunty brought cups of chai up to my room and we got to talking. After a while, I took the plunge. I told him I had an idea about getting into an arranged marriage with a nice Sikh lady. It was the first time I had actually said it out loud. Doing so made the fantasy seem suddenly real.

To Bunty, it was realer than real. If you are an American and you want to marry an Indian lady, all you have to do is ask. I learned that later. Nevertheless, he frowned.

"Why do you want a wife at your age? Just have an affair, old man!"

I laughed, thinking he was kidding. But he wasn't, and he asked again.

"Why not find an American lady?" he asked. "One who is used to your ways, your culture?"

He was concerned about my being divorced. Divorce is a scandal in India. It just is not something where you bounce back and get a new spouse; it is the end of your life, your reputation, your family, your rights. It is the end of the world.

"A divorced man is not the best husband for an Indian lady," said Bunty, placing his chai cup gently on the cracked plastic table. "Even if he is an American."

"Listen, Bunty," I said. "It's just these American women, they kill me. I can't keep a marriage going with an American lady. It's impossible! But an Indian lady would be different. I'm a devout Sikh. A spiritual man. I'd never have an affair. That's not the way I operate. I just need a lady who understands the Sikh way. The way of grace and service to God. I've come all this way to find the right kind of lady—a spiritual woman, a traditional woman, not some free-thinking American."

"I see. The American ladies, they are not good wives?"

"It's a cultural clash, Bunty. I'm a Punjabi at heart, I swear I am. They don't understand me the way a Sikh lady would," I said, adding, "and they don't know how to cook paranthas either."

He laughed, like he was supposed to, but it wasn't really a joke. Part of my vision was of having fried Indian delicacies served to me piping hot by a smiling woman who was happy just to see me happy. Maybe I have seen too many Bollywood soap operas. I don't know.

"So, you want to hire a marriage broker?" Bunty asked.

A broker? *My God*, I thought. *That is exactly what I want!* Someone to broker the deal for me. After all, if it came down to romancing a woman on my own . . . forget it, I would not have the slightest idea where to start.

Bunty told me that, to arrange a marriage, ideally, I needed a go-between: a relative, or at least a family friend. But lacking that, a guy can hire a pro. One of these brokers.

"I know just the man," said Bunty, "Dadaji, the most famous matchmaker in the Punjab!"

Bunty put me in an auto rickshaw driven by a grinning jackal of a madman, pointed down the street, and said something to the driver in Punjabi. He slapped the side of the vehicle like Secretariat's flank, and we were off.

chapter 8

The driver zig-zagged drunkenly along the busy thoroughfare, polka-dotted with pedestrians. Beggars saw my white face bobbing along, sucking exhaust, and hobbled recklessly into the street, the better to display their deformities. The driver made an admirable attempt at murder-suicide for a good half hour, before we wended down a stinking back alley and stopped. An old man in a tattered turban and drooping, colorless clothing sat in a cement alcove, surrounded by his things. The driver yelled something at him, and the old man smiled and nodded.

The old man, Harjinder Singh by name, claimed, in broken English, to have the best marriage bureau in the Punjab, then sat grinning as a mouse ran behind his desk.

Along the back wall of the alcove was a bed with a man lying on it. The old man introduced me to the man on the bed, his son, who moaned incessantly and had his head wrapped in bloody bandages. Apparently, he had been in a motorcycle accident. The son worked as our translator, though he had to stop frequently to wipe away strings of red drool.

"What is your age, sir?"

"Fifty."

"I see. You are a widower."

"No, I'm divorced."

"Divorced? Divorced?"

"Yes, but not from an Indian lady. From an American lady."

The son lay back on his bed, exhausted. He lolled his bandaged head back and forth and rolled his eyes. I was not sure if he was thinking or having a seizure.

Harjinder finally said something to his son, which the son did not translate. They began a conversation in Punjabi, then seemed to come to a conclusion.

"But you are American?" asked the son.

"Yes, I'm American. American citizen."

"Okay," said the son. "We will find you a good match. Doooooooon't worry. But first, why did you get divorced?"

"My ex-wife? She wasn't a good Sikh," I told them.

This wasn't true. Sat Siri Kaur was as devoted a Sikh as you will find anywhere in 3HO. A total vegetarian. Her prayers were immaculate, her chanting bold, and its cadence perfect, she was also a world renowned astrologer. She had served Yogi Bhajan with total dedication from the very beginning and never missed morning sadhana. But the old man and his son did not need to know all that.

I continued: "She was not devout. I am Gursikh and must have a woman who is very devout and prayerful. A vegetarian, too."

Of course, I didn't mention I had actually been married and divorced twice. It didn't matter though, because I was sure the third time was going to be a charm. This time through, I felt sure I could make marriage work.

chapter 9

Harjinder Singh claimed to know many devout ladies from good families. Then his son, on the bed, gave out a long, pathetic moan. Membership in the matchmaking service would cost 2,200 rupees, about fifty bucks. I produced 2,400 in large bills, and he kept the change.

In a couple of days I got a call through the hotel telephone. Bunty listened, talked, then hung it up.

"It was a man named Harjinder Singh, for you."

"Yes! That's the marriage broker!"

"Harjinder Singh? . . . not Dadaji?"

"Well, he said his name was Harjinder Singh. That's where the driver took me."

"My God!"

"What?"

"That's not Dadaji! You didn't give him any money, did you?"

"Yes, of course. I signed up to be part of his matchmaking thing."

Bunty covered his face, as if in despair, "Guru *Sant* Singh, how much did you give him?"

"2,000 rupees," I lied.

He sighed with despair, "Okay, well, you paid, so you might as well go."

"Go where? What did he say?"

"He said he has a bride for you. A lady is waiting."

"Waiting? Now? This minute?"

"Yes. She is waiting. Why don't you go and meet her?" he suggested blandly.

Then I described it all to Bunty, the whole adventure—how it must have taken half an hour to get there, how the auto had squirrelled its way through a maze of alleyways. I had no idea how to find the place again.

"My God!" Bunty replied, shaking his head as if at an incurably stupid child.

But for some reason, Bunty was still dedicated to helping me. He had taken me on as his charge—an obligation perhaps akin to owning a very bad dog. He asked his father to man the hotel's front desk, and we jumped on his scooter.

I directed him this way and that, sending him across town and back again, down all kinds of strange back alleys, trying to find Harjinder Singh's dirty little alcove—all the while, suppressing laughter. I figured it was all a wild goose chase. But eventually, miraculously really, I recognized the dirty rag and splattered wall and found Harjinder Singh in his alcove. He was looking off into space, ignoring his two guests, while his son moaned incessantly.

The candidate sat in the place of honor, receiving a primitive face lift from the deafening fan. Her mother sat by her side. We engaged in a shouted conversation, inexpertly translated by Bunty.

She was a very angry, 34-year-old lady, either divorced or a widow, who had a son living with a relative. She submitted her basic information—age, living relatives, caste—like dropping a handful of gravel in my lap, then waited for a decision.

I tried conversation.

"Do you live far from here? What's your son's name?" and so forth.

She frowned and looked at her lap. The mother rolled her eyes and sighed heavily.

"What is your demand?" said the mother.

"Um. A good cook? A good Sikh?"

"WHAT IS YOUR DEMAND!" hollered the mother.

"I'm very devout. I want a vegetarian lady . . ."

She looked at Bunty, exasperated.

"She is asking what you want for a dowry," Bunty explained.

I hadn't even thought of it! At fifty, I figured I would be lucky to get a woman at all. I was certainly not after any money.

"No! Nothing!" I protested. "I don't want anything!"

She didn't believe me, but I kept it up.

Eventually, the mother smiled and said, "You are very kind."

Anyway, I didn't want this woman. I told them I would have to think about it, but the son, still lying on the bed, encouraged me to take her.

"She is good enough," he said. "Why not marry her?"

The whole experience made me miss Yogi Bhajan acutely. Looking at this woman's hard, impenetrable eyes, I knew she could never fathom me, nor would she ever try. I suddenly felt deeply lonely. I realized anew that Yogiji was the only person who had ever truly understood me or ever would. As I sat there smiling and nodding, a hollowness grew inside.

"Why didn't you?" asks Sobha Singh, as we peer out through the prison bars at the darkening sky.

"Why didn't I what?"

"Marry her? She was good enough, as the man said."

I can't believe what I'm hearing. I answer, "I guess I wanted someone . . . I don't know, nicer, I guess. Prettier. Happier."

Sobha Singh furrows his brow beneath his enormous cobalt turban.

"She didn't even speak English," I add.

"Oh, yes! That's true!" Sobha Singh says, then, "You want a high-caste wife! Of course. You can afford one, so why not?"

"She doesn't have to be high caste. It's not about that."

Sobha Singh raises his eyebrows in disbelief. "Oh yes, she does. I know what you're looking for. You should have just told the man, 'Hi Fi.' You want a Hi Fi girl. That would have saved you a lot of trouble."

I drop the subject. Meeting that woman was such a depressing experience, I don't even want to remember it. Later, I would meet many more equally depressing women, but the first was a real shock. She reminded me of myself, before I became a Sikh. That depression. That sense of being adrift in the world, completely alone, desperate for something, but not sure what. I did not want to be anywhere near that vibe. It might rub off.

chapter 10

In 1980, I was 23 and had been living at the 3HO ashram in Eugene, Oregon for about a year or so.

My bad dreams were no longer bothering me but I was still able to leave my body after a particularly powerful yoga class or at the end of our morning devotions. I would lie flat on my back in *Shavasana* or, as we called it, Corpse Pose, close my eyes, and I would find my awareness out of my body, wandering around in the astral realms. It was great fun.

One day, I had just slipped out of my body when I felt myself in the presence of a powerfully spiritual being. I asked and was told it was Guru Ram Das, fourth guru of the Sikhs and special favorite of Yogi Bhajan. He reached out to touch me and seemed to say: "Right. You've had your fun. Time to take all this spiritual stuff seriously." And that was the end of my astral travelling.

I received my spiritual name in the fall of 1979 after one of my typical, spontaneous-but-life-altering decisions. My friend Sat Kir*pal* Singh was running across the ashram lawn with a suitcase.

"Hey, Clark! Want to go see Yogiji in Anchorage? I have an extra ticket!"

Every weekend, Yogi Bhajan jetted to a different ashram to grace the people with his presence and give a tantric yoga course. In preparation, they would scrub every wall, every floor. They would paint the whole ashram, inside and out, and also cook and bake up every possible delicacy for him and his entourage. Devotees would spend weeks preparing for a visit. Weeks. Full time. This was in addition to three-and-a-half-hour morning yoga sessions and, in many cases, twelve-hour work days.

I had always wanted to go to one of these things, so I got in the car with Sat Kir*pal* Singh and went, just like that. I was wearing a t-shirt, jeans, and Birkenstocks. Pretty soon we were in Anchorage, and it was forty below.

Alaskans in the airport stared rudely, as if I had three heads or a giant growth on my nose, but this time it was not because of my turban—it was because of my clothes, or lack thereof. Sat Kirpal Singh had to find a taxi and make it drive right to the airport door. I ran straight into the vehicle. If I had been outside five minutes, I surely would have lost my toes to frostbite. But God protected me, and pretty soon I was in the warm ashram, doing my obeisance to Yogiji.

Typically, what the ashram would do was set him up in a room ornamented with tasseled pillows, silken swags, and yards and yards of fresh flower garlands. It would be anointed with scented oils and incense. Fit for Krishna. Then the devotees would file in. With their fingertips, they touched his feet, then their foreheads, to transmit his sacred *darshan*.

Most folks had done it a bunch of times already. In fact, there were people that devoted every weekend to following Yogiji around the country, just to sit at his feet all day—gazing on him, or waiting on him. If he needed a glass of water, they would all scramble to be the one to bring it. I did not run in that circle, though. I had only met him once before, and didn't even know if he would remember me. So when I got there, I was a little nervous.

I had been told that, outside of giving his lecture, Yogiji rarely spoke. He might grunt at someone once in a while, but mostly the great man ignored everyone. He would sit in his big chair, feet out for the supplicants, talking on the phone in Punjabi. He was deeply involved in Indian politics, so it was always some crucial thing. People said he was always yelling on the phone and gesturing wildly.

Also, he would watch TV: soap operas and wildlife shows. The people filed in, knelt, bowed their foreheads to the ground, touched his feet, and heard, "This family of hyenas has driven a mother lion away from her kill. . ."

So imagine my surprise that day in Anchorage when, after I did my obeisance, he spoke to me.

"You're a skinny son of a bitch, aren't you? When I was your age, I ate fifteen chapattis a day! You should eat fifteen chapattis! Go get some meat on your bones!"

Envy bloomed in the breast of every ashramite within earshot.

Encouraged, I handed Yogiji the slip of paper I had written on the plane and stashed in a pocket. It asked the teacher for a spiritual name. That was how we communicated with him, then. We never addressed him directly. Sometimes he would respond, other times he would toss the paper aside. Depends upon what was on TV.

He took my paper and asked my birthday. Did some computations on the back. Numerology. He wrote a name and handed it to me.

Guru Sant.

Guru Sant Singh Khalsa.

All Sikh names are androgynous. Men add Singh. Women add Kaur. That's how you know the gender. Then Khalsa. In 3HO, we are all called Khalsa. It means we are pure and follow the traditional path of vegetarianism, not cutting the hair, and chanting the daily prayers. The warrior way. No drugs, no alcohol. Our names carry a real sense of pride. Even though Singh is a name all Sikh men share, one doesn't omit it when saying someone's name. It is a point of pride to be a Singh, so the name always gets tacked on at the end, very quickly, almost like a verbal tic.

"Guru *Sant* Singh" people say, rolling the 'r,' emphasizing the Sant, and letting the 'Singh' out like a little puff of air. It's lovely. These names have a musicality that puts American names to shame.

I said my new name over and over to myself. Guru meant I was a teacher, and Sant meant I was a saint. *What kind of name is this? I must be someone very special*, I thought, *just as I have always suspected.*

When I got back to Oregon, I went to the federal building and changed my name. It was goodbye to Clark Harris—my father's son, a good-hearted but naïve Christian boy, and hello to Guru *Sant* Singh Khalsa, the spiritual warrior.

chapter 11

After leaving the bride of darkness behind at Harjinder Singh's place, Bunty and I laughed the whole thing off like a couple of school chums. He said he would take me to the real Dadaji and get me a good woman, not some used-up old goat, so we mounted the scooter again and Bunty dashed headlong into traffic like a man damned.

Across town, he parked on an uprooted piece of broken sidewalk in front of what appeared to be a three-story concrete mausoleum cum office complex. It looked like some bombed-out section of Beirut. The drab, grey building rose from Amritsar's dusty asphalt plain with the sudden intensity of a karst formation. It was peppered with festive blue, yellow, and red signs in both Hindi and Punjabi. Many listed to one side or flapped in the wind like dead limbs.

The edifice loomed up in a vast parking lot, where innumerable cars were haphazardly parked. One soot-smeared auto rickshaw driver had parked in the lot, jacked up his clownish yellow vehicle, crawled underneath, and seemed to be changing his oil. Next to the building, a deafening highway flyover sliced through the sky over a busy road. On the road, a succession of well-dressed women, rag-clad families, and lame, overburdened servants actively crisscrossed the heavy traffic, on foot. They were all making their way to a small dirt patch in front of the office complex's parking lot, where an endless succession of long-distance busses seemed to be arriving, loading up, and roaring away in clouds of stinking exhaust.

Bunty introduced me to the office complex, which he called "the city center," with a proud, sweeping gesture. He took special pains to point out the local movie theater. Windows were broken and stuff was hanging out of the air ducts. I didn't see a marquee, but did notice a naked, unlit sign on the side of the building, where light tubes hung like dead gray snakes.

Bunty pointed out that, although the electricity was off for blocks around, Dadaji's battery-powered neon sign was still blazing away. We entered his glass-fronted office, where we faced an unmanned desk. It held nothing but a paperweight: a rose engulfed in clear plastic, embossed with the words "love through marriage." Toward the back of the long, narrow room, a matching living room set filled the space. No throw pillows, no carpet, no framed print on the wall, no knick-knacks, no vase of flowers, no end tables, no doilies, nothing like that, but by Indian standards, the living room was opulent, just for having an upholstered couch and matching chair. These furniture items were still partially covered with the torn plastic wrapping that proved they had once been factory-fresh. I would soon come to recognize such shreds of dirty plastic as status symbols.

As we entered, we were immediately engulfed in smoke. I looked at Bunty, ready to stop, drop, and roll, but he just smiled. A little butterball appeared through the haze, all dimpled and pink. She held out a tray of hot, fried paranthas.

"Eat!" she insisted.

We snacked and waited for the lights to come on. A filthy chai wallah, in the requisite filthy maroon vest, wandered through the gloom with his thermos. Then a stocky, mustached man, wearing an elegant suit, at least by Indian standards, bustled through the front doors--Dadaji. He shook our hands, bought chai from the wallah, and sent him on his way. The lights came on. Dadaji awkwardly spoke a few English words of greeting, then halted speech with a dour expression.

In Hindi, Bunty explained to him that I wanted an educated lady, someone under forty, and no kids.

"Virgin?" asked Dadaji.

I shrugged, "Not important."

"Good!"

Payment was complex. There was a membership fee, a 'first meeting' fee, another fee if I actually got married. Money for advertising, money for expenses, who knows what. Many forms had to be filled out. A real bureaucracy.

I suggested Dadaji get a profile on each lady before calling them in—recent portrait, spiritual affiliation, family background, age, that kind of thing. Weed out the unqualified applicants. I was thinking scientific method, progress, results. Applied Aristotelian logic.

"Yes, yes!" Dadaji beamed, his eyes alight with a strange fire. "Yes! Yes! Of course!"

After that meeting, I had to wait a few days for him to get the ball rolling. And anyway, I had a lot of time to kill. I still had a month's worth of dental appointments to make, so I was at loose ends. The rest of the week I spent as much time as I could at the Golden Temple.

The Golden Temple—its proper name is Harimandir Sahib—holds a special place in the heart of every Sikh. Its beauty and spiritual power are overwhelming and I felt privileged to be able to meditate there to my heart's content. Most of its visitors are Sikhs; still there are plenty of tourists--European, American, Japanese.

Most of the Sikhs who visit want to take a dip in the nectar pool. The pool is considered sacred and there are many stories of people being healed from different diseases by bathing therein. Men and boys strip down to underwear or swimsuits which are always modest. They change happily on the marble walkway using towels to preserve their modesty. For females there are plywood enclosures built by the side of the *sarovar* to give them complete seclusion as they change and dip.

After their dip, people walk around the marble causeway stopping at various points which have historical and spiritual associations, to offer prayers.

Inside the temple grounds, clean, white marble is everywhere, even though the dirty, sweltering, polluted, noisy city of Amritsar is right outside. Within the Golden Temple's sacred walls you can sit in silence, bathe at your leisure, and enjoy pleasant walks surrounded by beauty. It is crowded, sure—this is India and everything everywhere is always crowded—but this crowd is a respectful one, and mostly made up of Sikhs.

That week, I spent most evenings sitting and admiring the temple, enjoying the cool breeze off the nectar pool and the sacred music from inside the temple. One can only do so much meditating and I was looking for ways to pass my time. I decided to take on the role of gentleman tour guide. I would wander around, just enjoying the vibe, until eventually I would spy some good-looking tourist. She would be walking along, flipping through her guidebook.

"Hello! I noticed you look lost. Can I help?" I would ask.

"Oh! You . . . you're a Sikh?"

"Yes, yes. I'm a Sikh, from America."

"I . . . is this your job or something?"

"No, no, no! I'm just being friendly. Don't worry. I'm not Indian. Not looking for a tip!"

"Sorry."

"Not at all. Were you looking for the museum?"

We would invariably start chatting and I would tell her how I am whiling away time for a month while I get all this dental work done. She would then realize that I was legit, but also bored and looking for company. I don't care how tough a lady is, being a single female tourist in India is a very tricky business. You have to be constantly on your guard. Having a male companion who knows his way around is invaluable. So a guy like me—polite, knowledgeable, with time on my hands and plenty of money—I was the perfect tour guide.

I spent a few days honing my expertise at my newfound profession. It was easy enough. I developed a kind of standard Golden Temple tour. The most interesting part, for me, was when we got to the museum.

Sikhi has a great tradition of martyrdom and sacrifice, not only for the Sikh faith, but also for the protection of all faiths in India. The Sikhs are justifiably proud of this and various artists have immortalized the best known of these heroic deeds in paintings. The paintings tend to be rather graphic with lots of blood and gore. The Sikhs don't have a problem with this—in fact they are quite happy about it. To the unsuspecting Western tourist, especially of the female variety, the sight of these paintings was disconcerting to say the least.

Seeing some women's reactions to this stuff really made me realize that perhaps Sikhi doesn't have the universal appeal I had once thought.

Singh--the name given to all male Sikhs--means lion, and that sums up our culture: very forceful and aggressive. At least that was Yogiji's interpretation. He was like that to the core. Beyond forceful, really, just absolutely intimidating. He would say, "Send your children to Miri Piri Academy! Don't give me this bullshit about how you are attached to them! Be a good boy and do the right thing!" Or he would demand money, maybe your life savings, and act like you were a fool if you did not hand it over immediately. Yogiji never asked. He told. He ordered. That was his way. Then the next minute he would be smiling and laughing, hugging you and patting you on the back.

Yogiji was unlike any other spiritual teacher I have ever heard of. I remember when I was at the University of Oregon, I saw Ram Dass speak. Not the ancient Guru Ram Das, but the Harvard Professor, also known as Richard Alpert, who wrote "Be Here Now." He was too namby-pamby and touchy-feely for me. I could not get into him at all. I have also heard of this Indian teacher Ammachi, who goes around. She is what we in 3HO call a Jupiter teacher—all about hugs. People get in these mile-long lines to be hugged by her!

Not Yogiji. He was a Saturn teacher all the way. The people who gravitate to Ammachi may be soft New Age types, but those that followed Yogiji had to be confident, serious, dedicated. You had to have a lot of inner strength to have a tough teacher like that, and we were always proud of that.

chapter 12

Conducting these tours, I would get to enjoy some lady's company for an hour or two, just long enough to start fantasizing about marrying her, then she would go off to a new adventure and leave me with nothing better than a handshake. I enjoyed it though. I started to actually feel kind of suave. Me! A suave, single guy just picking up women left and right. I never would have imagined I could pull this off.

One day I met an attractive Japanese lady. I know what Japanese ladies like. It's simple: they like to shop until they drop. I began by impressing her with my smattering of Japanese, and things really took off from there. After touring the Golden Temple, she let me take her around the city to boutiques, restaurants, shopping malls, bazaars, you name it. For five straight days I met her at her hotel and took her somewhere new.

She helped me with my Japanese all this time, which improved my pronunciation a lot, and this also gave our relationship the feeling of a fair-trade arrangement—my tour-guiding services for her Japanese-teacher services. I was not sure if she was thinking about us romantically. I couldn't get a read on it, but I know I sure was. She did not exactly fit into my scheme of an Indian wife, but that's okay. She was exotic enough. I could have made it work. She had that very polite, very cute way about her that Japanese ladies have. It just kills me! As far as I'm concerned, Japan is paradise, real "mind candy."

Her name was Akemi, and I really saw a future there. On the

fifth day of our acquaintance, my cell phone rang a hole in my pocket. It rang 12 different times, but I was with Akemi, helping her barter for clothes in a loud, bustling bazaar, so I didn't bother to answer.

It was Dadaji.

As it turns out, a prospective bride had come from Chandigarh to meet me—four hours by train, then four hours by bus. Just like that, with no warning. Eventually, I dropped Akemi at her hotel, checked the messages, and took an auto rickshaw to Dadaji's, but the Chandigarh lady had left the office after waiting four hours. I guess four hours was her limit for everything.

Chandigarh was coming back the next day. I didn't know when, and I didn't want her to come. At this point, I felt like the whole idea of working with a marriage broker contradicted my new image as a suave, tour-guiding bachelor. It also broke my momentum with Akemi.

By the next morning, I wanted out of the whole arrangement, but felt obliged to meet the Chandigarh woman after she had come so far, *twice*. I called Akemi and tried to put her off for just one day, but she lost interest, said she was going to take the train to Delhi. That was the end of that.

Suddenly, I was sorry I had ever signed up with Dadaji! But anyway, I went in to meet this lady from Chandigarh.

Sobha Singh stops me. "Did you ask this Akemi to marry you?"

"No," I reply. "I didn't."

He throws up his hands in despair. "You let her get away!"

I sit cross-legged on my blanket, listening to the whining of mosquitoes and chirping of crickets as the bars of the cell make long, even shadows across the stained cement. Dusk comes upon Amritsar prison without much fanfare, and I find myself missing New Mexico's startling fuchsia sunsets. I smell the distant chance of rain. If it comes, it will truly be a mercy—washing away the perpetually airborne dust. I suspect the Punjab's famous monsoons will soon be upon us. I mention this to Sobha Singh, but he doesn't care. He still can't get over Akemi.

"Why didn't you ask her to marry you?" he demands.

"Well, it's just. . . western women don't do it that way. It takes more than five days. Except for the Sikhs, of course. If Yogiji had been there . . ."

"Yogiji this and Yogiji that! Can't you do anything without this Yogiji?"

I look at Sobha Singh, aghast. "He is my spiritual teacher," I reply. "His full title is Siri Singh Sahib Bhai Sahib Harbhajan Singh Khalsa Yogiji! (Yogiji had added a few embellishments to his name over the years) He is an ascended master, a mahan tantric, and the leader of Sikhi in the Western Hemisphere."

My friend harrumphs. "Never heard of him."

I can see in his eyes that Sobha Singh has never met Yogiji, never met anyone even remotely like him.

"I'm sorry for that," is all I can say.

"Yes, well, never mind. Continue, continue . . ."

So I do. I tell him about the women.

I sat in Dadaji's office, day after day, meeting the women that came in an endless river. His assistant, Alok, cooked for me upstairs. That way I didn't have to take a lunch break. All day long, she fried everything in the world and shrouded the place in smoke. With the hot peppers she threw in, it was like mustard gas, but the food was great.

I developed a crush on Alok. She was completely roly-poly. She was always smiling and laughing, but also smart and opinionated. She would boss me and Dadaji around.

During a typical interview, Alok would stand in the doorway, dimples engaged, arms crossed over her ample breasts, impatiently muttering, "What's it going to be? Marriage or no? Move it along!"

I asked Dadaji about her, but he said she was engaged to be married. Damn. I actually caught myself wondering if the engagement could be broken. I wanted that girl and I wanted her now! It's embarrassing, but I frequently catch myself thinking like this.

Perhaps it's the legacy of the British Raj that causes many Indians to become deferential and obsequious when they see a white face. Black is not beautiful in India, and no one pretends it is. Lighter skin is associated with higher caste and, tragically, caste is still everything. Maybe it was ego that caused me to believe that these women were genuinely impressed with my looks. I started to believe that my beard had a lot to do with it.

Most Punjabi men aren't baptized Sikhs, they're just born into it. Their grasp of the beliefs is tenuous and they do not recite the *Banis*, our prayers. They just wear long hair out of custom or perhaps habit, and many cut their beards. Some shave, some trim, and some wear their beards long and uncut, but gather them up in these little nets that go over each ear and under the chin. Some grow their beards but tie them in a knot, for convenience's sake. With my long beard hanging straight and proud, I stand for a lost way of life to a lot of these Punjabis, I really do.

This is the traditional, spiritual way of life that Yogi Bhajan brought back with 3HO. Yoga, prayers, *Banis*, chanting, and the strength of the Sikh warrior. I am proud of who I am and what I represent. I don't mind wearing my beliefs on my sleeve. In fact, I like it. It is why I figured some of these Punjabi parents might want me to marry their daughters. They might see me as a bona-fide, white-hatted "good guy" out of a Sunday matinee. A sure thing. That was what I was hoping for. In America, my look garners stares and whispers, but in India I got nothing but respect everywhere I went—before the arrest, that is. I got used to it.

As a white Sikh in India it's easy to think you deserve to cut to the front of every line, and get the freshest mango in the cart. Waiters fought each other over who got to serve me. Mad dogs kept their distance from me. And the people in the street, amid their daily comings and goings, they just stared, stared, stared—went home and told their families about me and my white skin, turban, and long grey beard, and probably got called liars.

The first actual candidate to show up at Dadaji's was a lady named Mehpreet. She couldn't speak English, and there I was without an interpreter.

"Dadaji," I said, "What's going on? The applicants should be educated and speak English!"

"She is speak English! Lady is saying she is speaking English!"

"When?

"On the telephone!"

"Did you talk to her in English?"

Dadaji shrugged and turned away. I got it. He barely spoke English himself, so how could he be the judge?

Alok ran upstairs to another business in the complex and brought down a girl, Kushi, from a travel agency. She was nineteen, cute, and very flirtatious. How could I even keep my head on straight? She tried really hard to translate for us, but her English wasn't much better than Dadaji's. Eventually, we all cracked up. I hadn't laughed so hard in a year. We ate some paranthas together, then Mehpreet left, laughing out the door.

Hell, with her sense of humor, Mehpreet might have been the best of the bunch. And Kushi? I could have gone for her, too, but she skipped back upstairs and out of my life.

Dadaji had a sign painter whose job was to go around and paint advertisements on the grimy, poured-cement walls of various buildings around Amritsar. The latest sign said, "American born Gursikh boy, age 50." Then just DADAJI. Everyone knew who he was and where to find him.

Every day, they came.

chapter 13

Dadaji didn't screen the women. He just let them come, day after day. Many were terribly, terribly sad.

One lady came with her sister and son. The trio waited hours for me one day, but I was off somewhere. So they went to the Golden Temple and prayed and came back and waited some more. The patience of these people is unbelievable. It is supernatural.

They brought back *prasad*, a religious offering—a sweet cereal wrapped in moist green leaves. When I arrived, the woman bowed her head and handed it to me in a humble, ceremonial way. I was touched. Then she started crying.

"Please, sir. I am not divorced. I am not a divorced lady. I am not married also. I am abandoned. I had one husband. I was married at age twenty-one, and my husband went to Italy for a job. Then I had my son. He is here."

Her son was there with her, and he was such a good boy, too. Very polite, very quiet and sweet.

"My husband never came back. I raised my son by myself, with my parents. It has been ten years and my husband is gone. He is completely gone. I am a good wife. I gave him no cause to leave me. Please believe me. My son is a good son. Please marry me. Please!"

She and her son were trying to live a spiritual life, against the odds, in spite of the poor woman's disgrace. She told me they prayed every day, made offerings at the Golden Temple as often as they could get into the city. I believed her, too. She was very, very sincere.

"PLEASE don't reject me," she pleaded. "PLEASE!"

But she was too sad. I just couldn't take it.

There were so many other ladies, too. Some were obnoxious as hell. They acted like they had won me at a county fair, and why wouldn't I just come along peacefully?

Dadaji would always prep me, saying, "This one is coming with a very good family. Hi Fi! Hi Fi!"

Hi Fi. I just kept thinking of a loud stereo that you couldn't turn off.

Another lady, Dadaji proudly announced that she was Hi Fi and also "a fatty." Punjabis are well fed and proud of it, so they call someone who is a little chubby, "healthy" or if they're really overweight, "a fatty."

There she was. A real fatty.

"I'm a politician," she said. "The best politician in the Punjab!"

"Oh?"

"Haven't you seen my name on signs?"

By then, I had learned to ask each woman to write her name on a sheet of paper, to see if she was literate. Some of the village ladies just looked at the paper like it was cow dung.

This fatty, she took the paper and wrote me an essay about her political career, aspirations, family, material possessions, everything.

Then, when Dadaji wasn't listening, she whispered, "Give me your phone number."

A piece of time passes. I don't know how long it is. It feels like a day. For me, the sun sets, darkness comes, the sun rises again, and the world remembers again to suffocate me with heat, shower me with dust, and overwhelm me with ever-smiling nonsense. I take a deep breath and say, "No, thank you."

People die in India, left and right. They are always dying, and will die at any age, just like that. A guy gets a little sick, or hit by a car, and boom, he is dead. Frequently, the survivors blame his wife for putting a curse on the house and ostracize her completely. They might as well shoot her in the head, for all the chance she has at survival. So there are a lot of young widows out on the street, or living off the charity of relatives, and they are utterly lost.

One woman was only 28, but a widow. A village girl, uneducated, with clothes about 30 years behind the times. She came with her brother, who was dressed completely in red. Red turban, red shirt, red pants! A gaudy gold necklace swung from his neck like a Crackerjack prize. He turned out to be a physician, with perfect English.

His sister and her two kids had moved in with his family, so the doctor was anxious to unload her. He kept interrupting our conversation to holler out her best qualities.

"What a cook! You should taste her chapattis!"

"She is really obedient, this girl. She'll do whatever you say! I promise!"

Eventually, the brother took me aside for a man-to-man.

"Listen," he said. "You're a good Sikh. A good man. You know the right thing to do."

I stood there, choking on Alok's cooking smoke, as usual.

He started speaking really slowly, like I might have been a little retarded. "All . . . You . . . Have . . . To . . . Do . . . . is marry her!"

Another day, a lady showed up at Dadaji's office with no one in tow but her sister. This meant she hadn't a single living male relative—a desperate state of affairs. But this sister had perfect English and a master's in business. She was a real go-getter.

What a saleswoman!

"Why don't you marry her? Give me one good reason not to," the sister demanded.

I stammered that I planned to meet a variety of women before I made up my mind. But that wasn't good enough for her.

"Give me one specific reason why not!"

"She's a very nice lady, but I'd like to think about it for a couple of days."

"That's no problem. Go ahead. . . *Then* you'll marry her?"

She was a born closer, this woman.

Once you say yes, that's it. If you don't follow through, they can bring a lawsuit—have you arrested, humiliated, cast out of society. No joke.

I said I would like her sister to learn some English.

"Learn English? No problem! That's all? You can teach her English; she can teach you Punjabi. That's nothing. Okay, let's do it!"

This went on into the night.

A 50-year-old Hindu lady was there one day, escorted by a servant. She was dripping with gold chains and jabbering on, in English, about how rich she was. As it turned out, she wasn't even single—she and her husband were only separated. That didn't seem to be an issue for her, though. What she wanted me to do was escort her to Europe.

"What security do I have that you won't divorce me, huh?" she nagged.

I replied that if I decided to marry her, she would have my word.

"Oh, no," she replied, "I want you to deposit ten lakh rupees in my account before I marry you!"

That's about $28,000.

Dadaji tried to hurry these kinds of women along, saying, "Do you really want to talk to her? Let's get rid of her!" But I was having the cultural experience of a lifetime. I wanted to meet them all: the rude, the sick, the sad, the desperate, the young, the old, everyone. They were my way into India. Their lives formed a bridge that took me far beyond anything that could be found in the Lonely Planet handbook, and even far beyond anything I had experienced on Yogi

Bhajan's guided "spiritual tours." These interviews took me right into the true grit of the Punjab—the Sikh Holy Land.

Looking back it's hard for me to believe that I could be so detached in the face of all these emotional people with their unrealistic expectations of how their lives might change because of me. It was like I was the center of an Indian TV soap opera, only this was real. I still feel sad when I remember the pain of these women and their families.

chapter 14

In the midst of my interviews with would-be wives, I was still meeting with my dentist periodically to get major dental work done, and that dentist chair did a number on me. Pretty soon, my neck was in agony, so I found a physiotherapist who could work on me with one of those electrical stimulation machines. His was a clean, private office that was reasonably hi-tech, with lab-coated assistants, magazines in the waiting room, and modern equipment. By Indian standards, he must have been making a mint.

My physiotherapist, Dr. Jagdesh, was Hindu, had an enormous half-moon of a smile in his full-moon of a face and spoke perfect English. Of course, he wanted to know what I was doing in India and how I had become a Sikh, so the first time we met, we talked for hours. Meanwhile, a queue of patients waited—just waiting, waiting, waiting with that infinite Indian patience that defies all Earthly forces.

When I told him about Dadaji and the women, Dr. Jagdesh perked right up. He didn't care about the women I met at Dadaji's, but started grilling me about the ones I met at the Golden Temple. He wanted to know more about western ladies.

Dr. Jagdesh was married but cheating on his wife, which he considered no big deal. The thing he did feel guilty about was the fact that his wife was a devout Hindu and he, secretly, was an atheist. He constantly worried she would discover this terrible secret. Dr. Jagdesh had an Indian girlfriend who lived in America, he was always bragging to me about, but his greatest dream of life was to go on a sex tourism spree to Thailand. For some reason, he just assumed

I would be up for joining him in this. I humored the guy. He was disgusting, but he was nice to me and never overcharged me or tried to scam me in any way. That alone was enough to make someone a friend in my eyes. Over the next few weeks, I met with him many times. Finally, Dr. Jagdesh invited me to his house for dinner.

His house wasn't much more than a little concrete bunker—a typical urban Indian row house. There were shabby, blue-flowered curtains hanging from the interior doorways, instead of doors, and just one window, directly on the street, accessing a bedroom. The living room was in the middle of the house, like a courtyard. A grate in the ceiling let sunshine in, as well as rain during the monsoons, I presume. This central area was furnished with a couple of hard wooden beds, a clothesline, a small television, a plastic chair, and a bougainvillea. Strings hanging from the ceiling supported the scrawny plant's snaking tendrils.

To receive the Jagdesh family's hospitality, the idea was to sit cross-legged on one of the beds in the living room as his wife served her husband and me little stainless-steel plates of spicy eggplant and fresh, warm, unleavened bread, called chapattis. I loved the way the two of us could sit there discussing politics, religion, business matters, or anything in the world while getting served, just like in a restaurant.

Then, on another silver tray, she served us tiny cups of chai and little white sweets for dessert. The sense of hospitality was great. A little formal, but not too much. I liked the tray. It lent a little pomp and circumstance to each simple offering. Unlike any American woman who was ever born, his wife did not resent any of this. It was just a normal day for her. I met his grown son and daughter-in-law as well, who lived with them, in the traditional way. After being introduced, they sat on the other bed, watched the TV, and ignored us.

The sense of family, the sense that everyone knew exactly where they stood in the pecking order, really impressed me. I loved that his wife had that quiet grace and confidence Yogi Bhajan had always talked about. And the fact that Dr. Jagdesh and I could sit and peacefully talk about our businesses and concerns, all with the support of his wife and kids who held down the home front but did not insist on being included—it was just as Yogiji had always said men should live! To me, it was like a beautiful dream.

With its cracked concrete walls half-heartedly smeared in stained, faded, yellow paint, it wasn't much of a home front, but that is the Indian style. I was not so much concerned with the aesthetics of the thing as I was with the nature of the relationships. I have never been particularly good at the intricate dance of gentle words and simple gestures that somehow keeps people together, so, to me, the situation was fascinating.

Over the next few weeks, I saw Dr. Jagdesh often—sometimes for help with my neck, sometimes I would just stop in for the hell of it. He would make his patients wait while we sat in the office and talked about everything from the bizarre sexual maneuvers he was desperate to try with a Thai prostitute to my adventures with Dadaji and the marriage candidates. He always advised me to stop what I was doing with Dadaji, to just quit meeting the women. He would lecture me on the sanctity of marriage, on how Indians don't go in for divorce and that I should not expect to be able to just end this third marriage with the facility that I ended the other two. He was very concerned about me.

"You must stop, Guru *Sant* Singh. You must!" he would say.

"But why?"

"Dadaji is playing with you! You are going to get yourself into serious trouble!"

"Oh, Dr. Jagdesh, it's nothing! These women want to meet me and I want to meet them! What's the harm?"

Once, Dr. Jagdesh leaned across his desk at me, his head shaking almost imperceptibly from side to side. "Marriage," he said, "isn't a thing you play around with. Not in India. It's serious business."

"It's fun for me!" I replied. I knew I sounded flip, childish. It wasn't what I meant, but at the time, "fun" was the only word I could use to describe the fact that these women were stripping away illusions about India that I had worshipped for decades.

"Watch your ass!" Dr. Jagdesh said, "Marriage isn't supposed to be fun!" Then he changed the subject back to his American mistress and his dream of the Thai prostitutes.

"Marriage is a serious lifestyle," he told me once. "I make money and hand it over to my wife. I don't even know how much it is. She manages everything. The household, the food, the kids. All I have to do is work, then go home . . . whenever I like. I get treated like a king. All the money is hers to spend, like a queen! But no matter what, Guru *Sant* Singh, we won't divorce. Never!"

"Perfect!" I said. "That's what I want! A manager!"

Though neither of my previous wives had been willing to work with me like that, I knew what it was like. After all, my dad had had it. As far as I could tell, the arrangement had been sheer perfection, until my parents' divorce that is, but even that had been his doing, not hers.

chapter 15

When I was a kid, dad was a deacon at the Church of Christ, on Town Avenue. I loved the place. Everyone had a smile for me. Everyone knew me. We had church socials and picnics and pancake breakfasts. My mom sang in the choir, and man did she ever sing beautifully. I mean just thinking about her singing "I'm washed in the blood of the lamb" or ringing out something else around the house, just any old time, oh man, it's a great memory. Good old Mom. She was the ultimate housewife and just lived for me and my brother. A typical fifties mom, really. In those days it was always "Father knows best," and Mom went along with that, no problem at all.

According to the Christian belief system, Dad was closer to God. He filtered the information down to Mom, and she followed it to the letter. Us kids did as we were told, and if we fell out of line, we got beaten with a belt. Once Dad beat me senseless. Utterly senseless. I don't even remember what it was for.

Then, when I discovered 3HO, in my twenties, I learned Yogiji's system. It was different from Dad's, and seemed better, kinder to me. Yogiji's system was based on the fact that women are smarter than men, but men have to give them spiritual guidance. Conveniently, in the old days, if any couples got in an argument, they just brought their issues to Yogiji and he sorted everything out for them. Told them what to do! Now that he is dead, I don't know what people do. Some folks consult our holy book, the *Siri Guru Granth Sahib*, some consult the 3HO leaders currently vying for Yogiji's place. Me, I got divorced!

Since we don't have kids together, the divorce from Sat Siri Kaur was reasonably uncomplicated. Her son, K.P., is from her first marriage, and by the time we got divorced, K.P. was living on his own. But even if we had had young children, they wouldn't have been around to be traumatized by a divorce. The children in 3HO are sent off to this special boarding school in India, called Miri Piri Academy. That way they learn a stronger allegiance to Yogi Bhajan, God, and Sikhi principles than to their earthly parents. There, they learn reading, writing, and arithmetic, but also Sikh martial arts, Sikh history, Sikh spirituality, Kundalini Yoga, meditation, and, of course, all about Yogi Bhajan. His portrait hangs in the entrance hall of the school, looking down on all his little spiritual prodigies.

In a typical situation, the parents don't see the kids that often, so discipline is not really an issue for most parents. I know Sat Siri Kaur never concerned herself with it, as far as K.P. was concerned.

Yogiji really harped on the importance of sending the children away at a very young age—five or six years old, if possible. He always said the children were not our children, but the children of the Guru. He believed it was a big mistake for kids to form too strong an attachment to their earthly parents. He pushed these ideas very strongly, just like he pushed everything. He was so intense about it; I would say he definitely forced people.

I don't know what it was really like for the kids at Miri Piri. Many of the kids who went there are now grown and have some real horror stories. Stuff like inadequate food, overly harsh discipline, drinking, drugs, bullying and sexual abuse from some of the guardians. Some of the kids have serious psychological problems and many of them are very angry about their "spiritual" upbringing.

K.P. had a pretty bad time of it there, but he was a mess. His father had left 3HO and then spent years lecturing the kid on how he didn't approve of our lifestyle and since Sat Siri Kaur and K.P.'s dad shared custody, K.P. was torn between their constant fighting. Looking back, it seems K.P. sided more with his Dad's anti-Yogi Bhajan views. At Yogiji's Miri Piri Academy, K.P. was expelled for secretly taking a midnight train with some other kids to an undisclosed location in order to hide from the school's wardens. K.P. had been doing fine in Santa Fe schools before Miri Piri.

I am not sure what caused K.P. to go astray but I do know that 3HO kids surely had missed out on the kind of fun I had as a child. When we were little, my brother and I went to church camp every summer. It was great. Just typical camp stuff. We would run around outdoors for hours, then come inside and have arts and crafts with glue and cotton balls and, I don't know, popsicle sticks or something. We swam in the lake, rowed canoes, and played games of capture the flag. Fun stuff. I mean being raised Christian was great. I was very into it. Especially because one time I had this really intense experience of Christ.

What happened was, I was playing some game, trying to get a stick to whirl around by wrapping a string around it, then pulling. Well it flew up, spinning, and hit me in both my eyes. I was blinded! The doc at the infirmary said we would just have to wait and see what happened. I couldn't see a thing. It was terrible.

That night, my cabin mates took my hand and led me, stumbling along, to prayer meeting. It was the usual thing we had twice a week, and kids were getting into it—vowing to accept Jesus as their savior. Kids were crying, adults were crying, everyone was consumed with the passion. That is the way it usually went, but it seemed special every time. After all that crying and vowing and praying and surrendering and stuff, there was this intense feeling of family among us all. Anyway, I was blind and I felt my way from pew to pew and went forward before the congregation. I went forward to make Jesus my savior. Tears were streaming, streaming, streaming.

Suddenly I could see! The healing power of the risen Christ had healed me! I would swear it on a stack of bibles, I really would. Everyone came up and hugged me and said it was a miracle. Well, especially after that, Jesus was definitely the man for me. I promised him my everlasting soul many, many times.

Later, when I became disillusioned with the hypocrisy surrounding my church, I decided to release myself from these promises.

The end of it all was when I got kicked out of Texas Christian University for being a rebel. I hated the hypocrisy there. The "higher-ups" in the administration praised God even while they tried to suppress the underground newspaper I ran. I guess I had been affected by all the duplicity I had seen—both at my church and here at a supposedly "Christian" university and I was determined to expose hypocrisy and untruth wherever I saw it. Christianity and "doing good" had lost its charm for me.

But those early days, as a kid, they had been great. Just surrendering to Jesus. Trusting the church with every fiber of my being. I loved the feeling. Jesus was all there was for me, for Mom and Dad, for my whole family, and everything. That's the kind of family feeling I would like to recreate, with me as the head, just like Dad was. Only this time, a Sikh family. A Sikh wife. That's pretty close to what my vision is.

chapter 16

In the course of meeting Dadaji's many candidates for marriage, I found that sometimes the mother would come alone, to feel me out, before dragging along her progeny. That was the case with Lovleen Kaur.

I had brought a scrapbook in my suitcase. I remember feeling silly when I packed it, since I had no idea if I would ever even get to meet a lady or anything, but I was optimistic as usual. It had everything from pictures of my childhood to newspaper clippings about me to my vacation photos from Japan. I pulled it out to show the candidates I particularly liked.

Lovleen Kaur's mother got really interested in that, especially when she saw all my military awards. That was nice. The damn things were finally good for something.

She also spent a lot of time looking at my Golden Temple portraits. I had paid a guy to take a couple snaps of me meditating on the *parikarma* in front of the Golden Temple. There I was, all in white, with my beard flowing down, and the temple gleaming in the background, giving me a heavenly, 24-karat aura. I am serene, devout, trustworthy. I am the very man you want your daughter to marry. That was the idea, anyway. I had another shot of me without my turban, so Lovleen's mom could see how long my hair was. She was impressed by that. I also showed her some thirty-year-old snapshots of my mom and dad. The pictures are pre-divorce, and they are smiling and proud in front of their suburban home, with its white picket fence and perfect lawn. I think these shots were probably what finally convinced her I was "the one."

So Lovleen's mom went away and told her husband, and he came along a few days later. Seven hours on a bus. He saw the same things and liked them. I liked him, too. Their family seemed very devout. Honest farmers from a village, but educated. The most interesting thing was that they loved their daughter enough to do all this legwork. I was touched.

Ten days and thirty women later, the man returned with his daughter, a child of 18. Very cute. She could have had her pick of young, wealthy husbands, but she had one problem: she was already a widow. Used goods.

I was frank, "Lovleen Kaur, you're very cute. I do find you attractive, but why would you want to marry me? I'm fifty years old!"

I could see the shock register on her face, but her father said it was okay, so she did a one-eighty.

"Yeah! Let's go! Let's marry!" she said.

I imagined going to bed with her. Her parents' pleading eyes encouraged me to continue that train of thought.

Good God, I had to get out of there! I leaped up and started gathering my bags. She jumped off the couch and ran to my side.

"Can I help you with anything? Anything at all?"

I nearly knocked the poor kid down as I sprinted out the door.

Meeting Lovleen Kaur was scary. I mean, the very idea that someone was offering me a willing eighteen-year-old . . . it felt deeply wrong. But then again, they wanted me to take her. And in a certain sense, she wanted it too. More specifically, what she really wanted, more than anything, was to be humble before God and serviceful to her father.

That incredible humility is such an Indian trait and so incomprehensible to most westerners, I think. It comes from centuries of spiritual teaching which is uniquely Indian. At the same time Indian culture—especially Punjabi culture—is driven by *izzat* (family honor) and *haumay* (personal pride). Punjabis can totally change their attitude from one minute to the next. Like Dadaji, for example. One minute he would be issuing commands in an imperious voice; seconds later he would be the epitome of obsequiousness.

Both America and India are ego-driven cultures—and India is making great strides to catch up with the US. The difference is that few Americans can comprehend that crucial factor of Indian culture: total humility in service to God and family. Yogiji tried to teach us that and in many ways he succeeded. He taught us to be obedient in such a way that most of us, even when what he was teaching or doing was clearly wrong, acquiesced to his commands.

But imagine what the ashramites in Española would say if I brought Lovleen Kaur home as my bride! Oh God, I would never live it down. Meanwhile, to her parents, the union was perfectly logical. They just wanted to ensure she would be well-cared for. I am not a violent man. I had not made any unreasonable demands. It worked for them. Of course, I am not the handsome young prince Lovleen Kaur probably once dreamed of, but once she became a widow, she probably stopped dreaming at all. She was probably just glad her village didn't stone her. Still, the American in me couldn't marry a kid like that. I just knew no good could come of it.

Day after day, I met more women. It made me feel important—like I was a shrink and they were coming to tell me their troubles. They would pour out their life stories and always finish with a plea:

"Please take me away! My husband beats me every day!"

"Take my one-legged daughter please! I can't afford to feed her anymore!"

"I have come three days on a bus. Please marry me. I am here now, and you can marry me. I have brought my things."

I really wanted to help. Honest to God. I couldn't marry all of them, after all, and frankly all their pain and sadness was starting to affect me. All I could think of to do was to recycle some of the spiritual clichés I had heard so many times from Yogiji.

"Look, the Guru is in your heart. Don't you see that? Look inside yourself for happiness! Be strong and self-reliant!"

In answer, one woman dropped to her knees, touched my feet, and began anew her litany of sorrows.

"I am nothing but a widow, kind sir. Please have pity on me. Please marry me. I will be a good wife for you. I will do all that you ask."

I wasn't expecting that type of reaction. I felt even more unsettled. So I decided to keep things simpler. "Always remember, the Guru is in your heart! The Guru is in your heart!"

In the West, "guru" has become a word that can be tossed around and used like any other. We have Investment Gurus, Political Gurus, Golf Gurus. All it means to Americans is someone who knows their specialty better than most. In India "guru" still carries a huge charge, particularly amongst the Sikhs. There is even a word *nigura*. It means someone who doesn't have a guru and even today some people will not associate with a *nigura*.

Guru is a particularly important word to Sikhs; after all the founder of Sikhi was *Guru* Nanak. He was succeeded by nine more saintly beings (one of whom was only a child during his reign). At some point the guruship became hereditary, passing to the most deserving son. The tenth master, Guru Gobind Singh, lost all his four sons to the Mughal oppressors. When the time came for him to leave his body, the Sikhs asked him who would be his successor.

Guru Arjun, the fifth guru, had collected the spiritual writings of the first four gurus, to which he added his own. Uniquely amongst world religions, Guru Arjun had included writings by Hindu, Islamic and Sufi saints to this volume. The book was known as *Adi Granth Sahib* (Revered Primal Book). Guru Gobind Singh, who had added his father's compositions to the *Adi Granth,* commanded that this volume would henceforth be the Guru for all Sikhs, and so it became known as *Siri Guru Granth Sahib.*

Thus, instead of a human guru, we Sikhs have a written Guru to guide us without the prejudices and failings that might be part of any mortal man. A leader like Yogi Bhajan could only be a spiritual teacher in the Sikh tradition, never a Guru.

When I talked about the Guru to these Sikh women they all knew I was talking about *Siri Guru Granth Sahib.*

I would say all this stuff and the women would smile demurely. Probably they were just thinking about going home and cooking up some chapattis, but I thought maybe it helped them. I thought I might be doing a little good for once.

I wanted to so desperately.

chapter 17

In the early eighties, NLP was big in Oregon. Neuro-Linguistic Programming, also known as hypnosis therapy. People used it to quit smoking, lose weight, overcome depression, all that kind of thing. It's very effective, but also a type of mental manipulation, so it can be used for anything. A salesman can use it to make customers want to buy. A politician can use it. A con man. Anyone. I had been at the Oregon ashram a year or so when Sat Kir*pal* Singh decided someone in 3HO should learn NLP. It was just the type of thing that was sure to come in handy for 3HO's altruistic scheme toward world domination. He didn't know why, exactly. He just had a feeling. So I took the course in Santa Cruz California where I was certified by the original NLP founders, Richard Bandler and John Grinder.

Pretty soon, I started thinking I could become a counselor, a brilliant psychologist. I could do good. Save people from themselves. For the first time since I was a kid in Christian camp, I really felt it in me: God. God's love. Love for humanity. The desire to help, to serve others, to do *seva.*

"So, Guru *Sant* Singh. You are a counselor. A man who helps others," says Amrik Singh through the dense, inky darkness of the night-time jail cell. "That is very good. You are a good man, I think!"

I appreciate his faith in me, but have to admit I never really did work as a counselor. Quite the opposite.

"No, Amrik Singh, I'm what's called a con man and a gambler." I tell him outright, though a bit shamefaced.

I moved from Eugene to L.A. with the intent of joining the central 3HO ashram, being closer to Yogiji, and helping people with NLP. In L.A., I was granted another audience with the great man, during which, like some eager freshman, I told him about all the good I planned to do in the world.

Yogi Bhajan shocked me by saying, "A counselor? Bah! You'll never make any money at that! Go work at GRD!" He dismissed me. It was always about money with Yogiji. Soon, I was out on the concrete, in the piercing L.A. sunshine, head spinning. A pair of joggers huffed past in matching pastel outfits. Palm trees looked down on me like demi-gods. I looked at the slip of paper he had handed me before I left. It said "Hari Jiwan Singh," and had a phone number on it. I went home and called it.

Hari Jiwan Singh ran the boiler room at GRD, or "Guru Ram Das Enterprises." This guy was unbelievably rich. A Jewish guy. I mean, he was a converted Sikh, like me, but damn if he wasn't a Jew—his voice, mannerisms, personality—all pure New York Jew, even though he was apparently from the Mid-West.

I met Hari Jiwan Singh at GRD Enterprises, which was just a basement full of telephones and Sikhs—what they call a "boiler room." During my interview, Hari Jiwan Singh asked me if I had sales experience.

Did I ever.

By the age of fifteen I had the beard of a lumberjack. I looked enough like an adult, so Dad got me working in his mobile home dealership. A young couple came in and made me an offer on a trailer. It sounded good. My first commission! It was a terrible deal. I robbed my dad blind accepting that offer, but he didn't care. He saw my eyes light up at the cash, and knew I was hooked. In no time at all, I became a real hustler. By sixteen I was dodging taxes with property investments in Mexico. Seriously.

Dad was one of those Christians who idolize the whole prosperity movement; "bear fruit and multiply" or something like that. His philosophy was to make people happy with the mobile home they bought and then provide excellent service so they'd tell their family and friends and then they'd come and buy more. To that end he worked hard and long. Dad may have cut a few corners on his tax returns and used a bit of high pressure tactics with a few of his sales prospects, but he was honest in his dealings with his customers and that was my idea of how business should be.

With his support and guidance I became just a bitch of a salesman.

***

Hari Jiwan Singh put me right to work. Yogi Bhajan would frequently visit the office and always leave us with this cryptic statement: "Remember, there's no karma on the telephone!" I took it as God's truth and put my conscience under wraps.

I do my shtick for Amrik Singh and Sobha Singh:

"Ma'am? Hello, my name's Bob Robertson. I'm a Vietnam veteran with a record of distinguished service. In fact, I lost both my legs in the war. . . That's right, Ma'am. Thank you, and you're welcome. . . You're very, very welcome. . . I'm working for Golden Circle Products now, and I was wondering if I could interest your company in purchasing several boxes of our copier toner? It's a high quality product. The Golden Circle brand isn't well known as of yet, but we are considered a 'company to watch' by Fortune 500 magazine. . . Oh, don't worry about the cost, you can just bill it to your company. Everyone needs office supplies! And I'll tell you what, if you give me your home address, I'll send you a new TV set just for ordering a year's supply of products from Golden Circle. After all, you'll need to order them eventually anyway! . . . Now what was that address? Can I put you down for six cases of typewriter ribbons too? And what about ball point pens? I bet you're already running low on those! . . . Ouch! Oh, that was nothing. I just felt a twinge in my left stump. It happens sometimes. Now, where were we?"

The toner cartridges and typewriter ribbons were ten times the price they could buy them for in their local office supply store. In the late 90's when I worked with Harijiwan Singh (Yogi Bhajan's other "right-hand man"), who was later dubbed "The Toner Bandit", we would change the name of the company every couple of weeks from names like Central Office Supply to Central Distribution etc. When we racked up huge phone bills we would just change from AT&T to MCI or Sprint and then put the account under the new company name in order to avoid paying the bills. No one could track us. I was a genius with that type of stuff.

I certainly had my doubts about the morality of the whole thing, but I was so good at it, I figured it was meant to be.

There was a girl I had a crush on at the time. Unfortunately, she turned out to be off-limits, as she was one of Yogi Bhajan's secretaries, who were all celibate—or so we were told. I told her about GRD and asked what she thought of it all.

"If Yogiji condones it, then why question? His consciousness is Krishna consciousness," she said. "Anything done in the name of Krishna is OK." Yeah! So I went with that.

Our whole organization was changing. We had started off trying to be Healthy, Happy, Holy. Now money became the priority. Even though our morning *sadhana* (spiritual practice) from 4 to 7am was still considered the most important part of our day we salesman were excused at 5am to take advantage of cheaper calling rates to the East Coast where school offices were open at 8am. The whole emphasis of saving the world through our yoga and Yogiji's teachings shifted to "make money, make LOTS of money." And, if the methodology was unethical at best and nauseating to anyone with the slightest sense of morality, well it was OK, provided you were sending your *dasvand* (tithe) to Yogiji.

Sobha Singh laughs at this. "You are a real hustler, my friend!"

I never needed to use NLP to work my magic. The hustle came naturally to me.

With forty-nine women down, I was looking forward to making it an even fifty. What the hell. But first, my cash was starting to run low, so I placed a call to my stateside lawyer, John Aragon.

The financial situation between Sat Siri Kaur and myself was—to say the least—a bit of a mess. Despite the divorce, we still owned a couple of homes together. We also owned a huge strip of property in New Mexico, on the intersection with two major highways, north of Santa Fe.

In 2007, the governor decided to widen the highway, so the state was expected to seize that strip of land and pay us compensation. Before I left, Sat Siri Kaur had agreed that once the case was settled, which should happen while I'm in India, we would divide the money evenly between us. That is why, all the time I have been in India, I have been throwing around cash like candy at Mardi Gras. On the phone, I asked Aragon if the case was settled yet, but he said no. I just had to wait.

The news got me cranky, and I took it out on Dadaji. I had been pissed off at him for a while, anyway. As far as the marriage angle, I just wanted an educated woman between thirty and forty, with most of her teeth and decent looks. I wasn't asking for the moon, but he could not seem to come up with this simple thing. Instead, he had me meeting every gypsy in town. Ninety percent of them didn't even speak English. How could I make wives out of them? It was ridiculous.

"Can't you get a profile? A photo? Some basic information before they come? Make a form for them to fill out. It's easy!" I told him.

I thought it was Matchmaker International. You know: videos, testimonials, essays about yourself. Everything on file.

What the hell did I know? This is India. There are no videos, for God's sakes. There are no files! Except in the police department. Their files go way back.

"Let them come!" Dadaji would say. "If they want to take the chance on meeting you, then let them come! What's the harm?"

In the end, it did not take much for Dadaji to get me back on board. After all, the Punjab was my spiritual motherland, and I wanted to get to know it. If I call myself a Sikh, why shouldn't I? And if the ladies had to travel a couple of days to meet me? Spend long hours on buses without upholstered seats or shocks of any kind, getting hemorrhoids and tiny fractures in their tail bones? Spend their life savings on a train ride from Delhi? Even if they couldn't speak English? Even if they had six kids already? It was reminiscent of working with Hari Jiwan. All I had to do was put my conscience on ice and blot out any thoughts of the effects my actions would have on other people, particularly sad, lonely women with enough problems already. Of course, for spiritual people, the Universe generally gives you enough rope to be able to hang yourself. I didn't realize I was about to get hung out to dry.

Dadaji was so much like Yogi Bhajan. Pushy, pushy, pushy. He pushed his viewpoint on me so hard it would have been murder to resist it, so I'm ashamed to say I did the easiest thing. I went along. It was just so easy to get swept up in marriage fever.

"Let them come. What else have they got to do?" Dadaji used to say.

"Yeah," I'd reply, laughing and eating another parantha. "What else?"

chapter 18

One day, before my first wife, Prem Kaur, and I were married, we were standing in the Los Angeles Gurdwara, flirting. Yogi Bhajan passed by, so I asked him if I could marry her, right in front of her, like I was asking for a pencil. She looked at me like I was an idiot, but ended up marrying me anyway. I never took her out to one candlelit dinner, a show, dancing, or any of that, that's not my style. So at Dadaji's office, as I continued my surreal search for wife number three by doing formal interviews, I felt pretty ridiculous, but it was as good a technique as I have ever had. Thank God for arranged marriages.

The Indian belief is that one arranges a marriage for money, convenience, and family status, and then love grows based on familiarity. In India, a woman cannot just strike out on her own and get an apartment, and a man hasn't any social status until he is married, so the arrangement keeps the couple together, for a while at least, based upon mutual need. Despite the fact that American society is totally different, Yogiji attempted to use this tried and true system to make finding a mate easy for us in 3HO. I, for one, appreciated it! No lengthy courtship period was necessary. At ashrams in San Francisco, Chicago, Tallahassee, Boston—wherever he traveled—he would just tell people whom to marry. Within days, it would be taken care of.

I knew a man who got matched to a woman twenty-five years his senior, with kids his age. Guys married strangers all the time. Some guys got a looker, other guys didn't. Once, there were two couples that ended up having affairs with each other's spouses, so Yogiji simply switched the marriages over.

"Why make a fuss?" he'd said.

As ashramites, we didn't have to "work" on our marriages the way other Americans supposedly do. All that psychological stuff about talking out problems and getting to know each other's inner drives or whatever it is. We just laughed at that! We figured, if Yogiji put two people together, then all you could do was wait and see how it would play out. Maybe you would fall in love. Maybe have children. Maybe you would get divorced or have an affair. It was all the will of God. It was all about surrender.

The first time I tried it was at Solstice. I met this beautiful blonde girl and asked Yogiji if I could marry her, kind of as an experiment.

He said, "Sure, why not?" But she declined the offer. I didn't even know you could do that.

But soon, Prem Kaur came along and I was suddenly a married man! I never doubted arranged marriage was the system for me. So, to me, it makes perfect sense that I would eventually come to India to seek out the source of the magic.

"But Guru *Sant* Singh, you are telling us that after meeting fifty women you could not find one woman to make your wife? Not one?" asks Sobha Singh. He and Amrik Singh exchange a glance.

"Arranged marriage . . ." adds Amrik Singh, "Like you said, it is a matter of convenience. You can make such an arrangement with any woman! No need to be picking and choosing until you end up in the jail!"

"Oh, yes," I reply. "Dadaji did finally find me a lady. A perfect lady!"

It breaks my heart even to talk about it, but I go ahead and tell them about her: Sukhvinder Kaur.

I walked into Dadaji's office to meet my fiftieth lady and just hoped to God and all things holy she could at least speak English. The fiftieth girl walked in with her mom, cousin, brother, and brother's wife, who was holding a newborn. And the girl was cute! I mean really really cute and young, too. Too young, really, about twenty-five, but after meeting all those teenagers and having their fathers beg me to take them on, she seemed perfectly mature.

Sukhvinder Kaur looked me in the eye, so that was a good sign. She didn't just stare into her lap, like a package of meat behind the butcher's glass. She wore traditional Indian clothes—the loose pajama pants, knee-length top, and enormous shawl draped modestly over the chest. But she had a hip denim jacket thrown over the ensemble, and a modern plastic watch on her wrist. Her cell phone rang, she checked the number, and put it back in her purse. She was no illiterate jungle child.

I asked if she was a Gursikh, meaning a vegetarian, a tee-totaller, and one who chants the prayers every day. She said yes, but started fiddling with her fingers in her lap. I thought, *HERE WE GO! She'll probably turn out to be hopelessly neurotic.*

But those eyes! Rimmed with lush, dark lashes. She had a thick rope of jet black hair, too, pulled back in a stern braid. I wanted to loosen the elastic and let it fall around her soft, sweet face.

I handed her the Sikh prayer book, the Nit Nam, and asked her to read something from it. Obediently, she took it, but didn't open it. She recited a prayer from memory, perfectly:

Ek Onkar

Sat nam Karta-purakh

Nirbhau Nirvair

It means *God is the true creator. He is without fear. He is beyond birth and death.*

This alone was impressive. I liked her. She was number fifty. I was fifty. Fifty sounds like a lucky number. Why not?

"Do you like her?" asked Alok, at her usual station in the doorway.

"Yes," I said, to Alok's obvious surprise.

Dadaji watched the proceedings from a plastic chair, frowning.

"Do you want to marry Guru *Sant* Singh?" Alok asked the girl.

"Yes! Yes!"

I felt kind of sexy.

"Why?" I asked.

She gave me a look at once quizzical and amused. It seemed to say, "Why *wouldn't* I?"

There was still the matter of literacy, and since she hadn't opened the Nitnem, I was a little suspicious. I asked her to write a paragraph about why she wanted to marry me.

Dadaji declared the meeting over and told them to return with the assignment completed. The family filed out. I tried to catch Sukhvinder Kaur's eye as she passed—a wink, a sidelong glance, anything to establish some special connection between us. But no, she looked straight ahead and marched away, the obedient daughter.

I told Dadaji I wanted her.

"She doesn't even speak English!"

"Yes she does!"

"What did she say?"

"'Yes.' She said, 'Yes!'"

"Anybody can say yes. She doesn't speak English. Don't jump in too fast. Don't be a fool."

"Too fast? After fifty interviews? I want her! Arrange the marriage!"

"She must learn English first!"

I had to bargain with Dadaji over terms? I didn't like it.

"Fine," I told him, "Get her some English lessons if you want to, but I want to marry that girl."

They came back again the next day: Sukhvinder Kaur, her mother, her cousin, her brother, her brother's wife, and the newborn baby. We all sat and exchanged pleasantries with Dadaji's inexpert translation. The mother explained she had a relative in Virginia who could help Sukhvinder Kaur learn English and make the transition to America. She grabbed Dadaji's phone and dialed the guy up.

I spoke to the relative on the line, and he confirmed this was true. But I had already imagined the high times we'd have, me pointing to a table and saying, "table!" Pointing to a wall and saying, "wall!" She would earnestly repeat each word. I would sagely tutor her each day, then she would prepare yet another delicious meal. We would eat and laugh over the silliness of it all. What memories we'd make!

I didn't want anything to do with the Virginia relative. In fact, I did not even want to go back to America. I wanted to make a life for myself in India. I wanted to study with spiritual masters, worship at the Golden Temple, and have a jolly Indian family and a big Bollywood wedding. What did I have to go back to in the U.S.? The wrath of my ex-wife?

I hung up and smiled at the family.

"The thing is, I might want to live in India," I stated flatly.

Dadaji translated, and the mother, cousin, brother, brother's wife and newborn baby all looked at each other quizzically.

"No! No! America!" they chorused.

For the first time, Sukhvinder Kaur cast me a lengthy glance with her big, wet eyes. A loose strand of ebony hair fell gently over her forehead.

"Well, maybe. We'll see," I said.

That seemed to satisfy them. I showed the family my scrapbook, then. All those newspaper articles about me. They must have thought I was famous and rich.

During the meeting, Dadaji retreated to his desk to do some

paperwork, so I took the chance to slip a gift to Sukhvinder Kaur's sister-in-law.

I wasn't supposed to give gifts. Dadaji was afraid the families would take it as an implied promise. But I figured it would be safe to give one to the sister-in-law. She wasn't the prospective bride, wasn't the mother, but had influence. It was a nice Punjabi suit—the knee-length dress with matching pants. They are a one-size-fits-all kind of thing and come wrapped in these flat little packets. It could only win me points, was my logic. Plus, I didn't care if they took it as a promise. Maybe it would force Dadaji's hand.

A couple of days later, I was sitting in the office yet again, snacking on Alok's latest fried delicacy, and talking awkwardly with candidate number 51—an older divorcee. The door swung wide and here they came again, this time without an appointment. Sukhvinder Kaur, her mother, her cousin, her brother, her brother's wife, and the newborn baby. I looked up in surprise, grease on my lips and crumbs in my beard.

They paraded right up to Dadaji, mother at the helm, and started talking in rapid Punjabi. Voices became strident. Everyone hollered back and forth. The cousin joined in, the brother shouted something, the sister-in-law got hysterical, then the newborn baby let out a wail.

Suddenly I remembered that in the Punjab—actually, all over South Asia but *especially* in the Punjab—there was that little something called *izzat*. *Izzat* means family honor and is taken very seriously by Punjabis, especially men. An insult to the family—especially to one of the women—cannot be tolerated and *must* be avenged, if necessary by killing someone. I wondered: had I done something to offend Sukhvinder Kaur or, worse yet, her father?

Sukhvinder Kaur broke off from the pack and turned sharply toward me. I remember it in ecstatic slow motion. She met my gaze.

Was it my long beard that had seduced her? Was it the devotion to God and Guru that emanated from my every pore? Could she see my purple aura, radiating an inspired state of being? My future as a spiritual teacher? Ah! She was a deeply religious girl with an ethereal bent. She knew true devotion when she saw it and wouldn't let anyone stop her from being united with an equally devoted man. She longed to pray with me. To share my bed.

To join voices in unison . . .

Sukhvinder walked over to me in three long, commanding strides, and threw an envelope at my chest. It fluttered into my lap. I looked at it. A love note? My name was written on the front, in graceful Punjabi.

When I looked up again, number 51, the divorcée, was standing and yelling at Dadaji, complaining that her meeting was being interrupted.

Dadaji told her if she didn't like it she could leave!

Fire in her eyes, the woman marched out the door; meanwhile, Sukhvinder Kaur rejoined her family in the ongoing harangue.

"WHY CAN'T I MARRY HIM RIGHT NOW? I WANT TO MARRY HIM!" Sukhvinder Kaur shouted.

So she did know English!

Finally, Dadaji calmed down and smiled. He patted the mother's hand reassuringly and spoke some soothing words. The mother's eyes turned to slits. She jerked her hand away, then led the family out the way they had come, everyone shouting curses over their shoulders.

Dadaji explained to me that the family was very eager for the marriage, but the girl had not taken a single English lesson. It was too soon.

"These things take time," he said. He laughed it off and insisted the family would calm down in a few hours. He assured me it was just a typical Indian family drama.

"I don't care if she doesn't speak English," I said. "I can teach her!"

"No. No. No. These things take time. It's the Indian way."

I told him my visa was only good for another month.

"Just you meet a few more women. Maybe a queen will come along for you!" he replied.

Dadaji was the master of a gleaming downtown office and, according to Bunty, the most respected matchmaker in the Punjab. He had brokered the future happiness of hundreds, maybe thousands, of young people for more than a decade. He was a seasoned veteran of hysterical mother/daughter scenes. I trusted him. What choice did I have?

chapter 19

The next week, it was Lohri—a big midwinter holiday for Hindus and Punjabis alike. Bonfires blazed everywhere: in the streets, on sidewalks, in parking lots. The local businessman's association set up a tent in the parking lot of Dadaji's office complex and had an enormous party for everyone that worked inside. It was a massive feast. Television cameras filmed the festivities, and Dadaji was on top of the world. He got on camera as many times as he could.

He introduced me to his business chums, really acting like a king. He also introduced me to S.H.O. Mohander Singh, the chief of police, who was partying it up with the rest of them. Dadaji made sure everyone knew I was his big American client. Pats on the back and handshakes went all around. Everyone smiled and laughed and danced around the place, but I could not get into it. There was so much meat being served. There was whiskey and wine. Everyone was drunk. It was gross, like some spring break bacchanal.

The next day, I returned to Dadaji's office to meet more women. The detritus from the party was still there. Emaciated dogs fought over scraps of food, garbage littered the scene, and liquor bottles clinked into the gutter.

Clearly nursing a hangover, Dadaji introduced me to the latest applicant.

"This is the girl, and this her friend," he muttered, with effort.

They were an unusual twosome. First of all, the friend was a black man, seemingly of African descent, which was very odd. The girl was a light skinned Indian and looked about twenty-two. She wore makeup and seemed quite sophisticated. They both spoke perfect English.

"And this is her mother," added Dadaji, gesturing at a half-blind old lady with one tooth, who nodded like a bobble-head doll.

Dadaji wandered back to his desk to collapse. I asked the girl if she was a Gursikh. She replied no. In fact, she was a Hindu.

What the hell was this shit? Damn it Dadaji! I had already found the girl of my dreams and here he was wasting my time with Hindus.

I asked if she was a vegetarian, and she said of course. She told me she was studying business and wanted to go to the U.S. and get an MBA.

"Do you want to marry me?"

"Yes!"

"Why?"

"I want to go to the U.S. and get an MBA!"

"That's all?"

I was disappointed. Sukhvinder Kaur may not have spoken English, but she saw me for who I was. She wanted a spiritual husband. She wanted me. She loved me. I could see it in her eyes.

"So, if I were a Hindu gentleman, an Indian gentleman, would you want to marry me?"

"No!"

"I see. Do you want to marry an older man? I'm fifty, you know. Is that what you want?"

I tried to get into an honest discussion with her about the whole thing. I thought she could handle it. But it didn't matter. The bitch was in heat. When she saw me, she saw the two sexiest words in the English language: Green Card. They might as well have been stamped on my forehead.

In the middle of this exchange, something strange happened. Policemen began to file in. They wore olive green uniforms and turbans and carried black submachine guns. Most were smiling, beaming, really showing their teeth. There were five, then ten, then twenty of them. They filled up the place!

Then S.H.O. Mohander Singh entered the office. He sat right beside Dadaji, at his desk, and they talked in low tones. But the MBA girl and the black man just kept on talking to me. They remarked that India was really growing, and in the future it would be an important international business hub, and so forth. They were completely unfazed by the police.

Then a TV camera crew came inside and started filming me and this girl chatting away. They also pointed the camera at Dadaji and filmed him, surrounded by police, looking one-hundred-percent miserable.

Then Mohander Singh said something to Dadaji, and Dadaji pulled a bunch of files out of his desk drawer. One by one, he showed the officer photos of all the ladies I had met.

Finally, the MBA girl seemed to have had enough. She checked her watch, mid-sentence, then, without comment, got up to leave. The black man and half-blind mother followed, but a policeman intercepted the girl and spoke to her in a low voice. She returned to her seat on the couch, her companions in tow, then she and the black man attempted to continue our conversation as if nothing had happened. The cameras kept rolling.

S.H.O. Mohander Singh wore a khaki colored turban, like the other officers. He also had his dark, curly beard mashed up against his chin with a beard-net. I had come to recognize this as a tidy, professional look for Punjabis whose beards were particularly long. He approached me, smiling, and said, "You should come with me."

"Do I have to?"

"Yes. You should come."

Mohander Singh's officers led Dadaji and me outside, back

through the scene of last night's debauchery. The other business owners in the building had come out of their offices by then. They clustered on the sidewalk, on the balconies, and leaned out their windows to see. They watched the police lead us away. Dadaji was looking down, trying to hide his face, and shaking.

The officer who had my elbow escorted me to a little car that looked like a circus clown's contraption. He crammed me into the back, between himself and another officer. Three more officers squeezed into the front, and off they drove.

The ones in front kept on staring at me over their shoulders and grinning.

The little police car careened through the streets until it got stuck in Amritsar traffic, just like everyone else. The driver toggled the siren and laid on the horn, but it made no difference. We veered off onto the sidewalk, around the traffic jam, and back into the road, barely missing a long-horned water buffalo that had ambled over the median, searching for a meal of street-side garbage.

In the twilight, some hobos along the road had started little fires to keep warm—a common practice. By now, it was dinner time, and they were roasting something to eat, I guessed, by the smell of it. Also, the Lohri bonfires burned in every alley and sidewalk. People kept adding wood, dung, and random junk. Here and there, the flames rose and fell and rose again. Popcorn and puri vendors by the roadsides had their own fires, too. Then there were the garbage fires. These blazed away every few blocks—a typical Indian method of waste disposal. On top of it all, the Hindu temples we passed burned great piles of incense, as usual, which hung in the air like something you could cut and eat. It was like a scene from Dante's Inferno, and me in the clutches of five demon tour guides—Cheshire smiles bobbing in the haze.

During the ride, I learned that the girl had been a plant. A television reporter. The black man worked at the TV station too, and the "mother" was just some lady they picked up off the street. The policemen were so proud of their clever orchestration of the thing, they told me all about it. It had been a sting operation, meant to bust Dadaji and I as co-conspirators in a marriage fraud racket—the kind where the man comes from afar, marries some girl, takes her dowry, and then jets back home, alone, with his ill-gotten gains. Usually he also assaults her on the wedding night and takes her virginity for the hell of it. Disgusting!

When we got to the police station on Rambagh Road, they took Dadaji off to an interrogation room. I will never forget the doomed look he gave me as the officers led him down the hall. They were eerily over-polite. "This way, please," they said to him, like it was Sunday brunch.

Me, the officers kept in the main station room.

"Are you thirsty? Would you like some juice? Perhaps some mineral water? Still, or sparkling?" Mohander Singh asked me. I said I wouldn't mind some bottled water, so he sent some underling to a corner store to get it.

They inspected my stuff, took inventory, and took it all away, including my passport and laptop computer. But Mohander Singh wanted to see the computer. I honestly don't know if he had ever seen one before. There wasn't so much as a calculator in the place. Every desk was as clean and clear as a freshly poured foundation. So they gave me the laptop back, as well as my cell phone.

On the computer, I showed Mohander Singh videos and pictures of my travels. I also played him audio files of my kirtan—Sikh devotional music. I have been playing and singing this music for thirty years, and it was great to show it to a real Indian Sikh. The officer nodded sagely, thoughtfully, as he listened. He commented that my pronunciation was excellent. This arrest was turning out to be a wonderfully validating experience for me, and I got the feeling Mohander Singh was the most devout Sikh I had met in India so far.

"You are age fifty, and you still want marriage?" he eventually asked.

"Yeah. Yeah! I still want to. I want a Sikh lady who understands me as a Sikh, you know? I can't find that in America."

"You are Sikh for how long?"

"Thirty years. I'm Gursikh."

Mohander Singh looked at me for a long time, sizing me up, then changed the subject. He told me he had some relatives living in Texas.

His cell phone kept ringing, and every time he answered, it was like a little ceremony. He would hold it aloft and raise his eyebrows, like the thing was a NASA transmitter for alien frequencies. Eventually he showed me his call history and pointed out a number.

"This one is from United States!" Sure enough, it was a Texas area code. He was as proud as if his phone had lost its virginity.

We sat there in the station house all night, and I entertained him with my computer the whole time. His English was not good, so this was less of a conversation and more of an extemporaneous one-man show, on my part. I produced every piece of evidence I had that might prove my sincerity in this search for a wife, but eventually I ran out of ideas. I broke down and just asked Mohander Singh what the hell was going on.

"Did Dadaji take money from the women? Is that what this is about?"

"Yes! Yes! He took money!"

"Did he promise some lady I'd marry her?"

"Yes! Yes! He made promise!"

Then, as an experiment, "Did he want to marry one of the women himself?"

"Yes! Yes! Marry!"

Bullshit. I realized then that he couldn't understand a thing I was saying. After all, his English was atrocious. So I waited a while longer.

Mohander Singh kept saying, "You're our honored guest here! We want to observe all your human rights!" Then, "What do you want? Some mineral water? Some juice?" All night, policemen kept finding excuses to get into the station room. They wanted to meet me—the white Sikh, the '*gora*,' as Punjabis call Yogi Bhajan's followers. Each man would say *Sat Siri Akal*, a Sikh greeting meaning 'God is the ultimate truth,' and I would say it back. Then he'd blush and scurry away.

By eleven o'clock that night, we were still sitting there. Nothing had changed. Nothing had been decided, and I hadn't seen Dadaji in nearly 5 hours. Another officer entered. I would put him at about 30. He spoke perfect English. He told me it was true: Dadaji had been taking money from each lady for the privilege of meeting me.

No wonder Dadaji, the bastard, had not wanted me to marry Sukhvinder Kaur; it would have ended the gravy train.

"This is legal, however. This is his business," added the officer.

Apparently, as long as every woman gave the money of her own free will, and nobody promised her marriage, there still wasn't, technically, a crime committed. The officer couldn't, or wouldn't, explain exactly what the crime was that Dadaji and I were being questioned about. He said it had something to do with someone lodging a complaint. That is all he would say. I suspected Sukhvinder Kaur and her family. They probably had grounds.

chapter 20

In the station house, I got to talking to the young officer some more. I asked him, "So, do you mind my asking? Did you have an arranged marriage?"

"Yes, of course. My parents chose."

"And are you and your wife happy?"

"Yes, yes. We are very happy. She has given me a boy and a girl. Both very good children. We are very happy indeed!"

I told him I wanted that, too. Just a typical Indian wife. A serviceful woman. One who would quietly serve with inner contentment and happiness just to be a wife. One who would never question my edicts and always be at my side, uttering encouraging words and offering fresh vegetarian food prepared with loving kindness.

He gave me a sidelong look.

I smiled serenely.

Then he took my laptop back.

Then Dadaji finally reappeared. There was no blood. No bruises. I concluded he hadn't been physically tortured, but he did look like a ruined man in every other respect. Mohander Singh led the two of us into a policemen's off-duty room, and admitted that he was obliged to arrest us both, but was still unsure what to charge us with, so he was going to lock us in there over night. As he left, he smiled and told us we were famous. Apparently, our arrest had been on the six o'clock news.

The next morning, they let us out to freely wander around the station room. Apparently, arrest in India is both deadly serious and quite casual, all at once. Everyone was friendly. It was like a big happy family: the guards, the prisoners, the policemen, the commanding officers, the criminals getting dragged in, and their families, who came along later to plead for release and bribe the officers with fried delicacies. It felt like we were all brothers playing at some cops and robbers game—policemen and criminals alike. Of course, there was a lot of family drama—hysterical wives, weeping mothers—but it seemed like a show. Nobody seemed that upset, really.

Most Indians don't have internet access. The police station itself doesn't have a single computer. So, if a business owner is going to hire someone for a job, he is not going to stand in line all day at some government office to get a background check. That would be a ridiculous waste of time. And even if you did, you might have to go through a year of hassle and paperwork to get any government official to cooperate with you. So, the way I see it, a guy's criminal record is basically his, his family's, and the police's business. No one else ever has to know.

I ask Sobha Singh if my analysis is correct. He shrugs as if to say, *of course*. I don't think he knows what I'm comparing it to—the American system, where a criminal record can ruin your life. I keep thinking about my stepson, K.P. He fancied himself a 'graffiti artist,' and was dumb enough to deface some state property. In America, that's a felony, so when he got caught, he did jail time, and now he has a criminal record.

At the age of 27, he can't get a job and none of my ex-wife's relatives wants anything to do with him. The kid has no support system at all except for his mom, Sat Siri Kaur, and all she gives him are astrological forecasts.

The Indian justice system isn't perfect by any means, but I really get the impression it allows people to start over. When the punishment is over, it is over. My weeks in jail with Dadaji also taught me that even when a guy is in jail, his mother, father, aunts, uncles, and other family members never abandon him. They bring homemade food, they visit him, they reassure him that when he returns home, there is a place for him. In America, it is every man for himself. No one has any such assurances. I don't like that.

Yogi Bhajan introduced me to this strong idea of family Indians have. It is the source of my fascination with Indian culture, really. Even in jail, I saw a sense of familial responsibility, a sense of loyalty, a dedication that people have for each other. My own family is not strong. My brother and I are estranged. My parents are divorced. My mother helps me when I need it, but is married to a man I never liked. Although we have now grown much closer as a result of this whole Indian experience, at the time all this happened my relationship with my father was tenuous at best. During my jail time I felt a deep longing for that kind of family caring.

I have always wanted to get this thing Yogiji was always talking about. This support. These people that would never leave you. Never. I want to be part of a culture like that.

That morning, in the station house, Dadaji's son showed up with a homemade breakfast. It was better than a restaurant! As I shoveled it in, I looked out the window and saw a guy in the police yard below, getting beaten senseless by officers with sticks. No one else seemed to notice. Later that day, some officers took Dadaji and me to see a judge and arrange bail.

"After that, they threw us in the slammer overnight, then we had that ridiculous press conference, then they brought us here in chains, and here I am!" I tell Sobha Singh and Amrik Singh. "I don't know who lodged the complaint against us, but I hope it wasn't Sukhvinder Kaur. I really loved that girl, though I suppose she probably would have left me when we got to the U.S. Would have got her precious green card and just left me!" I laugh it off.

Sobha Singh and Amrik Singh exchange a look.

"You probably won't believe me, Guru *Sant* Singh, but you were very lucky to get arrested," says Sobha Singh.

"You almost made the biggest mistake of your life," Amrik Singh adds, laughing into his shirt. There is a joke on me somewhere in here, but I don't get it.

"Oh Guru *Sant* Singh," Sobha Singh says. "Don't you know? No Indian woman would ever leave her husband."

"No?" *Is there still a chance for me and Sukhvinder Kaur?* I wonder. A tiny sparrow of hope flutters in my breast.

"She would never leave you," says Sobha Singh. "What she would do, most certainly, is poison you."

chapter 21

Poisoned? Is he serious? Would that lovely Sukhvinder Kaur actually poison me if I were to marry her? My fantasies about Indian marriages are being demolished, one by one. Sobha Singh, seeing a look of total confusion on my face, begins to explain.

"Guru *Sant* Singh, try to understand. In India, marriage is not only a man and a woman coming together; it's a business deal. If the deal starts to go sour—or maybe someone doesn't fulfill their obligations—there has to be a way to get out of it."

"But....but, what about divorce?"

"Divorce is of course legally possible. But the stigma attached to divorce in India is huge. *Izzat*, family honor, simply does not allow for divorce. The shame would be too great. People do get divorced but I think you now know how divorced women are treated."

I sure do. I remember all those sad and angry divorcees I had encountered at Dadaji's.

"So what happens?"

"That depends on the circumstances and the family. Maybe the bride has an "accident" with a kerosene cooking stove."

Later I come to find out that what is euphemistically called "Bride Burning" accounts for around five thousand or more female deaths per year in India. Also that "Husband Poisoning", while not as common as Bride Burning, is not exactly unknown.

I sit in shock for a while then Sobha Singh resumes the conversation.

"Yes, my friend, you were truly framed. Truly framed!" says

Sobha Singh. "This man Dadaji was taking money from those women, that's all."

"Oh, no, he wasn't! He just took the regular fee."

"Guru *Sant* Singh," says Sobha Singh, "Don't be a fool, man! That Dadaji has a bad reputation to begin with! He just wanted to keep on taking and taking money from every woman. He was never going to marry you to that young woman. Never!"

"Luckily!" adds Amrik Singh.

I stiffen. I don't want to believe any of it. And even if it is true, I don't care. Until that last moment, when he left me with nothing, Dadaji treated me very well. I have survived prison reasonably comfortably because of him. I don't want to hear any more.

"But I want to know about this GRD telephone scam," says Sobha Singh. "You can really make anyone do anything, eh? A charmer! I think you are a charmer!" He laughs again. Then he whispers something to Amrik Singh. I would think this was rude, but this is India. Whispering and staring are not considered rude. Or else people just don't care about being rude. I never know which it is. Social protocol has never been my strong suit, anyway, and this *is* prison, after all.

"You are a man who likes a bit of trickery, are you not?" asks Sobha Singh.

I don't know what to say. "No one has ever put it that way before," I answer. "But yes, I guess I do."

"You are, how do you say . . . open for a game."

I laugh. It's too true. "Yes. I guess I'm open for a game, as you say. But really I didn't like doing that stuff in the boiler room."

"Yes, you did!"

"No, no. You've got me wrong. I hated it. I did it for Yogiji. I did it for the money, too. But sitting in that boiler room with that plastic phone pressed up against my ear? I hated that. I like action, you know?"

"Action. Yes. I think you like some kind of trickery. But you like it to be . . . how can I say? . . . man to man."

"Yes, I like to be in the middle of things. I think you know what I mean, Sobha Singh?"

"Yes, I do. I like to be in the middle of things, too," he says, and wags a finger in the air. Then he sidles up and pats my leg, getting too close—the Indian manner of showing friendship between men.

"Tell me more about this GRD," he asks, with strange eagerness.

"Well," I tell him, "I finally got a break from the phone sales when Yogiji pulled me into a different scam—a much better one."

In 1977 a scathing article about Yogi Bhajan appeared in Time Magazine. It suggested—amongst other things--that he was a womanizer and lived a sumptuous lifestyle while most of his students lived in penury. Then, in the early eighties, some Indian Sikhs started publishing articles about 3HO and Yogiji. They called us "Bhajan's borgs" and 3HO a cult. These things weren't widely read, and of course we "borgs" thought it was a complete joke, but then things escalated.

The Time article quoted a well-respected Sikh scholar and historian Dr. Trilochan Singh who said "Bhajan's synthesis of Sikhism and Tantrism is a sacrilegious hodgepodge." Dr. Trilochan Singh spent several months with Yogiji and eventually published a book called "Sikhism and Tantric Yoga: A Critical Evaluation of Yogi Bhajan's Tantric Yoga in the Light of Sikh Mystical Experiences and Doctrines." If the Time article had been scathing, Trilochan Singh's book was devastating in its assessment of the validity of Yogiji's teachings.

The book was never distributed in the US and very few of Yogiji's students ever heard of it let alone read it. Certainly it was unknown to me. The few of Yogiji's students who read it dismissed it in this manner: *"This guy, Trilochan Singh, knows nothing of the spirit, consciousness or grace of the Siri Singh Sahib's teachings. He is looking from a very narrow perspective. He is an intellectual Sikh who only values the rituals and ceremonies of Sikhism but not the spirit."*

Certain people who styled themselves as "cult deprogrammers" started circling around some of our members. They actually came to 3HO homes a couple of times and dragged some ashramites away, kicking and screaming. We always expected the victims to come back as soon as they got a chance, but they never did. Tension was definitely building around the ashram.

All of this criticism of Yogi Bhajan was starting to affect his reputation, both in the US and India, and he simply couldn't afford to lose the support of the big high muckety mucks at the Golden Temple. Yogiji had to do something to win back respect among orthodox Sikhs and the general public. That was where I came into the picture.

One day, at the Gurdwara, in 1982, I met a woman named Krishna Kaur. Sometimes they called her Black Krishna because she was black and because there was, of course, another Krishna Kaur in L.A. The other Krishna—Pink Krishna—was said by Yogiji to be the reincarnation of Queen Elizabeth I of England.

Black Krishna was vivacious and attractive. In her previous life she had a career on Broadway. She sang "The Age of Aquarius" in Hair, toured with the musical, and she is right there on the original cast recording, belting it out! She gave all that up to join 3HO and become one of Yogiji's Mukhia Singh Sahibs. That's what we called the big muckety mucks. Mukhia Singh Sahib—"Respected Elder." She was one of the very few blacks in the whole organization, at the time.

She approached me one day after sadhana and invited me to her office for tea. She called me Honey. That was her way. Black Krishna was very motherly, very sweet and lovey dovey, with a kind of down-home southern manner. It was "sweetie" this and "darlin'" that while we chatted about who knows what. Ordinary things.

Then, out of the blue, she said, "So, Guru *Sant* Singh, I understand you can shoot a gun?"

I told her I sure as hell could, wondering whom she wanted me to shoot.

Just the thought of shooting made me sit up straight in my chair, and I was surprised. I thought I had put all that behind me, but the old me, the 12-year-old military school commander, came to the forefront ready for marching orders. It wasn't that I was bloodthirsty; it was just that I was so damned good at it.

Black Krishna asked about military school and my dad being an ex-marine. I didn't know how she had found out all this, but I was not that surprised. No one can keep a secret in 3HO.

"We've been looking everywhere for someone just like you!" she said, smiling hugely.

Most of Yogiji's followers were peaceniks. They would rather carry a venereal disease than a rifle. Black Krishna couldn't believe her luck, finding a guy like me in a crowd like that.

In those days, Reagan had his political regime in full ops, and conservatives reigned supreme. There was no tolerance for fringe groups in America, and the army had just revoked its exemption allowing Sikhs to wear beards and turbans in the military. Truman had put the exemption through ages ago, but Casper Weinberger, Reagan's Secretary of Defense, ripped it out, I suppose just to prove what a real true Christian he was. Black Krishna was looking for someone to make a stink about it: to try to enlist in the army, get rejected, and then raise hell. The idea was to hit first and hit hard, before the moral majority quietly snuffed out our entire movement.

It sounded like a smart move to me, so I listened as she laid out a plan. It never occurred to me that I was a pawn in a much larger game.

chapter 22

The first step in Black Krishna's plan was that I had to reconcile with my dad.

He had disowned me two years before in a big, painful scene that left us completely estranged.

What happened was, about 1980, after I had been a Sikh for a few years, changed my name, donned the turban, and all that, I moved back to L.A. That's when I started working in the boiler room. My parents had divorced by then, so I went and saw my mom, who was her usual loving self, then I decided to go and see my dad.

Mom warned me, "Your father has been backsliding, Clark. So don't be surprised if he is not the same man you remember."

I didn't have a car, so I took the train to Pomona, which took an hour or so, and arranged for a couple of local ashramites to pick me up at the train stop. They drove me another hour to his house in upscale Claremont, and dropped me off at the curb. But as soon as I took one step over the threshold, and Dad got a look at my all-white outfit—turban, Indian tunic, and baggy cotton trousers, he started ranting.

"You look like a weirdo! I can't introduce you to anyone!"

He accused me of idol worship, disavowing my family, rejecting the family name, all kinds of stuff. It lasted long enough for him to stub out one cigarette, light another, throw some rocks into a glass, pour three fingers of Red Label, and down it.

"You . . . You . . . You aren't Clark. You aren't my son!"

And that was that.

I picked up my suitcase and duffel bag and walked out. I wandered around the neighborhood in a daze. A phone booth appeared, so I called the ashram. Someone drove all the way from Pomona and picked me up. I wish I could remember who.

The next day, I was back at the L.A. ashram, trying to get back into my sadhana routine, trying to shrug the whole thing off. I had not told anyone about the incident except my old friend Sat Kir*pal* Singh.

It was a Friday, so that evening I joined the others in going to see Yogi Bhajan off at the airport. There must have been a hundred of us, making a scene at LAX in our white outfits and turbans, just wishing him well. He went away to teach tantric yoga every weekend, but those weekends without him seemed so empty. How could we even think without him? We always made a big occasion of his leaving and his return.

Before getting on the plane, the holy man turned around in front of all those people, pointed at me, and hollered, "That guy there! That guy has more faith than anybody!" For me, that single moment made it all worthwhile.

I don't know how Yogiji knew about my dad disowning me, but, of course, like the others, I had always assumed Bhajan was psychic, so I took that moment as proof positive. He was psychic, and therefore holy. That was all there was to it. That day, Yogi Bhajan renewed my faith one-hundred-fold.

Thinking back on it, back in that Claremont phone booth, I probably called the ashram switchboard. I don't know what I said to the operator, but she had probably had to ask around until they found someone willing to spend several hours to come and get me. At the end of the day, I suppose there were hundreds of people that could have known about it. Maybe Yogiji finding out was not so miraculous after all. But so what? He said I had more faith than anyone, and it was true.

By the time Black Krishna asked me about trying to reconcile with Dad, two years had passed without a word between my father and me. But what the hell. I called him up. He said he felt really bad about it all. Since then, he had stopped his backsliding and gone back to the church.

I told Black Krishna everything was clear on the Dad front, so next thing I knew, 3HO got me a publicity consultant. I spent two weeks with this guy rehearsing what I would say, how I would answer questions. If someone asked, "How long have you been a Sikh?" I was to say, "I have always been a Sikh. A seeker of truth." If they asked, "Is 3HO a cult?" I was to respond that even Christianity was considered a cult when Jesus was first martyred on the cross, and that Sikhism, or Sikhi as we say, is a 500-year old Indian religion. We knew they would try to paint me as a weirdo, and the idea was to put both the media hounds and the Army to shame by establishing the legitimacy of 3HO, Sikhi, and our way of life.

In the end, if we prevailed, I might actually have to join the Army, but I was okay with that. In fact, I looked forward to it. I could fulfill those old heroic fantasies.

So, in full Sikh regalia—Indian dress, turban, steel bracelets, ceremonial dagger hanging at my side—I entered the local U.S. Army recruiting station. I told the fellow there I would like to join up but would not cut my beard or hair, as they were articles of faith.

I loved it! The drama!

I was a champion marksman, a graduate of military school, former vice-president of the University of Oregon student council and a former aide to a U.S. Congressman in Washington D.C., but they said no thanks.

"We don't want your kind."

That's when the fun really began. The consultant arranged newspaper interviews and press conferences. He mentored me through the whole process. One press conference was a particularly big one at the Los Angeles Press Club where eminent leaders like President Harry Truman had spoken in the past. The consultant drove me to this legendary Hollywood institution, coaching me all the way. But when we got there, Hari Jiwan Singh was already there—the same guy that headed up the boiler room. He acted as my spokesman. He was basically Yogi Bhajan's right hand man and did not let me get a word in edgewise.

I was a puppet, obviously, but I didn't care, as long as I got my picture in the paper. And what a picture it was—Hari Jiwan Singh and I sitting side by side at a table, with TV and radio microphones clustered in front of us like summer mosquitoes.

Los Angeles Times
Sikh Adherent Does Battle With Army's Dress Code
December 23, 1982
By Joy Horowitz, Times Staff Writer

As a modern-day warrior, he doesn't drink, doesn't smoke, doesn't eat meat and dresses in white—symbols of purity. Piled on his head and tied in a knot beneath a white turban, his long hair is wrapped around a small sword, mandatory articles of faith.

His religion, the 500-year-old Sikh faith with its history of warriors and martyrs, exalts the sword and a "righteous path." So while he rises each day at three a.m. to pray and practice yoga, he also is an expert marksman (and a firm gun control opponent) and proudly wears the badges he's earned from national championship shooting competitions on his white cotton jacket.

The son of a retired Marine Corps officer, he has changed the name his father gave him twenty-five years ago from Clark Alan Harris to Guru Sant Singh (lion) Khalsa (the highest station). But, he says, the values his father transmitted to him "of serving God and country" have not changed; nor has his indefatigable dream of becoming an officer in the U.S. Army.

There's one glaring problem, however. Uncle Sam won't have him—

unless he gets rid of his turban, chops off his hair, shaves his long, reddish-brown beard and stops wearing his steel bracelet, a Sikh symbol that one's strength of purpose will be tested.

"That would be a disavowal of my religion," Khalsa said, sitting in the front office of the Sikh storefront headquarters that is wedged between a sign company and a mirror outlet on Robertson Boulevard in West Los Angeles. "It's religious discrimination."

After 24 years of permitting followers of the Sikh religion to wear articles of faith, such as untrimmed beards, turbans, and steel bracelets, the Army decided last year to abolish its dress code exemptions for Sikhs and not to accept any more enlistees of the religion whose 15 million adherents include soldiers in the Indian, British and Canadian armies.

So when Khalsa tried to enlist at the Santa Monica recruiting office last month, as a result of the revamped "appearance standards." Sikh demonstrations across the country followed on Pearl Harbor Day . . .

"I think it is really silly the government is prosecuting people who won't register, and here they won't let me in when I'm committed to serving my country," said Khalsa, an office supplies salesman who plans on returning to the University of Oregon next month to complete his degree in Political Science.

"This country was founded on religious freedom. There shouldn't be any conflict between God and country. I believe it is my duty to defend our country if attacked. My father inspired me to serve my country and protect what we have; I am willing to lose my life for that. I mean what do they (the Army) want?". . . Sikhs believe in one God, rejecting the Hindus' worship of idols as well as their caste system; they teach service and are known for physical prowess and hard work . . .

Khalsa, who was raised in Claremont, said he first donned a turban as an undergraduate at the University of Oregon, where he took classes in Kundalini Yoga and was introduced to the Sikh faith.

"I found it really fit in with my life," recalled Khalsa, who first began shooting at age 11 as a Boy Scout and then went on to win the U.S. National Junior Pistol Championship and to train at Ft. Briggs with the current director of the National Rifle Assn. "The principles and values of living righteously fit in with what my parents taught me.

"Sikhs are warriors and have been for 500 years. We relate to weapons as a form of worship and learn how to respect weapons.... We are a peaceful people. I voted for the nuclear freeze. But it's not a conflict to stand for peace and promote defense as well. Basically, it's standing for righteousness and standing for truth."

Khalsa's father, Bill Harris, said he still calls his son Clark but supports his challenge to the Army's dress standards "all the way."

"We kinda grew apart a little at first," said Harris, a mobile home salesman. "Now I'd say we have a good relationship. I picked up a book on different religions and realized it wasn't a weird scene and wasn't a cult.

"Now, I'm really proud. He lives a strict life with real quality moral people. Once you get by the long hair and beard and dress, you realize it's too bad we don't all stand for what they believe in—being honest, working hard and especially defending your country. They're probably the best citizens we have. I'd rather have a dedicated soldier than worry about length of beard and wearing a white turban."...

My dad was impressed with all this fuss about his son. He had to admit our organization was impressive. With these quotes to the press and his 14 years of service in the Marines, Dad's endorsement definitely added to my cache.

They printed that press conference photo in the L.A. Herald Examiner, funnily subtitled, *Army reject Guru Sant Singh Khalsa, left, and Hari Jiwan Singh Khalsa.*

After that press conference, the 3HO administration took this business about me joining the army one step further. They really wanted to bring 3HO out into the open and create an aura of legitimacy, and even martyrdom, where otherwise we would surely be seen as nothing but a freakish group that had somehow survived the sixties. So Hari Jiwan Singh declared December seventh a day of national protests, and Sikhs came out in droves, all over the country. Carrying signs that read *For God and Country,* and *Let Sikhs Join*, Sikhs picketed federal buildings in Houston, Los Angeles, Boston, San Francisco, Phoenix, New York and Chicago.

In truth, most of these so-called Sikhs didn't know anything about the true Sikh religion, how militant it really was. Nevertheless, they would do anything for Yogiji. He was clairvoyant and a spiritual teacher and almost a god. So, a decade after they protested the Vietnam War, ashramites found themselves protesting that they were not allowed to enlist in the US military. The streets filled up with hundreds of Sikhs dressed in the all-white garb of purity. The men with bushy, outrageous beards, the women swathed in gossamer veils that went over their turbans, down around their shoulders, and trailed off and blew in the wind.

The L.A. Times printed a great photo of me in my shooting jacket, festooned with badges and honors. I'm looking dreamily off into the distance, and a portrait of our first Sikh Guru, Guru Nanak Dev Ji, hangs in the background.

I bought two of every paper that covered my story and clipped out the articles.

"I kept one for my scrapbook," I tell Sobha Singh and Amrik Singh, "and I always posted the second to Bhindranwale."

"BHINDRANWALE?" my fellow inmates chorus with wide eyes.

"What? You knew the great Bhindranwale?" stage-whispers Sobha Singh, through the darkness.

"That's impossible!" shouts Amrik Singh.

"Preposterous! The great Sikh martyr? You knew him? How can this be?" adds Sobha Singh.

I want to tell them the rest of the story about suing the army. I want to tell them about the ACLU getting involved, but they won't have it.

"You must tell us about Bhindranwale," insists Sobha Singh. "I don't believe you. You never knew the great Bhindranwale. That is not possible."

In truth, I feel very privileged to have spent time with a man who was probably the most important figure in Sikhi of the 20th Century.

chapter 23

Indian Sikhs struggled, throughout the seventies, against a vicious government regime that carved up the prosperous Punjab into separate states and exploited the agricultural wealth Sikhs had built over hundreds of years. In response, a coalition of Sikhs eventually moved to secede. They dreamed of a homeland called Khalistan—Land of the Pure, but these dreams sparked a kind of underground civil war. By 1984, the Punjab had become a killing ground. Sikhs were killed, raped, and even scalped in Indira Gandhi's anti-Sikh campaign. Eventually, her own Sikh bodyguards shot her dead. In my youth, I was almost a part of it.

When I first joined 3HO, in 1977, I knew nothing, and I mean nothing, about the Khalistan movement or Punjabi politics. We ashramites were as removed from modern India and its twenty million Sikhs as if the 3HO belief system had been transmitted directly from Mars. Looking back, I realize Yogiji never really encouraged his American Sikhs to form friendships with Indian Sikhs. The reason for it is clear: it has to do with that book and those articles that came out against him—the ones that had been the catalyst for my attempt to join the U.S. Army. Fact was (and I learned this many years after the Bhindranwale experience) to the extent that the great Yogi Bhajan was known in India at all, he was considered a charlatan: a low-level customs officer turned spiritual con man in America. The Indians, frankly, didn't understand him. Didn't grasp the depth of the love he had to spread. Sometimes it's like that.

Spiritual con men are a dime a dozen in India, only most don't make it all the way to fame and fortune in America. But Yogiji did have a fortune, so, despite his reputation, he actually wielded plenty of political clout, both in the U.S. and India.

Nonetheless, Indian Sikhs laughed at him, his ideas, his yoga, but most of all at us, his "gullible" followers. I can still hear the criticism:

"Yoga? Sikhs don't do yoga. That's Hindu shit!"

"Decorating the Gurdwara with portraits of himself, golden idols of yogis, Hindu gods? In real Gurdwaras, Sikhs don't portray living things. Not even plants!"

"Meditating on his picture, performing fire pujas? Is that a joke?"

I didn't hear any of this claptrap until I came to India on my first yatra. And what a time that was.

Traditional Sikhi doesn't require adherents to go on yatras, or pilgrimages, but people do it anyway. Everyone loves to come to the Golden Temple to pray and experience its beauty and peace. So whenever Yogiji said his devotees needed to go on a yatra, we always just bought tickets. Never asked questions. A hundred or more white Sikhs would dominate a 747 and descend on the Punjab in a great cloud, like the Mongol hordes.

But in 1982, strangely, there were just three of us that wanted to go. I didn't know the other two. A couple middle-aged ladies. Nobodies. Yogiji himself wasn't even going. It was unheard of! I didn't watch television or read newspapers. All I did was chant the Lord's name, sing kirtan, and accompany myself on the harmonium—a spiritual instrument like an accordion in a wooden box. Seriously. Did I wonder why the yatra was so small this year? Yes. Did I question it? No. Of course not. Since joining 3HO, I had never yet questioned God's will. Or Yogi Bhajan's.

Most ashramites were less isolated than I. They knew. You would think somebody might have grabbed me and hollered, "You're walking into a bloodbath! Get your ass off this plane!"

But as I boarded, everyone waved and said, "The Guru will protect you."

Protect me from what? I thought, as I waved.

Once we were in India, the two ladies and I had a guide: Baba Nam Singh, an American Sikh who had been living there for years. He had been able to learn Punjabi and, with the advantage of his suntanned skin, basically go native. Baba Nam Singh was known to travel under the protection of Yogi Bhajan, so despite the ongoing turmoil, he was able to safely get us in cars and take us around Amritsar to the typical pilgrimage sites. But when we got to the Golden Temple, it was a war zone.

A holy man named Jarnail Singh Bhindranwale had moved into the compound with several hundred of his followers. Although often associated with the Khalistan Movement, he neither opposed nor supported the formation of Khalistan. However, he did consider Sikhs as "a distinct nation", where nation means a community united by common history, geography and culture. In the labyrinthine world of Indian politics, Indira Gandhi's ruling Congress party had initially given Bhindranwale tacit support—and it is rumored that he also received covert financial support from them--as a counterbalance to the Sikh based *Akali* party in Punjab. Feeling that he had outlived his usefulness, Mrs. Gandhi allowed the Indian feds to accuse him of murder, theft, weapons trafficking, and any other charges they thought would stick. By 1982 he and his followers were wanted men. They hid out in the Golden Temple complex—specifically the Akal Takhat, the second most sacred building after the Harimandir Sahib. It was their fortress. There, Bhindranwale stockpiled weapons and oversaw the entire revolution.

People protested for Sikh rights everywhere, shouting and

screaming in the streets. Indira Gandhi gave her officers strict orders to shoot anyone in an orange turban (the devotional color), no questions asked. Sikhs fought this injustice, of course. People found bodies in alleyways all over the Punjab—Hindu and Sikh alike. Cops and soldiers aren't legally allowed inside the Temple grounds, but on the street outside, there was gunfire at night. You would see policemen grabbing anyone with a turban and hauling them away. Cops viciously beat guys right there on the pavement, while bystanders just watched. One night, a Punjabi Police captain was machine-gunned to death right outside the gate to our guesthouse.

In spite of all that, India was still India. When Indian Sikhs saw my turban and white skin, they all wanted to meet me. Sikhi is a proud culture but it is still small enough to have a bit of a club feeling to it. Typically Sikhs are born, not made, so a white-skinned convert is definitely an item of fascination. Several times I noticed someone see my face across a crowded room and start walking toward me as if he had no control. He would get to me and not even know what to say. He would just stare.

Baba Nam Singh and I were birds of a feather: born rebels. Unlike me, however, he had been separated from Yogiji so long that he actually had thoughts of his own. A rogue! Much as I felt obliged to obey Yogiji, I was impressed with his independent thinking.

Baba Nam Singh was not a political animal; he felt that Khalistan was not his issue. He simply loved hanging out with Bhindranwale's men and befriended many of them. He would go with them to the Harimandir Sahib every night, just after midnight, to do the seva of cleaning the floors. From there they would go to the Akal Takhat for more seva. The Indian media portrayed them as goons and terrorists; Baba Nam Singh said that he found them to be intelligent and devout men who were there because they believed in their cause.

When he explained the Khalistan movement to me I was excited. I wanted to be one with Indian Sikhs. Fight with them. Die for them. I was back to the old militant mindset, and it felt good.

So Baba Nam Singh got an idea. Bhindranwale happened to be residing in the same rest house that we were staying at, Guru Nanak Nivas, so we climbed up on the roof where Bhindranwale spent much of his time. Up there, the great man sat cross-legged, drank chai, and watched the carnage on the streets below. He was surrounded by beefy armed guards with AK47s. I had never laid hands on an assault rifle before, but always wanted to. The guards liked my white skin, and I liked their guns, so right away we had stuff to talk about.

All kinds of visitors climbed up there. Important people. They would sit cross-legged and talk at length to the holy man. Then they would leave; new visitors would come.

Sometimes voices were raised and then subsided. As far as I could gather, negotiations were taking place. People came and went all the time. They treated that rooftop like some government office.

I trembled with the thrill of war, itching to get my hands on a gun. So close to power! I thought of all the great revolutions in history. I thought of Washington and Jefferson, of Robespierre and Lenin. I even thought of Mao Tse-tung.

Down with the bourgeoisie!

I thought of Castro and Guevara dismantling Batista from their mountain stronghold—nothing but a Belgian 12 gauge and a couple of Springfields for their whole little rebel army. And now Bhindranwale. But this revolution was even better than those. It was bigger than politics. As Sikhs, we had God on our side.

This was destiny.

This was living!

Forget about the daily grind in L.A., I thought. *I want to hide out on rooftops with guns! Boldly pursue a great cause! High-level negotiations, code words, secret handshakes… Oh God, what a dream come true!* And to fight for my adopted culture, my lifestyle, my spiritual practice—what could be more profound?

I wasn't afraid of it. I was born for it.

When I came into my adolescence I developed the attitude of a skeptic and a rebel. I had been obedient to God, obedient to the church, obedient to my officers at military school. I was still OK with being obedient to God—and it was hard to be anything but obedient to Yogiji -- but my experiences at my church, at Texas Christian University and in the business world had taught me that those in power seldom had the best interests of others at heart -- least of all those whom they were supposed to be serving.

The world has this image of India as the home of Gandhi, the world's largest democracy, and a wonderfully spiritual place—the light of the world. Actually, even though India doesn't make it into the top twenty of most corrupt countries in the world, it's an incredibly corrupt place. Not as corrupt as North Korea, Sudan, Afghanistan and seventeen or so others but that's small comfort.

If all the politically correct people in the West knew how India treats its minorities and smaller religious groups—like the Sikhs—they would be up in arms. The essentially Hindu central government, however, is very image conscious and does whatever it can to promote the image of goodness and spirituality that most people associate with India. They also do what they can to discredit Sikhs within the diaspora, in places like Canada, the UK and the States. The Sikhs don't seem to have the wherewithal to promote their image to the world and so their sufferings go unnoticed. That is until an event like the Oak Creek massacre fills the front pages.

Hearing about the deliberate actions taken by the Indian Central Government to weaken, discredit and undermine the Sikhs made my blood boil. My righteous indignation was full to overflowing. That and my desire to get my hands on one of those AK-47's.

I imagined I would die in service to the cause—a great warrior to be remembered through the ages. That was how I wanted to go. *Bring on the action! The sooner the better!* My blood rushed with possibility. I could have lived that way, died that way. Could have joined them. Except for the language barrier, of course. I didn't speak word one of Punjabi.

The final barrier to my insane fantasy came when Yogiji wouldn't allow it. I called him from a pay phone, told him I thought I could be useful to the cause and wanted to stay in India a bit longer. He said no, knowing I would obey. Truth was, Yogiji never did support the Khalistan movement.

Nevertheless, I had fourteen days to entertain myself behind the walls of the Golden Temple. Baba Nam Singh and I went up to the roof frequently, just to visit. Usually Bhindranwale was busy—talking to all those people, holding his appointments. Finally, I got a chance to speak to the great man himself, with Baba Nam Singh translating. I told Bhindranwale how I became a Sikh and all about the great Yogi Bhajan. He had met with Yogiji there in his rooftop lair but didn't seem to be particularly impressed with him. Bhindranwale told me of his desire to bring the Punjab back to fundamentalist ways: uncut hair, no alcohol, no tobacco.

"I don't drink, smoke, or eat meat!" I proudly proclaimed.

He sipped his chai. "I see you have a long beard. This is very good," he replied, through Baba Nam Singh.

"I never cut my hair! Never!" I was not done impressing him, though. I went on, "I chant my *Banis* every day, and sir, I'm a crack shot with a rifle!"

Bhindranwale looked off into the distance and I noticed Baba Nam Singh hadn't bothered to interpret what I had said. He was looking at me funny. So I mimed shooting police officers below—first with a submachine gun, then I lay prone and showed him how I would do it with a target rifle. Bhindranwale got it. He smiled. Thinking back, I was just some wide-eyed kid full of Waheguru. He humored me, but that was the end of the conversation.

Once I got back to L.A., I wrote the holy man a letter. I said I wished I could have stayed there with him to fight for Khalistan. I said I was sure the Guru would give him victory in the end.

He was martyred two years later, in a violent siege, called Operation Blue Star, which destroyed the sacred Akal Takhat. I wasn't *exactly* jealous. I mean, the man was dead. But he had gone down in a blaze of glory. That, I admired. I had to. It was the ultimate fantasy I had played out ten thousand times with plastic green army men in the mud battlements of my mother's rose garden. Most importantly, his sacrifice meant something to millions of people. This had not been any random war, it had been a just war, with what, for me, were clear-cut lines between the good guys and the bad.

I tell Sobha Singh and Amrik Singh all about it, especially about how Bhindranwale and I had that brief correspondence. They are suitably impressed, but I immediately regret it. After all, I'm hoping to get let out of prison within the week, and, for all I know, my association with Bhindranwale, the wanted man, could have been classified as a crime. I quickly try to steer the conversation back to my story about trying to enlist in the U.S. Army.

"Bhindranwale never responded to those letters with the newspaper clippings, but I'm sure, a few months later, he followed the story about me suing the U.S. Army," I say.

What Sikh leader wouldn't follow a story about a man standing up for Sikh rights against the military might of the world's greatest superpower? When it all started, a couple months after that yatra, Black Krishna assured me Sikhs all around the world were following the case, and that I was big news in India. I pictured it: people talking about me and my bravery everywhere, framing my photograph and festooning it with flower garlands. The whole deal! All over India, Sikhs surely knew who I was, I thought, at the time.

"But listen", I tell Sobha Singh. "After my attempt to join the army had been in the newspapers a few times, some respected advocates gave me a call." I can tell it's hard to get his mind off Bhindranwale, but I'm putting my all into it. Of course, the "respected advocates" were actually representatives of the ACLU. They volunteered to represent me pro bono in a discrimination suit against the U.S. Army. I remember, in the moment, putting my hand over the phone receiver and letting out a bloodthirsty battle cry. I told them, "Let's screw that jackass Weinberger to the wall!"

But we lost the case.

The court decreed that the army could do whatever it wants. I appealed, took it to a higher court, and got the same result.

It didn't matter though; at that point, Black Krishna told me Yogiji was tired of the whole thing. I tried to propose more ideas. Lobbying congress? A press junket to Gurdwaras around the world? More protests? I was so into being a Sikh, I didn't see how anyone could consider this less than the ultimate cause on the planet. But no. She said it was over. Yogi Bhajan had made his point, had silenced both his Indian and American detractors, and had emerged, if not triumphant, then at least having established 3HO as a legitimate religion. But this opportunity lost had, I believe, tragic consequences.

If Bhajan had followed through and pressured the Reagan administration enough to allow Sikhs to join the armed forces it is arguable that the Oak Creek tragedy might not have happened.

There has always been bigotry within the US Army and other services. Had Sikhs been allowed to integrate it's arguable that Wade Michael Page—the Oak Creek gunman—might have known Sikhs from his army service and might have understood that they were not the Taliban and had nothing to do with 9/11.

America can clearly see the result of the US government's racist policies. The U.S. military must fully embrace what they profess to teach: respect for religious diversity. The US Government urgently needs to change their policy of religious discrimination and allow Sikhs to proudly join the ranks of US soldiers serving the United States of America.

And as for me? Well, it was hard to give up my dream of single-handedly raising the banner of international Sikh righteousness, but with Yogi Bhajan's guidance, I came down from the media high and rejoined normal life.

chapter 24

I survive the week in the company of Sobha Singh and Amrik Singh, but it is awkward. I still enjoy the relative freedom of being able to come and go at will and walk around the grounds as I please—an arrangement made by Dadaji's relative, and apparently still in place. The two of them, however, have no such privileges.

By the second week, I simply can't be far from a toilet at any time, so I stay put and meditate. The dysentery I had feared, when Dadaji enthused about the purity of prison water, has arrived in force. These Indian toilets are just a hole in a concrete floor. You squat over them and splash water on yourself afterward. Toilet paper is unknown and actually considered unclean. The plumbing couldn't handle it anyway, and there is no system of garbage disposal. In cities, as far as I can tell, all they do is burn the trash. Also they have street sweepers who sweep up about half of the street detritus every evening with brooms made out of lashed-together twigs. Imagine if Indians used toilet paper! Used toilet paper would be everywhere! All over the city! Those twig-broom-sweepers would never be able to round it all up! A little thing like toilet paper could destroy India itself. Destroy it.

I'm practically living in that little concrete bunker of a latrine, with its spiders and flies and just a horrible, horrible stink. The prisoners on latrine duty throw water around the bathroom until every wall and floor is thoroughly drenched, which seems to be what passes for cleaning. Occasionally, they even scrape the spider webs out of the corners.

The prison is overcrowded and these latrines just were not ever meant to service so many people. Out in the fields, the sewage bubbles up where buried pipes are broken, and great muddy puddles of shit seep to the surface. Some of the newer bathrooms just have open sewers flowing out of them, which is gross but actually more efficient. Going to the bathroom as many times as I do in a day, I have to hold my breath. I just have to. It takes all my will power, but I resolve to survive the dysentery without vomiting. I simply refuse to vomit. Sometimes I feel the spasms coming, the heaving. I clench it down. I refuse.

At first, the squatting is fine. I have been to India before. But with this dysentery, it gets to be tiresome. I'm in there for an hour at a time. My Achilles tendons do not stretch like that. They don't stretch at all, in fact. They are like concrete. Indians, they have these gymnast's legs. I once saw a guy selling street food, sitting on his little cart. His legs were skinny and twisted. I thought he was a cripple, but he hopped around on his folded legs like a jumping frog, and I realized he wasn't handicapped at all. Some Indians are just like that. Their legs are like insects' legs—all spindly and bending every which-a-way. I'm getting charlie-horses just from squatting over the toilet, and I wonder, sometimes angrily, how thirty years of yoga never prepared me for this.

I am resting in the cell when Wall Eye finally comes to tell me I am free to go. I am thrilled, but the prison of my dysentery is something I will have to take with me. Sobha Singh and Amrik Singh lighten the mood by giving me high-fives and then accompanying me to the gate. As we pass through the prison yard, they yell out to other prisoners that I am getting released. Everyone gathers around to pat me on the back! Even the burly man who first washed my clothes is here. They all wish me well. We're like a big family, and, in a way, I am sorry to leave. After bidding my fellow inmates goodbye,

I step through a small, man-sized door cut into a massive iron one that could be for elephants or ox-carts. I enter a cavernous enclosure, filled with guards. As usual, they loll about.

Someone hands me a paper, and I sign it. My briefcase is handed back to me. Another guard gives me a date and time when I should appear at the Amritsar courthouse, for my hearing. He tells me my passport has been confiscated until my hearing, three months from now.

Someone hands me a telephone. I stare at it, wishing I could call Mom, Dad, or even my ex-wife Sat Siri Kaur. I start wracking my brains, trying to think of someone in India who would be glad to hear from me. After the way he left me in prison, I don't want to risk calling Dadaji.

Then I remember Dr. Jagdesh. I find his number in my bag and call him.

"My God, man! Where have you been?" he asks with real concern. I tell him.

"Oh Guru *Sant* Singh! Guru *Sant* Singh! Why didn't you listen to me?"

I tell him the situation, and he says he will come get me, throwing in a couple of reprimands for good measure. I can't believe what a good friend he is, this perverted physiotherapist. I send up thanks to God for having met him.

I take the long pedestrian path back up to the road. Linking the bustle of Amritsar traffic to the high walls of the prison, the path is bordered with scraggly trees, overgrown weeds, and unused outbuildings. It's an unremarkable journey back into the world, and feels like a walk of shame. Prisoners in chains are escorted past me, in the other direction, and they stare, stare, stare.

A smiling, beturbaned guard lets me out at the gate, and I wait by the busy highway. Eventually, Dr. Jagdesh drives up. He says I look thin and tries not to say, 'I told you so,' yet again. The difficulty of this seems to be contorting his face.

"I guess you were right about Dadaji being trouble!" I say, with a laugh, to ease the pressure in his skull. He nods humbly. Dr. Jagdesh drops me off at the Golden Temple, urging me to come visit his office as soon as I can.

I get a pilgrim's room in one of the Temple's inexpensive boarding houses, called a *Nivas* (rhymes with 'tree moss'). My room is just big enough to pace back and forth, so that is what I do. As I pace, I realize that without my passport I am between a rock and a hard place. A foreigner cannot even check into a hotel in India without a passport. You definitely don't want to be caught on the street without it. The police are very strict about this. *So how*, I wonder, *am I to survive?*

chapter 25

I resolve not to leave the Golden Temple campus for the duration of the wait. I'm safe in here, and they serve free food twice a day. I can survive. But I'm furious! I am a Khalsa! A mighty Khalsa! Yogi Bhajan taught me I was among the most proud, most holy people on this planet! How could I have sunk so low? How could the Punjabi Police be so disrespectful of my status as a holy man?

Some of the world's greatest holy men have become martyrs, I reason. Perhaps that's the road I'm on: the road to martyrdom. I stop my pacing and pray. I meditate until the sun goes down. Eventually, I realize I have to connect to the international 3HO network. These people have power and money, and I'm one of them, whether they like it or not. They must rally around me. They *must.*

The trouble is, I'm not sure whom exactly to contact. The obvious choice is Hari Jiwan Singh. Hari Jiwan—who used to run the boiler room in L.A, and who acted as my spokesman when I was trying to join the U.S. Army—moved to New Mexico about the same time I did and by now has practically taken over the Española ashram, Hacienda de Guru Ram Das. If he could, he would style himself to be Yogi Bhajan's successor, but he just doesn't have the charisma. He doesn't have the Sikh authenticity, either. Oh, he has the glamour. The jewelry he wears, just like Yogiji! But he doesn't have the kindness, the loving tenderness, the spiritual side. He's more of a business man than anything else, and since most people don't know about the gem-stone fraud he got nailed on, in an FTC (Federal Trade Commission) sting operation called "Project Field of Schemes", he is able to control most of the starry eyed Bhajanistas.

I do remember one other friend who has some pull. Her name is Mukta Kaur, and she is head of 3HO public relations. She travels to India frequently and might even be in Amritsar right now. I have known Mukta Kaur for 25 years. We practically grew up in 3HO together. At least, we've grown old in it together. I know her ex-husband, who eventually left 3HO, and her kids, the subjects of a bitter custody battle. She is politically connected and has been to the White House, met a couple of U.S. presidents. She is a powerful woman, but, unfortunately, also friends with my ex-wife, Sat Siri Kaur.

I don't have her phone number on hand, but I know where to find it, so I go to the closest 3HO stronghold: Miri Piri Academy, Yogi Bhajan's international school.

It's lovely to look at: big decorative gates are set in a high white wall surrounding a pristine emerald lawn. In the center is a rambling, white building. Inside, the kids run around in their turbans and cloaks—the school uniform. I take a one-hour bus ride, then get a bicycle rickshaw to take me through the countryside and rural farms of outer Amritsar until I reach the walled enclosure of Miri Piri. There, a guard sends me inside to the receptionist, and she sends me to wait for the principal in a beautiful garden patio.

An hour later, the principal opens the French doors, both at once, like a lady in a Windex commercial—smelling the clean country air and seeing everything sparkle. Her clothes look pristine, white, and unruffled as if freshly from a steam bath, but her face is tight. Lips, eyes, nostrils—everything pinched. Instantly, she wants nothing to do with me. I ask if she will at least give me the contact information for Mukta Kaur, but she won't. She throws me out of the place without the least ceremony.

Days later, I actually spot Mukta Kaur and the Miri Piri principal strolling together on the *parikarma* at the Golden Temple. I try to talk to Mukta Kaur, but she looks away. I ask if she knows anyone I could contact—someone who could sort things out with the police.

"Just keep your nose clean!" she says, over her shoulder. "Stay clean! Stay out of trouble!"

"This affects all of 3HO!" I insist. "Not just me!"

It's true, too. My arrest could become an issue of 3HO's international reputation, not to mention Sikh rights.

They run away from me, then.

The bitches literally run.

The next day I consider another option: one that has been in the back of my head all along, but that, until now, I didn't dare consider: Bibiji. Yogiji's wife. She is still living in New Mexico, in the family palace, and still has some clout, though the trustees of Yogiji's estate are gradually stripping it from her, year by year.

To me, Bibiji is like a goddess: scary, but perfect. She always acted like the ultimate Indian wife, supporting Bhajan in everything he did, and standing in the background, ready to lend a hand, ready to serve him. At the same time, she is smart. She always knows exactly how to run her household and her affairs. Good luck to anyone who gets in her way!

Once she set me straight when I went to her for counseling just after she received her psychology degree. There is a strong will, an intelligence, a businesslike manner to her, and yet there is the traditional side of her, too. That side ensured that Yogiji himself was the only person who never got lashed with her sharp tongue. She is everything I have always wanted, but could never find, in a wife. Everything I am searching for now.

I dare to exit the Golden Temple grounds. Across the street, I slip into a long-distance phone center—what they, for some reason, call an "STD." Amazingly, Bibiji answers the phone but then gives me an earful.

"If you wanted another wife, I could have found you one! Why didn't you ask me? Instead you . . . you . . . Finding a wife . . . it's not a cattle call!" she screams through the line. "Families meet families. It's a very civil procedure. You meet one or two, not fifty women! You go through someone you know—a cousin or a friend. Someone like me! You don't just go out and meet strangers, you idiot. You Idiot!"

Immediately, I regret calling her, but then Bibiji surprises me. She tells me she will call the manager of the Nivas and use her connections for whatever they are worth. In the end, she convinces the manager to let me stay there for fifty rupees a night, less than $1.50.

I believe she did all she really could for me. Poor Bibiji. She doesn't have much political power, really, and never had. The woman certainly paid her own dues to Yogi Bhajan, putting up with his absence for nearly a decade. Back in the sixties, he came to America to make his fortune and she raised their kids in India, alone. Then, when he finally did send for her, she had to put up with all those "secretaries."

chapter 26

After suing the army, back in '83, I was so full of myself that I refused to return to the dreaded boiler room, so Yogiji gave me another job: chauffer for his team of personal secretaries.

It was definitely a promotion.

His secretaries were a handpicked team of women, always single, who traveled with him everywhere. The story was that they were celibates, having "dedicated all their creative energies to the lifelong service of Yogiji." Kind of a perfect hybrid of Charlie's Angels and the Stepford Wives. Like us all, they dressed completely in white, but added gossamer veils to their turbans. They were like angels, from afar, until you looked into their eyes.

The secretaries spent their time massaging Yogiji's feet, serving his food, fanning away flies. Whatever went on behind closed doors between them and Yogiji—they never talked. In return for their service to him, the secretaries had total control over who saw Yogi Bhajan and when. They also made decisions about ashram-owned businesses. They hired and fired. If one of them didn't like you, you would get the worst ashram housing, worst job, worst of everything.

They slept in the same room with him, too. One at a time, two at a time, or more, or so I've heard. No one knows what really went on, but we were assured by Yogiji himself that he was too pure for any sexual hanky-panky as he had committed himself to celibacy.

One of his secretaries in particular was the one who got me my job. Guru Ke Kaur. That voice! Angelic! She was so sweet, so soft-spoken—utterly feminine in every way. I'm sure Yogiji was as captivated by her as I was. Soon after taking her on as a secretary, he had an intuition that she had a certain "car karma."

Bhajan felt that if she drove herself she was liable to get into a horrible accident and die, so Guru Ke Kaur wasn't allowed to drive anywhere. I would pick her up and take her grocery shopping or wherever. Over time, we became friends of a sort, but only in the way that ashramites could ever really be friends: as fellow devotees, always turning their conversations to the exalted source, to Yogi Bhajan.

Although Guru Ke Kaur was my favorite, I ended up driving all the secretaries and developed a limited friendship with each one. This was as close as anyone got to them outside of Yogiji. In fact, I felt like I knew them even better than they knew each other. Although the secretaries, as a whole, presented a united front, believe me, they were not friends with each other.

Premka Kaur was Yogiji's favorite and above us all, even the other secretaries. Unapproachable.

A lady of great intensity, she was Yogi Bhajan's "Secretary General of Sikhs in the Western Hemisphere"

Sat Simran Kaur was a bossy Jewish girl that handled events and entertainment. She set up meetings with the Pope, the Dalai Lama. Heady stuff! She was hot to trot—always in the most expensive cars and designer kurtas.

Nirinjan Kaur was a spicy Italian girl. She handled everything about Yogiji's appointment book, living quarters, the kitchen staff, you name it. When you received an answer from Yogiji, she was the one who typed the directives from the great man.

Nirinjan Kaur would spend most nights with Yogiji in a converted garage in the back of the Guru Ram Das Ashram on Preuss Road. After my all-night security duty at the ashram, I'd see her walking Yogiji's white dog and white cat,

"Sat Nam, good morning Nirinjan Kaur,"

"Sat Nam Guru Sant Singh."

Shakti Parwha Kaur was the only secretary older than Yogi Bhajan and had been with him from the very beginning, even before he first started teaching yoga at Jules Buccieri's antique store at the top of Robertson Boulevard in Beverly Hills. Shakti didn't like to drive much so I would act as her chauffeur. Every week we would drive to the Wells Fargo bank on Wilshire Blvd in Beverly Hills, to retrieve a different set of jewelry for him to wear.

On my first visit to the bank, my eyes almost popped out of my head. Within the safety deposit boxes, I saw literally dozens of trays of expensive and ostentatious jewelry. Each week Yogiji demanded a fresh array of pendants, necklaces and rings; different kinds of gemstones to align his auric body with the vibrations of different planetary positions and conjunctions. It was highly scientific and Yogiji had it all figured out.

"Let's go get the crown jewels Guru Sant Singh."

"OK Shakti, will we be taking the Rolls or the Benz today?"

Siri Ram Kaur was a Harvard graduate who edited the ashram magazine, and Surya Kaur—also Jewish—was a short, pushy girl. I don't know what she did except incite conflict.

Then there was angelic Guru Ke Kaur. All she had to do was hang around and be sexy.

She did it well.

Some secretaries stayed with him for life, but over the decades, many came and went from his service. Some would eventually meet a guy and leave Yogiji to get married, others would pursue careers or simply leave for unexplained reasons. There were always more women willing to accept the honor.

Mostly Yogi Bhajan chose his secretaries for their intelligence or skill in some area. He had secretaries to write books for him, do his taxes, manage his businesses, and do his homework so that he could get his online Ph.D. One thing about his secretaries: all were smart as whips. Many had Ivy League degrees. The whole arrangement was a stroke of genius. He had a team of people with the best educations money could buy, and he got it all for free. They did it to serve God, and, I assume, for the status.

Bhajan used to say he kept the secretaries' auras aligned, like a "super husband", while Bibiji and their kids lived in a palatial estate nearby, almost forgotten.

Those secretaries spent a lot of time listening to Yogiji, taking down his every word for posterity. What they liked about me was that I actually listened to them. They always had plenty to say, but it never amounted to anything other than bitching about each other. It was like living in a big swarm of bees: everybody buzzing, everybody stinging, everybody after the honey. And if the lady got a drink of nectar—a little personal attention from Yogiji—all she wanted was more. Even Guru Ke Kaur wasn't above it. She would jump into the fray just like the others, stinging deeply with soft, delightful words.

It was lust. Pure and simple.

By denying or shunning one of them, he would only make her want him more. It was the same thing he did with all of us, only more intimate.

He once told a fellow disciple: "See these women?" He waved his arm around his living room which was full—as usual—with his staff. "They all want to fuck me but they know they can't because of my vow of celibacy. So you know what they do instead? They fuck with my head."

They tended to fuck with everybody else's head, as well.

chapter 27

My daring jaunt to the STD booth emboldens me, and I decide it's not too risky to grab a bicycle rickshaw and pay Dr. Jagdesh a visit. When I get to his office, he is enjoying his lunch of warm chapattis and okra stew, which his wife brought all the way from home. He ushers me in and asks if I have a new advocate yet. I tell him no.

"You won't believe what that cockroach did. That cockroach of an advocate Dadaji got for you; you know, Rajeev. You just won't believe it when I tell you."

"What?"

"As soon as you landed in prison he called me."

"You? How did he . . ."

"You must have put me as your contact person on the form."

"Oh, yes! I didn't have anyone! I'm sorry!"

"No problem, my brother. I know how to handle these assholes."

"This Rajeev, he said to me, 'If you don't pay an extra 33,000 rupees, I'll revoke the bail for Guru Sant Singh.'"

"My God!"

"I said he was a left-handed sisterfucker who didn't deserve to live, and I didn't care what he did. 'Get out of my face,' I told him. 'If I ever see you I will call the police and you and Guru Sant Singh can talk about it together behind the prison walls. What do you think of that?'"

"What did he do?"

"He never called me again. And I guess he didn't revoke your bail after all, eh? What do you think of that!"

"It's great! Jagdesh, I knew he was a slimy son of a bitch from the instant I laid eyes on him. And do you know how much I gave him already? 32,000 rupees!"

"Guru Sant Singh!"

"I had to!"

"Listen to me. That's not the end of it for you." Dr. Jagdesh gets up and paces behind his desk. "You are going to pay out a lot more in time. Rajeev thinks you are a walking ATM machine and so will the judge. You need a new advocate right away."

I tell Dr. Jagdesh about my trip to Miri Piri, approaching Mukta Kaur at the Golden Temple, and calling Bibiji.

"Why are your people not helping you? They are your family."

"Honestly, I don't know. Mukta Kaur acted almost like she was afraid of me. I don't know what to make of it."

"Guru Sant Singh," Dr. Jagdesh asks, stepping very close and looking straight into my eyes. "Have you any enemies? Here in India?"

"In India? I don't have any enemies in India! Sure, in America, sure I do, but not in India. That's why I can't figure out why Mukta Kaur and this Miri Piri principal hate me so much."

"Your arrest was on television, Guru Sant Singh."

"Oh, yeah. That."

"You say this Mukta Kaur is friends with your wife?"

"Ex-wife."

"And this ex-wife . . . is she your enemy?"

I slump into my chair a little too hard, and a crack in the plastic lengthens with a pop. I think for a few minutes. Is Sat Siri Kaur my enemy? I hadn't thought so. I thought the divorce was pretty amicable. But I can't forget one moment. I'm not sure of its importance exactly, but it just shows how unpredictable she is. I didn't think it was a big deal at the time, but to her, for some reason, it was.

It was just last year. After my first vacation in Japan I really grew to like it, so I began flying to Japan pretty frequently to get away from the mess of our marriage. Also, my neighbor, Siri Hari, and I were involved in a bitter lawsuit. Being in Japan was heavenly and being in New Mexico was sheer hell. The women in Japan just love American men. They smiled a lot, laughed at my jokes, and treated me like a king; that's all there was to it.

Although she had agreed to the divorce, legal proceedings with Sat Siri Kaur were not yet underway. To me, that meant I was free to at least look around. In Japan, I met this 30-year-old waitress named Yunmi and totally fell for her. She studied yoga at the 3HO ashram there, so we had some nice long talks about spiritual stuff. That was all we did together, though. I believe in marriage; I don't fool around. But there was something about her that really attracted me and I was under the impression that she liked me too. During my marriage to Sat Siri Kaur, I had become very influenced by astrology and thought I saw an astrological destiny for Yunmi and me. So I sent her an email, professing my love, supported by my astrological fantasizing.

Your Venus is in the 4th house of Love and my Mars and Venus are in the 10th house, which has a direct aspect to your Venus. My Venus is also directly conjunct your 1st house ascendant within 1 degree, this shows a strong Love connection. Ask any Astrologer.

And so on.

Somehow Sat Siri Kaur discovered the email. I don't know why I wasn't more careful, but I just didn't think it mattered anymore.

She confronted me, hollering, "How could you!"

"But you agreed to a divorce!" I replied. I didn't know why she was upset. There was a long silence, then she said, "You believed me?"

There's nothing you can say! Women! It's madness. I would

have taken the problem straight to Yogiji, except he was dead. So I just shrugged it off.

"Dr. Jagdesh," I say. "I don't think Sat Siri Kaur is my enemy. But I have never been good at reading women. Anything could be going through her head. Anything at all. But my ex-wife is kind of like me, you know. She doesn't get together with groups. She mostly keeps to herself. For fun, she likes predicting things, you know. She takes clients and does their astrology, or she buys and sells futures on the stock market. She reads books. She's not the type to go out and start an international slander campaign against me. She doesn't have that kind of drive."

Dr. Jagdesh leans against his examining table, looking at his shoes. He drums his fingers on its taught, vinyl surface. "Okay, so your ex-wife, she might be an enemy, but not a dangerous one. Who else? Do you have any other enemies? Guru Sant Singh, think hard. This is not a joke."

It's funny the way he always says to me, "marriage is not a joke!" "Your enemies are not a joke!" It makes me wonder if I am, unbeknownst to me, actually wearing a big red nose and floppy shoes. Is there something about me that suggests I think everything is a joke? To Dr. Jagdesh, there must be, but for the life of me I can't figure it out.

As far as my enemies go, the list is pretty long. Sat Siri Kaur is really the least of them. Jacqueline Forsythe, for instance. She quit harassing me many years back, but I don't think she ever forgave me. If she ever has the least chance for revenge upon me I'm sure she will move Heaven and Earth for it, and no mistake.

chapter 28

Back in L.A., in the mid-eighties, one day, I had a realization. It was obvious that the key to getting the love and attention I was so desperately craving from Yogiji was to make more money—a lot more money. The people who Yogiji allowed to be around himself and his secretaries on a regular basis were all extremely well-off. I desperately wanted to be a part of that inner circle and get the kind of attention that they got. So I figured that if I was able to up my net worth by a considerable amount I might stand a chance of joining Yogiji's "in crowd."

I didn't see any reason why I couldn't. After all Yogiji had told me that everything I touched would turn to gold, and I chose to believe it. In fact, I staked everything on it.

I was running an art gallery on La Cienega Blvd and doing well. But I was desirous of making millions.

Andy Warhol had just died and the value of his work went through the roof. I formed a "partnership" with Bob Goldman, a man with a rolodex full of art-dealer connections. Bob assured me that this was a chance of a lifetime so I gave him a big chunk of my own money to "invest" in these Warhol's. My intention was then to sell them for a profit—lots of profit.

Goldman always wanted all cash, I mean green dollars, no checks. In fact it seems many entrepreneurs we associated with back then dealt only in cash. While cashing a $50,000 check in the back room of Hari Jiwan Singh's favorite check cashing store in Santa Monica to pay for a Marilyn Monroe serigraph that Warhol had supposedly embellished, I ran into Baba Singh who was adding up a ten inch high stack of checks to be cashed from that week's telemarketing sales. Baba Singh was one of the first students to practice kundalini yoga and follow Yogi Bhajan. I had a lot of respect for the guy so when I said, "Sat Nam Baba Singh" and he ignored me, I wasn't sure what to think. Maybe he was just having a bad day.

Baba Singh had partnered up with Hari Jiwan to sell type writer ribbons on the telephone and was another of Yogiji's Mukhia Singh Sahibs out there making money for the Dharma but maybe Baba Singh just didn't like the fact that I was only 26 years old and trying to be like the big boys of the ashram, cashing six figure checks, wheeling and dealing with Yogiji's right hand men and all.

At any rate, I was becoming so successful and well known that when this deal with Goldman came along I sincerely believed this new chance to make really big money was a blessing from God and so decided to "spread the opportunity around." In my excitement and naivety, I wanted to help my friends and others share in these profits. Of course, the fact that I would make a commission on each sale was also a motivator but I genuinely wanted to share my good fortune with my fellow ashramites. Needless to say, Bob Goldman encouraged me.

Most of all I was looking forward to sending ten percent (or perhaps more) of these enormous profits to Yogiji as my *daswand* (tithe). Surely that would catch his attention.

Even so, it wasn't only that I wanted to impress Yogiji. I really believed in his teachings and what he said was his—and our—mission. Way back in the 60s, the cast of the musical "Hair" was singing about the Age of Aquarius" and the hippies were looking towards a radical change in the consciousness of society. Yogiji was a very shrewd operator and told his students that we were the "chosen ones" to lead the world into the Age of Aquarius.

Yogi Bhajan's Message at the Dawn of the Aquarian Age

THE AGE OF AQUARIUS BEGAN ON NOVEMBER II, 1991.

We are in the cusp period between Pisces and Aquarius.

The world shall change. A new world shall emerge beyond our expectations, imaginations, and situations.

Of course, when he first arrived from India, Yogiji had said the Aquarian Age would begin in 2005. But what's fourteen years between friends?

I genuinely believed all this stuff and felt that I could help fund this spiritual revolution from reselling Andy Warhol serigraphs.

Maybe I wasn't part of Yogiji's inner circle—at least, not yet—but 3HO people knew and trusted me. I had total access to Yogi Bhajan any time I wanted. I could just call him up. It felt like being God's little brother.

I wanted to believe, and my investors wanted to believe, too. Being Sikhs, raw faith was our stock in trade. We all had plenty of practice in it. After all, believing is a lot easier than asking tough questions, and it feels so good.

Hundreds of thousands of dollars I borrowed. Nearly a half million when all was said and done.

I'm embarrassed to say I also borrowed from my first wife's rich relatives.

Yeah, I know.

The first deal was legit: a Marilyn Monroe that I sold for a hundred grand. The next deal seemed legit too: an American Eagle embellished by Warhol. After selling these two, I think Goldman realized just how easy it was to pull money out of all these wealthy, turban-headed fools, so he just started taking the money and saying the paintings were coming along later.

He played me for a sucker all the way. Most of the paintings he supposedly bought and sold never existed in the first place, and neither did the fancy clients. I kept handing him briefcases full of cash, and he kept saying the buyers were just taking a little time to come through. I had to be patient because the money had to be wired from Switzerland, or some place, and there were international trade issues. So much horse shit.

Then the American Eagle painting turned out to be fake, and I got sued. There was even a Grand Jury investigation into possible criminal activities by Goldman and myself. The reason it all blew up so badly was because it's so difficult to prove fraud when an artist is dead, and what with Warhol and his Factory—he was always having other people embellish his stuff. It's impossible to know which paintings were actually done by him.

I couldn't pay my investors back, and people lost their savings. One lady, Jacqueline Forsythe, had taken a loan out against her family home to get in on the thing. I have to confess that I had done a very thorough sales job to get both her and her husband involved but they were as gung ho about the possibility of cleaning up as much as I was; in fact, more so. The money she put up felt, at the time, like the last piece of the puzzle. With that capital, I really thought she, I, and all the 3HO investors would strike it rich.

Yogi Bhajan told her the investment was a sure thing, so of course she believed him. Well, she lost everything.

In 1992 I had to declare bankruptcy. Jacqueline wasn't even the one I owed the most money to, so if I had had the money to pay anyone back, it probably wouldn't have been her anyway.

It was a very dark time in my life. The people who lost money with me were not shy in letting me know their feelings and I had to live with that. But what was worse was my own shame and guilt; not only the shame that so many people had suffered from my bad judgment and naivety, but the shame that I had allowed myself to be taken in by a conman. Even though I was still in my twenties, I had imagined that I was pretty hot stuff and destined for great things but I had had my ass handed to me on a plate. I was still ready to believe in Yogi Bhajan no matter what. He had told me I was destined for greatness, so I had felt free to take some risks—big ones, because it was a big promise he made me in return for a big sacrifice. After all, Yogiji had said, "You'll be ten times greater than me!"

Of course, the fall-out from this disaster went on and on. There were people who left 3HO because of it—Jacqueline foremost among them. It was a real mess.

That was when, to get away from the bad vibes in L.A., my first wife Prem Kaur and I followed Yogi Bhajan to the ashram in Española, New Mexico. He had bought land there and built a golden-domed Gurdwara, an executive building, and even an ostrich farm for gathering ornamental feathers. The whole thing was entered by gates so grand it could have been some eighteenth-century viscount's castle. Golden statues of giant Buddhas and Hindu gods flanked the driveway. All the bells and whistles.

This ashram, incongruously placed out in the scrub and sagebrush desert near provincial Española, "the low-rider capital of the world," was supposed to be the new spiritual center for 3HO. At first, tumbleweeds kept rolling spookily past the gleaming white marble Gurdwara, with its golden dome, but eventually we cleared them all away. Yogiji helped Prem Kaur and I get a new start by selling me a house. In truth, I asked my mother to buy it, since I was broke and had a lien on my bank account anyway.

But that woman Jacqueline tracked us to New Mexico like a bloodhound. Hell bent, she and her whole family, toting along her newborn baby, drove 900 dusty miles from Los Angeles to Española, crammed like sardines into a beat-up Honda. They holed up in some cheap hotel while she tried to sue me for the house, but of course it was in my mother's name. Her family picketed the ashram for days walking frenetically back and forth, like tigers in the zoo, in front of the ashram's huge doors, marble pilasters, and gold domes. Their signs said I was a crook. I started carrying my pistol.

Oh, she played the victim well, Jacqueline did. But she wasn't so innocent. Her mom had put the house in Jacqueline's name for a reason; it wasn't just out of the kindness of her heart. Those people were no babes in the woods.

Jacqueline had made the investment—without even telling her mother that she was doing it—because she was looking for a payoff; and there was no reason for her to tell her mother since she was the legal owner of the house. When the deal went south, Jacqueline's mother and brother were furious. Along with all the other enraged investors, I had my hands full.

When all was said and done, I finally was able to make about $24,000 in payments on Jacqueline's $80,000 house loan and I paid her a $10,000 lump sum too. She wanted blood, that's all. And she got it in the form of my reputation. She sued me and I countersued for defamation of character, but when my bankruptcy went through, the whole thing got sent to Federal court and I guess the Forsythe clan decided it wasn't worth pursuing me any longer. Years later I started making gifts of several hundred dollars a month to them even though I had no legal obligation to do so. I have to say it made me feel a lot better about myself.

Then, even though Yogiji had told me that she would never divorce me, Prem Kaur left me. She ran off to Mexico with her lover, and I sank into depression. I wished I had never married her, but there was so much pressure in 3HO to get married. The whole philosophy was about male and female relations, husbands and wives.

"Look where that philosophy got me!" I tell Dr. Jagdesh. "But the thing is, I still believe in it. I do believe I can succeed as a husband. That's why I'm here, in India."

chapter 29

Frowning, Dr. Jagdesh asks, "So, Guru Sant Singh, you are now telling me you do have enemies." He takes out a pencil and begins scribbling a list, "Your ex-wife, this Jacqueline woman, and who else?"

"Specifically?"

"What do you mean? Of course, specifically."

"It's just that . . . pretty much the entire ashram, back in New Mexico . . . when they find out I've been thrown in jail they'll probably jump for joy."

Dr. Jagdesh's jaw drops open. He raises his eyebrows as if to say, "Continue," so I do.

If there was one unwritten rule in 3HO that no one will mention, it was this:

Yogiji was never wrong.

Not only was he never wrong but, if you disagreed with him for any reason, you were in the wrong. His staff and other minions *would* never--and, it seemed, *could* never allow themselves to believe that anyone who disagreed with him might be right.

The funny thing was that even Yogiji would occasionally admit he was wrong or even acknowledge that someone--who happened to disagree with him—might be right. More often though, he would yell and scream at anyone who showed the slightest sign of disagreement, in order to browbeat them into submission.

My father was an ex-marine officer—a pretty tough guy—and he taught me well. I grew up trained to be a fighter. Not a physical fighter; that was not my style. But he taught me to stand up for myself and for what was right.

When I became Yogiji's student, it was easy for me to transfer this attitude to the organization. We were told that Sikhs stood for righteousness and Yogiji even hinted that the time was fast approaching when we might have to fight and die again—for "righteousness', of course. I loved all this. It was music to my ears and I felt like I was finally fulfilling my life's purpose: I was a spiritual warrior, ready to fight and die for a "righteous cause'.

That's what I believed then and that is how I still try to live my life. Amongst the ashramites though—particularly the ones who hung around Yogiji—there was always a feeling that Sikhi, particularly the way that devout Punjabi Sikhs practice it, was a little bit of a nuisance; something to be, if not actually sneered at, regarded as "uncool" for those who occupied the rarefied heights of the Bhajan presence.

It was these kind of people who would go to the weekly Gurdwara service in Española and—rather than going in to enjoy the Guru's kirtan—would hang around outside and gossip until Yogiji showed up to give his weekly lecture, at which point they would go in and bow reverently to Siri Guru Granth Sahib.

The fact of the matter is that most so-called "American Sikhs" took up their version of Sikhi because of pressure from Yogiji or because it was required if you wanted to get some of his "energy." Since his death in 2004, while the number of Kundalini Yoga students has increased hugely, the number of white Sikhs has been dwindling.

In spite of his followers, I still loved the man. I thought he was . . . divine, magical, or something like that. The resonance of his voice was so soothing. The love pouring out of him when he addressed crowds, so undeniable. It was crystal clear to me, at least, that he had a direct line to God. Sure, sometimes he acted just plain greedy and materialistic, like a regular man, and sometimes he was a regular man. And then other times he was imbued with the spirit, and he was a God. A God of compassion, tenderness, and pure blissful forgiving love. But his God-self was tied to his man-self, so what could I do? I had to stay with him.

And yet I was determined, really, determined, that I was not going to be played for a sucker again. Not by anybody.

Not even by . . . Yogiji?

In Española I have managed to make enemies. It would take an hour to tick off a list of the ashram's grievances against me, but most are just little personality conflicts. The real problem, why they hate me, is that house Yogiji sold my mother. That damned house.

Part of the deal was that it needed a kitchen remodel and Yogiji was going to pay me five grand to do that. Once my mom got the house loan and signed on the dotted line, once Bhajan had the money in the bank, then he would pay me back for the remodel, was the deal. I didn't know why he wanted to do it that way, but I trusted him. But then the secretaries got involved. All twelve of them.

Yogiji had sold me a car some years back, an old Mercedes that I really paid too much for but because he had used the car for many years as his personal vehicle, I paid Yogiji his full asking price. I had in mind to restore the car and someday display it in a museum dedicated to the master. Somehow the car got parked on the street and ended up being impounded by the city of Los Angeles for no registration. The secretaries looked at the books and said I still owed Yogi Bhajan money on it. The truth was that Shakti Parwha Kaur would not give me the title for the car which was required to retrieve it from the city impound, so why should I pay Yogiji anything? I wasn't going to pay for their stubbornness, so the argument ended in a stalemate.

It was never about the car, of course. It was about these secretaries, my former friends, who had decided my lousy reputation was bad for business and wanted to push me out of 3HO. If only they had known me better. Trying to push me out was exactly the right way to ensure I would stay, come hell or high water. Just to spite them, if for no other reason.

I never did get the money for the remodel, but I went ahead and did it anyway: a real nice job amounting to about fifty grand in improvements.

After explaining all this, I pause for a sip of water, and Dr. Jagdesh scribbles "secretaries" on his list. "How many secretaries?" he asks.

"Twelve, I guess."

He scribbles again and bids me continue. I feel a surge of emotion and realize I'm getting some strange kind of pleasure from seeing this list grow longer.

Then came the crowning blow. Yogi Bhajan directed his long time yoga student and confidant, Dr. Alan Weiss, to sell the house next door to me to the Angleton family. James Angleton was a big CIA chief throughout the Cold War fifties and sixties—one of the founders of the CIA itself, as a matter of fact—a very powerful man, and one of Yogiji's government connections. With connections like Angleton, Yogiji wanted to make the Khalsa powerful and rich so we could start spreading our dharma (our philosophy) throughout the world.

Back in the seventies, Angleton's wife and two daughters had joined 3HO, and they had been loyal to Yogi Bhajan all these years, just like I had. Yogi Bhajan treated them like they were made out of spun gold, of course. Their mother was not around the ashram much, but the two girls were so close to Yogiji they could just walk in the back door of his estate any time; like I used to do.

What Yogiji wanted to do was actually give the Angletons an estate adjacent to his and join them together in one huge mega-estate symbolizing the absolute and total unity between himself and the Angletons, who had every political connection Yogiji could ever want in his wildest dreams.

I don't mind saying I resented it. Here Yogiji was next door to me already. He could have joined his estate with my property. It could have been me, but instead it was them. I might not be some blue blood politician, but I did a lot for him over the years. A hell of a lot. And my father had millions. They weren't my millions, but still.

As part of this idiotic scheme, Yogi Bhajan wanted to buy my house back from me. Hari Jiwan Singh from the GRD boiler room had come to New Mexico by then and, of course, had his finger in every pie. He saw the immense benefit for Yogiji in aligning with the Angletons, of course, and supported it wholeheartedly. He started a subtle campaign, trying to convince me to go along, for the sake of 3HO.

After all the renovations I had done, Bhajan offered me an insulting price for the house.

I told him no.

He would not let go. He was relentless. Every time he saw me he harassed me in public about it, reminding me that I had turned down his offer.

One day, out of sheer frustration I said: "Yogiji, if I sell you the house where do you expect me to live?"

"You can build a new house on that land that you own, down next to the highway."

Sure. I can sell my own comfortable house in a beautiful location, on which I've spent tens of thousands of dollars, for a pittance; then start again from scratch, building a new place right next to a noisy highway.

No, thanks.

Everyone at the ashram took Yogiji's side. He was furious with me but I didn't care. I was so angry. It wasn't just the slight, it was the absolute ruthlessness of his selling me the house and then trying to yank it back out from under me when I didn't fit into his scheme anymore. After all these years.

Around that time, Yogiji's chiropractic doctor and numerologist Guruchander Singh asked me point-blank, "Why don't you just leave? If you're so dissatisfied with Yogiji, just leave 3HO. Why stay?"

I couldn't answer him. I didn't know. I guess it was like being angry with your father. He is a son of a bitch, but he is still your father. The rumor mill being what it was, things got all mixed up in peoples' heads. They started saying I had stolen the house, that Yogiji was angry with me and that I was a crook. They said all kinds of vicious things, and after that, I was persona non-grata at the ashram. As far as my reputation, that was the end of me.

But still, I stayed.

Finally, though, I cracked.

By now I had done so much real estate dealing that I was very familiar with the zoning and density regulations of Santa Fe County. I saw that Yogiji was ordering alteration after alteration to his property without even trying to get the necessary permits and I became more and more incensed. I felt this was not the way a holy man should behave. When he had the guest house moved from the Angleton property on to his without any kind of planning permission or permit—as well as putting in an illegal laundry room, septic tank and road—I had had enough. He may have been my spiritual teacher but he was also my neighbor. Why shouldn't he be subjected to the same zoning laws as anyone else?

I reported Yogi Bhajan to Santa Fe County and the County attorney filed a criminal case against Yogiji in magistrate court. Yogiji's attorney, GTS (Guru Terath Singh) Khalsa, got the case dismissed on a technicality. Not surprisingly, any sympathy that I still may have had within the Española Sikh community quickly evaporated. Maybe I had friends elsewhere in the world; I certainly didn't have any amongst the Española Sikhs.

Before he died, Yogiji forgave me and told me to just keep the house. He didn't care anymore. That, of course, did not hit the rumor mill. There is no drama in forgiveness. The dirty laundry is what they are after.

Dr. Jagdesh adds "Angleton family" to his list, scribbling in "father, mother, two daughters . . . CIA connections." Then he looks at me long and hard. He adds, "Hari Jiwan Singh" to the list.

I smile. This is fun! "Don't forget the secretaries!" I add.

"I got them already," he grumbles. "Anyone else?"

"Just the entire community, you know. No one specific."

"Do you like getting into trouble?" he asks.

"Trouble seems to find me!" I answer, though I know the truth is quite the opposite. "But that's life. That's the fun of it!" I add. "What else is there to do?"

"Is that why you signed up with Dadaji, Guru Sant Singh? To seek trouble?"

"No! Really Jagdesh, I was sincere. You know I was sincere, don't you? I really wanted a wife. I thought I might find one, crazy as that probably sounds."

"Are you sure you didn't do it just for this fun, as you say? Just to stir up the pot?"

I know what he means. He still can't figure out why I took the risk of aligning myself with Dadaji and meeting all those women. He can't imagine why I would be so stupid. But only now, in hindsight, do I realize how wise Dr. Jagdesh had been when he warned me. Only now do I realize how obvious it was that I was bound to get accused of marriage fraud for what Dadaji and I were doing. I now see that Dadaji was using me, making big bucks off my desire for a wife. I can also see what it must have looked like to anyone else—like we were in cahoots on some kind of scam. It was just a matter of time before we were "found out" and arrested. And yet, even had I understood this at the time, I couldn't have stopped the meetings. I needed them.

Meeting those ladies made me feel like I was finally getting some answers I had been seeking for decades. Answers about what is really going on in India, behind the silken veils. Answers about who Yogi Bhajan really was, where he came from. I still haven't put all the answers together yet. Thinking about those ladies makes me feel like I'm holding a bunch of magnets, only their poles are reversed and they won't click together. If I could only figure out how to turn them around, I would feel everything snap into place.

"It was more than fun, Jagdesh," I begin. But I can't explain it. How can I tell him the most mundane aspects of Indian life are keys that unlock thirty-year-old puzzles for me? I finger a seam in the arm of the chair and don't finish the sentence.

"You really wanted a marriage, didn't you, my friend?"

"Yes," I say. "I really did."

"But after meeting fifty women, you did not find what you were looking for?"

"No," I reply. "I wanted a woman . . ."

"Yes? A younger woman?"

"No!"

"A light-skinned woman?"

"No! Not at all! I wanted a woman like Bibiji."

"Bibiji? Your guru's wife?"

"My spiritual teacher's wife. Yes. She's the perfect Indian wife. She stood by his side."

"But any of those women . . ."

"Jagdesh, I'm sorry. I can't explain it, but I needed to meet those women. Sure, they were all a little like Bibiji . . . yet completely unlike her as well. None were right for me. And now, God has put me in another situation, and I trust God to make things right."

He looks at the list of enemies and shakes his head, "Maybe you will be stuck in India forever, my friend."

"If it is God's will, I will happily submit," I reply.

chapter 30

At the *Nivas*, I meet a lot of Sikhs coming and going, but there is one fellow I always seem to see. He wears a blue turban and has a monstrous, waxed mustache attached to a little plucked-chicken beard. I don't know if he keeps "running into me" on purpose or not, but after learning my story, he tells me he has a cousin in the government. He assures me this man is very powerful and would surely want to help me. This cousin could get my passport back in the blink of an eye, he says. Supposedly, he will get my case dismissed like it never happened; his cousin is that powerful.

It would only cost me ten lakh rupees. That is about 28 thousand dollars.

I really want to believe him! I want this whole business to be over with so much, I actually consider asking my dad for the money. But then I see the gleam in his eye. I can't deny it's there. The way he promises me the world, the way he swears to the heavens he'll get my case dismissed. The way he says I'll be so happy when he is done with me.

When he is done with me.

"What if you take my money and fail? What if you can't help me, after all? What then?" I ask.

"That can never be!" says the man. "My cousin is very powerful!" He looks down at his shoes, off into the distance, anywhere but my eyes.

What kind of fool does he take me for? I walk away from his deal.

Seeking legal help, I contact the SGPC—the Golden Temple's governing body. I talk to some slick attorney there who assures me the whole business will blow over in no time.

"Doooooooon't worry! It is nothing! These things happen!"

He doesn't want to help me.

I have been staying in my cheap room at the Nivas for a couple of months now, but the manager doesn't like it. Those rooms are supposed to be for pilgrims who only stay one or two nights. Sometimes it is so crowded that people sleep in the hallways, and even in the elevators, huddled around their meager belongings.

The manager takes me aside one day and tells me it is time to go. I plead with him. If I leave, I will surely be arrested! He doesn't like it, but when I mention Bibiji's name, he sighs and lets me stay. It doesn't stop him from scowling every time he passes me.

There are several 3HO members in town. We are easy to spot, after all. Besides Mukta Kaur, there are only a few of them I know personally. I see Guruchander Singh, his wife and a few other Española ashramites worshipping and sight-seeing at the Golden Temple, but they pass me on the *parikarma* like strangers. They act like it's not obvious—from our pale faces and all-white garb—that we both belong to one of the world's most exclusive spiritual clubs. I try to say "Sat Nam", but they are prepared to ignore me.

I still don't know if this is some organized campaign to excommunicate me or if long-time acquaintances and perfect strangers alike, just hate me on a freelance basis. So I go to an internet café, go online, and check out the newsletter for Hacienda de Guru Ram Das Ashram, my community back in New Mexico. I view the issues of the past few months, but there is no mention of me or my plight. I can't decide whether this is good or bad.

I head to the counter of the internet café, where a young Indian man takes my money. His turban is black and tightly wrapped around his skull and topknot. It is more the suggestion of a turban than a real one, the kind little kids wear, but it does the job. His brown eyes are bright. I hand him a 100 rupee bill, and he gives me back eighty. He does not pretend he hasn't got any change.

The next day, I stop in again. I check out SikhNet, another website run by 3HO—an international news site for Sikh issues. I write in to the discussion forum:

My name is Guru Sant Singh Khalsa. I was arrested January 12th in India by the Amritsar police which stemmed from my involvement with a marriage bureau. I learned some valuable lessons. I would not use a marriage bureau again!

I am asking for your prayers. Please pray for all the facts and witnesses to come forward with the truth. I am reminded in Japji, Guru Nanak says:

They are judged by their deeds and actions in God's Court;
God and His Court are true.
The good and evil will be judged there.
(Satguru) Nanak says that these facts will become known in that court.

I feel better already! The young man behind the counter is helping a woman. She wears baggy harem pants and a revealing tank-top: an outfit unique to India's many young tourists. Her dreadlocked hair is wrapped in a frayed scarf, and her face, with its delicate nose ring, is young and lovely, but it is red. She is on the verge of tears, and her nostrils flare with the effort of holding back the waterworks. She talks rapid fire, in a Spanish accent, about how she has had enough of India's noise and insects and chaos and wants to go home.

The young man suggests she travel up to Rishikesh and get out of the heat. "There are many excellent ashrams there," he says. "You can relax and have good food at Little Buddha and make a lot of friends there, if you want to. You'll like it."

"Really?" she says. "Where is that?"

He opens her Lonely Planet guidebook and shows her the write-up for Rishikesh. She does like it. Her natural color starts to come back.

"How do I get there?" she asks.

"I can book you a bus ticket for just 200 rupees."

"It's a nice place?"

"Yes! You will love it! It's a very good place." He smiles at her. "Look, let me show you. See, here is the bus ticket website. In Rishikesh, you will be happy. Very happy."

From where I stand, I can see it's true. The ticket really does cost 200 rupees and he is not charging her any extra. She takes the ticket and leaves with a spring in her step.

When he finishes, the young man takes my money and gives me change and a smile. "Hello, Brother! You must be American!" he says.

"How did you know?"

"You are a Yogi Bhajan Sikh! A white Sikh! I have met some of the white Sikhs. They come in here. After all, this is the closest internet café to the Golden Temple."

"Of course," I answer, and leave him with a smile of my own. I am beginning to like this friendly little hole in the wall.

The next day, I'm back at the internet café, and there is a response to my post on SikhNet:

guru sant singh ji fateh

everyone on sikhnet is with you and praying for you, can u share present situation of case, im in amritsar can i help you in any way. we pray for your sooner aquital , have faith on guru.

plz remember following words of guru nanak:

Falsehood will come to an end, O Nanak, and Truth will prevail in the end.

No way I am going to contact the guy! By the fact he does not capitalize or punctuate, I can tell he is young, of the "texting" generation. He cannot be in a position to help me, and his inquiry could easily be the first part of a scam, but I am emboldened by the fact that there is a response at all, and I write back to him, returning my thanks and prayers.

For more than two months, I have done nothing but read my Nitnem and the *Gita,* meditate, do yoga, contemplate God, have the occasional chat with Dr. Jagdesh, and wander the grounds of the sacred Golden Temple. I no longer have an interest in finding a wife, and I have not been meeting any women or really trying to make any friends. I have just been communing with God and asking for answers. Today, I think I have one: I'll find the help I need through the internet.

I post my story on several different Sikh chat rooms, looking for an offer of assistance coming from someone I know, even remotely. I have been a member of 3HO for thirty years, after all. Even though I don't have a lot of personal friends, I know a huge number of people in the group. With each post, I go into more and more detail about my case.

It is a quiet day here at the internet café. I am the only customer in the place. The overhead fans are whizzing like crazy, but it is stifling hot. The young man with the small, black turban is half-asleep on a little couch, curled into a ball, in the compact, agile way that only Indians and kittens can curl. His father is here, too, balanced on another tiny couch, also half-asleep. They are holding hands. I tuck the money behind the counter and sneak out without waking them.

When I hit the pavement, the heat radiating off the ground takes my breath away. I have to stop myself from staggering backward. Experience has taught me that walking, even if it is just a few blocks, in the normal, brisk, American manner, will leave me overheated and dizzy. I slow myself down with a few deep breaths, then begin a languid, Indian-style shuffle and weave, gradually threading through the dense crowd. I navigate the few blocks back to the

Golden Temple, past innumerable shops, around a man selling fried snacks from a tray balanced on his head, and through a jungle of scarves hung over the sidewalk for display. Meanwhile, I ignore the various rickshaw drivers who skim the road's edge, insisting I jump into their vehicles: "Where are you going? Going to Golden Temple, Sir? Yes! Let's go! Get in the back!"

The next day, I am back at the internet café. It is not actually a café, which is to say there is no coffee or tea served here. It is just a room with some computers in it. Indians must have picked up this idea of a "café" from some visiting European and run with it, is my best guess. Amritsar is peppered with these simple, no-frills, internet portals, but I am loyal to this particular one.

The young man is there, as usual, and he and I strike up a conversation. "You are really a good customer!" he says.

I tell him a little about my situation and what I'm up to. He nods gravely.

"I don't like these kinds of people that are tricking people. It could be this man Dadaji, it could be the women, it could even be the police. Someone is trying to fool with you. This is not the Sikh way. To be a Sikh is to be honest. To be a good guy. An honest, prosperous business man. That is what I want to be. This Dadaji, I think he was, what do you say? He was . . . oh yes! . . . 'ripping you off.'"

I like the kid. He is a true Sikh, striving to do right by God. He gets it. We Sikhs work hard to help ourselves so that we can be in a position to help others, and we do it without sneaking and scamming and fooling people. That is the essence of our warrior way of life. Well, I can't say I have always been that way. I have had to do a few sketchy things to get ahead, sure. But I was in desperate straits. You do what you have to do. After all, Yogi Bhajan always reminded us that 3HO was going to uplift the world spiritually. We 3HO Sikhs were going to usher in the new age, and we just couldn't do it without a whole lot of money and power, so whatever we did to get there would be justified in the end.

For instance, one time, when things were really bad in New Mexico, I set up a partnership with that bastard from L.A., Toner Bandit Harijiwan Singh. He would send out bogus invoices to hundreds and hundreds of companies, charging them for office supplies and such. It's the oldest scam in the book. Most never got paid, others got paid without question and with others, the people would call the number on the invoice to see what was up. You had to have a number to call in a thing like this or else you would get reported for bogus billing right away. So they would call this billing inquiry number, which rang on my mobile phone. I would answer:

"Golden Circle Products."

"I just received an invoice, but we don't use your company for office supplies. There must be some mistake."

"Oh, okay. Your invoice number please?"

They would read out the invoice number, and I would say, "Sorry about that. There's another company with the same name as yours. Our mistake. Disregard the invoice."

"Okay. Thanks."

And that's it. I got a cut of everything Toner Bandit Harijiwan Singh made on the scam, and he avoided getting caught by the cops for years and years, until in 1999 he was arrested and spent 18 months in Federal Prison on several counts of mail fraud. What an operator he was. I didn't like doing it, but times were tough, so I just did it until I got my own thing going.

That is what I am talking about when I say I actually deserved to go to jail. When they picked me up at Dadaji's marriage bureau, I was almost laughing. I mean, all the stuff I have done that should have landed me in jail, and now I am getting arrested for Indian marriage fraud, of all things? It is too funny! Karma, that's what it is.

chapter 31

My story has gone viral, but most of the online comments are hateful. With their perfect English, I am pretty sure these comments are from 3HO Sikhs, not Indians, but they are people I don't know. They say things like:

This Guru Sant Singh Khalsa shouldn't dare to call himself a Khalsa. He is just a sick, lonely old man who is giving good Sikhs a bad name.

That fool deserves no sympathy at all. He is just one of the many, many westerners who go to India to take advantage of honest women. He should be ashamed. He isn't one of us.

Don't for a minute believe this man, Guru Sant Singh, or anything he says. Please, don't send him money or sympathy! The man is a known gambler and a cheat. His claim of being spiritual is complete bunk. He has done nothing but bring shame on the diaspora of western Sikhs. We are, frankly, embarrassed by him.

***

Then there are other comments, mostly from Indian Sikhs. They remind me of Dr. Sobha Singh saying, "Surely, she would poison you." I am shocked at the vigor with which these strangers defend me:

This poor man is just one such example of how the scheming Indian women will take advantage of any man having enough money. These women will sue him for marriage I think and bleed him completely. The law favors Indian women, no matter what they do. It's a disgrace.

Of course he is being sued! And probably all the women this man met are ganging together to get his money. Or else it is their [sic] fathers. One sincere man wanting a wife cannot trust any Indian woman. They are a scheming lot and take full advantage of the "marriage fraud" laws to bilk any man. Good luck to you, Guru Sant Singh, you are truly one victim in this case.

I laugh and laugh at all these comments. God certainly is playing a number on me this time! I wonder if the men who accuse these women of setting me up are correct. I hadn't thought of that angle, actually. I had thought it was Dadaji that might be to blame. And myself, too, for sheer stupidity. Or maybe the police for trying to make themselves look terrifically clever at my and Dadaji's expense. But could all those women have actually conspired to scheme against me? It's hard to believe. The kid that works at the internet café—I have learned his name is Shira—I show him all the comments and ask what he thinks.

"Why would these white Sikhs say such bad things about you? You were in jail, in prison, and, as you say, you did nothing wrong. I think this is very wrong of them to say such things."

I tell him, "I don't know!" But of course I do know. Besides the trouble I had with the art investments, Jacqueline Forsythe, the bankruptcy, the house—which by now is all largely forgotten—there are more reasons why the American Sikhs dislike me. Even people I don't know! It's because I am a bit of a publicity hound. I have been in the newspaper a few times, mostly for the lawsuits I've been part of. Back in the eighties, I was even on that T.V. show, The People's Court, a couple of times!

In 3HO there was always a feeling that Yogiji should be the only one to get publicity. It was OK to stand out for your achievements but only at his pleasure. If you made it to the newspapers or TV that was OK, provided you didn't do it too much—and provided it was a positive article. I was fine as long as I got my picture in the paper for trying to join the army. When I got publicity because of my various law suits, like the time when I sued my Blackjack teacher for accusing me to be a spy on behalf of the casinos, I was offending a lot of people.

Also, since Yogi Bhajan's death, many of his students are panic-stricken by anything that might be construed as bad publicity for 3HO. After all, the purity of our "brand," and of Yogi Bhajan's memory, is currency they take to the bank every time they sell a kundalini yoga class, a $5,000 weekend yoga retreat, a box of Yogi Tea, or a carton of Golden Temple breakfast cereal.

Then, there is my gambling, too. I was a sports better and played Blackjack for a living for years. Trouble is, I had the audacity not to hide it. Technically, gambling is against the Sikh spiritual code, so a lot of squares at the ashram had a problem with that; Yogiji, however, condoned it.

That's right, Yogiji seemed to be quite happy about it, and that was all that mattered to me. He actually invested in the project. In fact, when he found out what I was up to, he put me in touch with a couple of other 3HO guys, including his right-hand man Hari Jiwan, who were into trading, betting, investing, and stuff like that. I remember Yogiji said to us, "I'll call you the Four Musketeers!"

To me, playing Blackjack wasn't even gambling, because I was counting cards, which is a scientific process. And when it came to sports betting, I was merely leveraging probabilities. I just don't believe that's the same as the gin-soaked, back-room poker games that most people imagine when they think of "gambling."

***

I had already been betting on baseball games. Then I met Sat Siri Kaur, soon to become my second wife. She was the leading Jyotish astrologer in the country at the time and was wild to get into this scheme. We got more technical: we would spend hours looking over the pitchers' birth charts. Then I started reading up on risk management and probability theory. I learned about the binomial distribution, which is where you have to look at winning and losing streaks in terms of the long run. If you are a good gambler you come out on top, but you have to take a very long view of it.

Next, Sat Siri and I started looking into professional handicapping. The idea is that no bookmaker wants to be heavy on one side. They want their books to balance out, so if everyone is betting on the Yankees, the bookies are eager to take bets on some of the underdog teams, and they give you a nice price for them. Because of the way the baseball season works, it is practically inevitable that every team is going to win a certain number of games per year, so those taking the right underdogs are bound to win, eventually. There is money to be made in handicapping, but you have to understand the binomial distribution. So that's what we did. We developed a very complicated system for picking the teams—all based on astrology & straight mathematical statistics! I would pick one team a day. Things went well for Sat Siri and me for a while. But the more money I made, the worse my reputation got.

***

Among the 3HO Sikhs there has always been a division between the ones I call the squares—those that really buy into the yoga and spiritual stuff, take it at face value, and don't know anything about the boiler room or my Warhol art debacle or Bhajan's real estate deals or his friendships with gun runners, drug dealers or his mafia connections or any of the rest of it—and those, like me, that are in the inner circle. Those of us involved in making Bhajan's "magical" abundance manifest know exactly how it all happened . . . and it wasn't achieved through prayer.

Somehow Yogi Bhajan seemed equally sincere in every type of company he kept and miraculously managed to keep the squares completely innocent of all the nefarious goings on. That was the key to it all. It was an unspoken thing that those of us making the big bucks kept our mouths shut about how we did it. But I was different. I was a true believer. *If Bhajan sanctioned something, then how could it be wrong?* was my thinking.

I was quite open about everything I did. People didn't like that. Bhajan's devotees, especially the secretaries, preferred to maintain a certain sheen of "goodness"—as long as certain things are not spoken about, they are okay. But these things, like my gambling, were never "officially" okay. That means my life-style was never officially sanctioned and I was supposed to hide who I really was. Meanwhile, our spiritual teacher completely approved of what I was doing. I couldn't wrap my mind around that, and I caught hell for it.

Because I refused to lie about the scams I did, the law suits I started, the gambling, the used car racket I had going on, or any of the rest of it, the squares always took a distinct dislike to me. But why should I lie? This is who I am. My father would have been proud of each and every deal I made, each and every dollar I earned.

Whereas Yogiji's other students, despite how they made their money through scamming people, always liked to play it straight. They jumped when Yogiji said jump and made a career out of covering his tracks as well as their own. While Hari Jiwan Singh was pulling a phone sales scam selling supposed "crown jewels" to lonely old people, he was beefing up his image as Yogiji's personal yoga-teaching assistant at Summer Solstice. And while

Toner Bandit Harijiwan Singh was secretly running the invoice scam with me, he was becoming certified as a "Kundalini Yoga and Gong Master"—the go-to guy for anyone seeking true enlightenment.

The hypocrisy!

chapter 32

I get a call from Dr. Jagdesh. He says he has found me a good lawyer, a man named Puneet. Soon, I am across town, balancing on a school boy's wooden chair in Puneet's tiny cubicle of a home office. Puneet—which, ironically, means *pure*—has about a hundred cases going at once and could not stand still if you shot him with an elephant tranquilizer. While he talks to me in halting, incomplete sentences, he constantly runs here and there, answering calls, picking up faxes, talking to people on several phones at once. It's dizzying. His English pronunciation is good, but his grammar is so bad that I honestly do not know if he is going to try to convince the judge that I am not guilty of any crime, or try to find an innocent-seeming judge who, himself, is not a convicted criminal.

Suddenly, I get a brilliant idea.

I return to the internet café and ask Shira if I could hire him as my interpreter. It turns out the kid speaks both Punjabi, the local language, and Hindi, India's national language, and has actually worked as a guide before, for National Geographic photographers, no less. He already has a price: 200 rupees a day. That's four dollars. My God, I would have offered him ten. He owns the café with a friend, and his dad helps out too, so Shira has no trouble getting many months off of the job at once.

The next day, I return to Puneet's office with Shira in tow. Today, I have to stand because an old man sits slumped in the wooden chair. After some discussion with the two men, Shira fills me in. Apparently, this old man is Puneet's dad. Puneet is taking over the business from his father, who has already retired, so while Puneet runs around doing everything, his black barrister's robe billowing in his wake, the father just sits there, overseeing things. Through Shira, I try to talk to the old man. I ask him if he has any ideas for my defense, but he just says I should talk to Puneet, then goes back to staring into space. All the while, I can hear Puneet's kids playing somewhere in the background and his wife occasionally scolding them.

I don't learn a whole lot about my case today except that Puneet thinks it won't be difficult to prove my innocence. I suggest he submit evidence of the fact that I have plenty of money in the U.S. and that it makes no sense for me to work with Dadaji to scam women for what amounts to $20 a day. He nods. I suggest he try to prove that Dadaji was the one using me and that I was just as much a victim as the women. Shira talks to Puneet at length, seeming to be trying to interpret this idea. Puneet waves him off. He says he knows what he is doing. He says I should trust him. Again, I have no choice in the matter.

After the meeting, Shira and I head back to the Golden Temple neighborhood, find a clean-looking restaurant, and I buy us some lunch. Fronted by an ice-cream shop and a colony of flies, this restaurant, called Virsa, is tucked back away from the street and is mercifully windowless, dark, and cool. The menu is extensive, but I have a simple diet. I ask the waiter for a plate of plain daal and rice with a few well-cooked vegetables added. No one is offended when I pull a bulb of garlic from my pocket, peel off a section, and slice it, raw, into my rice and daal. Yogi Bhajan's personal bacteria-fighting regimen.

I ask Shira how he learned to speak English so well.

"From girls!" he says. "Oh, when I was a boy, my father wanted me to learn English so much. He beat me and beat me but I can never learn! Oh, I never, ever learned, and finally he gave up. He was so unhappy. But then, when I became older, I started to see all the tourist girls I wanted to talk to. They came into the internet café. I tried to talk to them, but I could not. Little by little, they teach me. Taught me. Then I go to Little Buddha Restaurant and oh! I meet so many girls there! American, English, Polish, Israeli—all kinds. They teach me little by little, little by little!"

"Shira, you should watch out for women. They will really trick you, you know."

"Trick me? Why like this? Why trick?"

"You should get married, that's all. Don't go with a woman without marrying her first. That's the Sikh way. You said you wanted to be a good Sikh? Well, that is the way."

"Oh no! I am not ready for marriage! Not me! I will never marry!"

"Shira, you should put your energies into meditation and *Gurbani.* Direct your energies to God, to chanting the Lord's name. That's where true happiness lies."

"Oh, okay, Guru *Sant* Singh. Okay."

Maybe I have gotten through to him a little bit. For the first time, I notice a tattoo around the kid's bicep. It's a simple, tribal design. Tasteful, I guess, if you like that kind of thing. A group of chattering young tourists walk past us and out the door. One of the young ladies in the group catches his eye, and he smiles at her discretely, like a pro. For the first time I notice he is really a good looking kid. Majestic Roman nose, light brown skin, big eyes—almost sad eyes really—and a wide toothy smile.

"Read your *Banis,*" I tell Shira. "Every day. You have no idea the bliss you can find in being close to God. It's just amazing. Do you sing kirtan?"

"What? Oh, Guru *Sant* Singh! No, I don't sing kirtan! But I like kirtan very much."

"Well, I've been singing kirtan for a long time. I'll play you some of it on my computer, later."

"That's great! I want to hear that! I have never heard white-Sikh kirtan, but it is very good. People have told me."

He seems sincere, and I believe him. The kid has layers.

"Listen," I tell Shira, as we finish our meal. "I want to buy you a mobile phone so I can call you whenever I need you."

His face brightens but then flickers, like a fluorescent light tube that has just been switched on. He is desperately trying to contain his enthusiasm, but failing miserably. It's charming. We go to a local store and make all the arrangements. In typical Indian style, this involves proof of residency, identification, next of kin, name and occupation of your father, and so forth. I just give him the money and let him take care of it. A lot of Indian youngsters have cell phones, so I didn't expect this to be such a big deal for him. He handles the paperwork just fine, and asks me, bashfully, to buy several hours' worth of talk time. He wants to call his friends.

"You've never had a mobile phone before?" I ask him, once we are out on the street again.

"Oh no, Guru *Sant* Singh. I do not have . . . no, *did* not have . . . no *have* not had a mobile before."

"But I thought all the kids had these things. I see so many young men with mobile phones in India."

"Not me. Oh no."

"But you have a job, right? At the Internet café? What do you spend your money on?"

"Oh no, Guru *Sant* Singh! I give the money to my mother! I do not need so many things, like phones and such. I do not need that. Just for you, I need this phone. But just working at the café, I do not need this mobile phone and things like this."

We run into a young man, a friend of Shira's, on the street. Shira greets him and introduces me.

"Oh, I see your shirt!" says the friend to Shira. "Did you go to the Full Moon Party?"

"Oh, no! Never! I just have the shirt!" says Shira, smiling with something like pride and youthful ambition. I realize this T-shirt is some kind of social status marker, but I can't imagine why. "Maybe someday!" says Shira, and his friend goes on his way.

I contemplate the "full moon party" silk-screen and its implications. I have heard about these parties—drug and sex-fueled orgies for kids that come to India to party and destroy their souls, instead of awakening them. But Shira is so innocent. Handing over all his money to his mother! His world is as traditional as Punjabi life gets. I am quite sure he really has no idea what a Full Moon Party is.

Neither do I, actually. I never did anything like that as a kid. That world, the one where kids smoked joints and had wild, loose sex, and went into states of false ecstasy—I never really experimented with that. I was an innocent and a serious kid. I think Shira is a little like I was then, back in the seventies.

chapter 33

I used to sneak in and use the teachers' restrooms in high school, so I wouldn't have to encounter other adolescent guys, with their toilet humor and their smoking. My friends were the teachers, not the students. I used to stay after school and talk philosophy and poetry with them for hours.

Later, in college, I was more rebellious. At Texas Christian University I started this underground newspaper called The Raven. The name was after that Poe poem: "the grim and ancient raven wandering from nightly shores . . ." It seemed like a mystical omen. I wanted it to feel threatening to the establishment. I was just another deluded young revolutionary, I guess, but I did succeed in rocking the boat.

My whole dorm got in on it, and we wrote articles about the most outrageous stuff we could think of: drug experiences and living off the land ideas and dropping out of society stuff. I didn't actually do any of that stuff. No way! I just wanted to piss people off. It was that old military school hate bubbling up. TCU was extremely conservative, so The Raven eventually led to me getting kicked out.

After that, for months, I just drove this Volkswagen micro-bus around the country, going from one shooting competition to the next, basically just trying to meet girls. During that time I went through a phase of trying to really get into the counter culture and be like other kids. What a doomed enterprise that was.

That was how I met Doreen Palmer. She was a national-level marksman, like me, and a spoiled rotten suburban rich girl. She got me once to smoke hashish while I drove her around Washington

D.C. at night, meanwhile she rolled around in the back of my micro-bus, scream-laughing like some character out of A Clockwork Orange. All those traffic circles, the Washington monument, city lights whooshing by and blinking and shining at us from every angle. I thought I'd puke.

I pretended to enjoy it, but I think she knew and secretly enjoyed my discomfort. After all, I was a square pretending to be hip. Maybe I deserved it. The drugs and driving and all that laughing—it was too much. Hanging around her, a person could get killed or arrested or something. Forget it!

Then Michelle came along. The army had recruited her and automatically made her an officer so she could win sharp-shooting medals for them in the Olympics. She didn't have to do boot camp or anything. It was a free paycheck! I was only 19, but Michelle was 29, a real woman of the world, a hippie that had lived through the sixties and taken lots of LSD. There was nothing army about her. She was married, but then she got into this book, The Zipless Fuck, all about free love. She seduced me in the back of that micro-bus. My first time.

When all was said and done, I felt I could take it or leave it.

We kept on traveling to shooting matches together: me, Michelle, and her husband. But it wasn't the same after that. It certainly wasn't "zipless."

After that, I lost interest in girls for many years. Too much trouble.

Frankly, I hope Shira never makes it to this mysterious Full Moon Party. The very thought of it scares me. Despite the tattoo, he is really pure, in a way. I head back to the Nivas and leave him to enjoy calling his buddies.

"Save some minutes for me!" I admonish the kid, playfully.

"Oh, of course, Guru *Sant* Singh! These minutes are only for you!"

chapter 34

A week later, I have Shira call Puneet and ask for another meeting. It's starting to look like if I don't pester Puneet, he'll just disappear into the woodwork and I won't see him until the trial. The fact that my passport has been confiscated and I might be stuck in India indefinitely doesn't seem to faze this advocate at all. The fact that I have served time already and that I am probably being exploited by . . . somebody or other . . . doesn't raise his hackles either.

This time, Puneet is at his other office, at the court house, so Shira and I grab a bicycle rickshaw and meet him there. These rickshaws have hoods that accordion up and over, if you want protection from the sun. I ask the driver to put it up, so he nimbly leaps down and maneuvers the rickety apparatus until it covers the back and top of the seat in an arc, like the top of a roll-top desk. I immediately regret it. I have to crouch, practically with my head between my knees, the whole way there. Shira, of course has no problem. He folds himself up like origami, and we are squashed together on the tiny bench like a couple of love birds. When I disembark at the courthouse, the sense of relief is almost like getting out of prison again.

The courthouse is unremarkable except for being a big, old, ugly building. More than anything, it resembles an urban school in America. I guess it's the rows of horizontal windows that open out on a crank, the stolid red brick structure, the peppering of graffiti here and there, and the few trees planted in front of it, growing miraculously within the neighborhood's general decay, like symbols of hope. There is no grand entrance, no Greek facade, nothing but a few dinged metal doors in front of which queues of patient, beturbaned men have formed.

A large crowd waits in front of a slide-across window, which opens as we pass. The people jostle their way to the front and each one leaves with a white paper, which they hold above the crowd, like flags, as they jostle their way back out. Everyone in line seems to have a limp or a crooked back or something slightly wrong about them. A man selling newspapers from a bicycle basket passes by. His voice is wonderful, really resonant, as he announces his wares. He doesn't carry any kind of bag. Instead, when he sells a paper, he tucks the money up under his kurta. I wonder idly if he is sticking it in his underwear or what.

Luckily, we don't have to join any of the queues; Puneet's office is out back.

Behind the courthouse stands a village of square, cement bungalows: advocates' offices. Dotted with large-leafed banyan trees, the compound might have once looked nice; quaint, even. But now it's overcrowded. Some attorneys sit beside the walkway, on apple crates, behind rain-warped plywood desks, under filthy, corroding canvas tarps riddled with holes. Others can be found inside the little bungalows, where a folding table and a couple of plastic chairs constitute all that is needed for a typical lawyer-client meeting. Signs stick out over the doors, proclaiming names and titles. In the dusty breeze, they creak on rusty hinges. Meanwhile, cows and chickens roam the area freely. It's like a decrepit kibbutz just for lawyers.

Shira and I pass a scrawny rooster, two cows tethered to a stump with chains, and a black and white calf with a dirty red kerchief tied on its head, milk-maid style. We meet Puneet in his bungalow. He wears a white dickey kind of thing that hangs outside his robe, like a bib. He assures us that yes, everything is on track for me to get my passport back and get out of India. I will be good as gold come April!

Grinning like a mad man, I thrust forward my hand, which Puneet doesn't seem to expect, and a second passes before he thinks to shake it. I'm so happy, and Shira is happy for me! We practically skip down the walk, past the bungalows, the roosters, some broken concrete slabs, a formica-topped desk rotting in the sun, a well-dressed woman with a furrowed brow, a busy fruit stand singing with flies, and some make-shift booths where men bang away on old Remington typewriters.

Finally, we slip out of the compound and into the street. I point out Dr. Jagdesh's physiotherapy office, right across the thoroughfare. "My friend has that place," I tell Shira. "Why not pay a visit?"

Shira shrugs. "Why not?" he says, in his typical blasé manner.

On the street, cars whiz maniacally back and forth, but Shira walks out in the road like it is a field of daisies. I follow him, trying to look like I'm not. The key, when crossing Indian traffic, is not to run or stop, but just to walk very slowly and deliberately across any street, no matter how busy it may be. This makes you predictable, so the tuk-tuks, taxis, cars, and bicycle rickshaws coming along can swerve around you at the last minute, just like avoiding a pot hole. I see an enormous Ambassador heading for me, and I panic. I run a few steps.

"Don't run!" Shira admonishes.

"I guess no one ever gets hit, do they? As long as they don't run?"

"Oh yes, they do. How do you think I got this limp?"

And with that, we arrive at Dr. Jagdesh's office.

Dr. Jagdesh is thrilled to hear my good news. He calls his assistant and orders chai to celebrate. I love that I'm drinking chai in this little office with my two Indian buddies. Suddenly I love India again. I feel embraced, included, appreciated.

"So, Guru *Sant* Singh," asks Dr. Jagdesh, "Have you given up on getting a wife?"

"Oh God, yes!"

"But Guru *Sant* Singh, why? Now that you are free of Dadaji, you can find a lady and take her home with you. It would be a shame to return to America without a wife, after all this, isn't it?"

"Sign up with another matchmaker? Are you kidding?"

"No, no! Guru *Sant* Singh, of course not," adds Shira. "You don't have to do that. Just put an ad in the Punjab Tribune. Use my mobile number, and I will talk to the ladies. I will test their English and get rid of the bad ones, then set up meetings with the good ones."

"You'd do that?"

"Why not?"

I laugh and shake my head. These guys are great. They are really good friends, and I can already tell I'm going to miss them as soon as I'm back on American soil.

"This is true, Guru *Sant* Singh," says Dr. Jagdesh. "With Shira's help, you might be able to find a Hi Fi girl. One who would make you a good wife . . . and an Indian citizen! You could come visit Amritsar any time, no visa required!"

I can't believe I'm actually considering it, but all the way back to the Golden Temple, Shira and I talk about the logistics. He assures me that because no money would change hands, and I don't seek a dowry, the police would have no reason to object. In fact, I think the fact that I'm persisting in this search would reinforce my legal claim to be sincere in seeking an Indian bride.

It's an intriguing idea, but my primary concern right now is with getting cleared of the charges. I do not entirely trust Puneet. Something about his facile demeanor. The way he makes it all sound so easy. By the next morning, I have thought of a way to double-check Puneet's story. I take a tuk-tuk over to the police station where I was arrested. Even as S.H.O. Mohander Singh was arresting me, he seemed genuinely to like me, and I suspect he will honestly tell me about any new developments in the case—Sikh to Sikh. I don't ask Shira to come along. I'm not sure why, exactly. Maybe I am a little embarrassed about my arrest. Maybe I think Mohander will open up more if it is just me. Something just tells me to go alone.

At the station house, things are quiet. The windows are open, but dead, hot air hangs inside the building and hovers over the room's blank, empty desks. A filing cabinet drawer is propped halfway open, and several officers stand around it, glancing at paperwork. A ceiling fan stirs the sweaty stew pot. I get the distinct impression it is simply too hot to fight crime today.

Mohander Singh gets up from behind his desk and greets me with a big smile and *Sat Siri Akal*. He immediately sends some lackey off to get me sparkling water from a corner store, and I sense everyone in the place is energized by my surprise visit. The other officers cluster around to watch us talk, like it's a show.

"Everything is quiet now, Guru *Sant* Singh! So quiet without you!" Apparently there is not much to do around the station house these days but berate petty thieves. "It is quite a dull business," he assures me.

I ask Mohander Singh about my case, and he replies enthusiastically, "The charges have been dropped, Guru *Sant* Singh!" His earnestness can only be borne of having finally done the right thing for a fellow Sikh. I will get the official confirmation, he says, at my April fifteenth hearing. I feel my body relax all over. My legs, my arms, my back, my neck—I melt into a chair like a rag doll. My relief is so intense, it crinkles my eyes and I feel a surge of love for all humanity.

Mohander Singh rattles open a metal cabinet and pulls out a chess board.

"Chess!" he says. "Do you play?"

"Why not?" I answer, adopting Shira's catch phrase.

We are well matched, but I let him win.

I was imprisoned in January. My visa ran out in February. It is now March. I await April, glorious April, feeling elated and confident. After leaving the station house, I return, ironically, to the city center, the scene of the crime. At the travel agency upstairs from Dadaji's now-closed office, I buy an airplane ticket to Albuquerque, New Mexico.

The next day, I am up at my usual time: four a.m. Yogiji used to call these "the ambrosial hours." I do my chanting, meditation, and yoga within the cramped confines of my room in the Nivas. I pop into the Golden Temple's open-air cafeteria for a little breakfast, and return to bed for a nap. The routine helps keep me centered on the fact that I am on a God-given journey, and none of this is really under my control. It helps me remember to submit to God's will in everything. Yogi Bhajan taught me that time and time again, and even though I'm an ambitious man, I never forget it. He drilled it into all of us, relentlessly.

Throughout the seventies and eighties, Yogiji ran his ashrams on a punishing spiritual itinerary meant to fast track us all to ultimate inner power, enlightenment, and world domination. It was the ultimate submission to God, and, by extension, Yogiji himself. In those days, I would be in the Gurdwara by 3:30 every morning, at 4:00 am we would recite *Japji Sahib*, the inspiring prayer, written by Guru Nanak and recited daily by all devout Sikhs. After that we would practice yoga, than chant the *Long Ek Ong Kar* mantra. This whole routine is called Daily *Sadhana*, and it is the core of the 3HO spiritual practice.

When we finally had our breakfast, it would be in keeping with whatever forty-day diet Yogiji had us on that month. Sometimes we could only eat white things, like white rice and milk. Other times, it would be just beets, or just celery. Yogiji told certain people to drink their own urine first thing in the morning. He once gave an entire yoga class a diet of just raw garlic, nothing else.

Most of the ashrams were funded by the proceeds from vegetarian restaurants or bakeries, where the devotees worked like slaves, sometimes twelve-hour days in addition to two and a half hours of sadhana. No one got paid. You got room and board and that was it.

They called him a Saturn teacher. Yogiji knew what each person needed for enlightenment and he gave it to you straight. If you didn't like it, too bad. Once, a lady disagreed with him over something. I remember, it was about how she was raising her son. He didn't bother arguing. He just punched her in the nose in front of all of us. He really did.

Once when I lived in LA I had witnessed Yogiji physically kick a depressed young man mercilessly around the large meditation area of the Guru Ram Das Ashram in LA while the boy just lay there helplessly. As far as I was concerned it was Yogiji's way of imparting some spiritual lesson to him. One of Yogiji's secretaries, Nirinjan Kaur, who witnessed the event, told me that he had done much worse to all of them and for me not to worry about it.

Yes, self-esteem was a trap for others. A delusion. What we had was better: submission to our teacher. We knew how to submit and be serviceful. It was something so un-American. We were proud of that.

We reveled in it.

Eventually I stopped going to group sadhana because I didn't do the regular yoga exercises anymore. Instead, after my morning meditation, I always did a special set Yogiji had personally given me, and these are the exercises I still do. They're for building my ability to see auras. Seeing auras is important because Yogiji said a man should never have sex with a woman whose aura is less than seven feet across. If you can't see auras, it makes choosing a wife on your own pretty tricky. So now that I'm thinking about marriage again, I'm exercising with extra vigor. Regardless, I have been doing this routine daily for oh, twenty five years at least. Pretty soon, I should start to see auras, I'm certain.

After my nap, I venture out to an STD booth and make a call to my American lawyer, John Aragon, hoping for good news about the settlement from the highway condemnation case. No luck. As far as he knows, it hasn't been settled. Sat Siri Kaur hasn't deposited anything in the trust account. This is odd. It should have been settled by now. No matter, I will investigate the situation as soon as I get home. Not long now! I while away the rest of the morning strolling the *parikarma* and marveling at the beauty of the Golden Temple. Several times, I stop to pray. I am really going to miss this place. India is truly my spiritual homeland.

By lunchtime, I have made my decision. I call Shira and tell him to go ahead and place the advertisement for a wife.

chapter 35

"Have the ad read: American born Gursikh boy seeks bride," I tell him.

"Boy? Why boy?" Shira asks.

"That's the way Dadaji did it."

"But you are not a boy . . ."

"Just do it that way. That's how Dadaji did it," I say.

"But Dadaji went to jail!"

"One thing Dadaji knows, Shira, it's how to advertise," I answer. "And he didn't go to jail for his advertisements. He was framed. We were both framed, they're saying, by these women."

"Maybe that's true. Maybe not."

"Or else it was just a big misunderstanding! Anyway, it's all over now. So just say 'boy.'"

I'm buying him lunch at our usual place, Virsa restaurant. We have found a cool, dark corner in front of a little plastic fan. Shira sips his coke and shakes his head. "Okay, Guru *Sant* Singh, but don't expect me to lie for you. I'm going to tell the truth to every lady and let her know you are fifty."

"Of course! That's fine."

"One thing I've been wondering, Guru *Sant* Singh."

"What's that?"

"Well, you say your first wife, she left you."

"That's true."

"And your second wife, she wasn't pretty."

"That's true. But it was more than that."

"Oh? What was wrong with her?"

"She just . . . she just . . . I didn't love her, that's all."

"And you think you can find a woman that you will love from an advertisement?"

I laugh. I see where he is going.

"No. I don't expect to find love through an advertisement."

"Then why, Guru *Sant* Singh, do you want to find an Indian bride? She will not even understand your culture. You should get a woman in America, some lady that is also like you. That will be the best match for you, I think."

"No, no, no, I'm through with American women. That's one thing I know for sure. Shira, I'm a spiritual man. You see, only an Indian woman can understand me. Indians are spiritual. Indians understand."

"Please don't be mad at me for saying this, Guru *Sant*, but really, I don't think any Indian lady will understand you. You are not Indian. You are not even like an Indian. You are American . . . or something."

"Shira, do you do yoga?"

"Of course not. I lift weights. That is all the exercise I need."

"You should do yoga and meditation, then you would understand."

"Understand what, Guru *Sant* Singh?"

"About inner peace. About the celestial connection. You would understand about really living a spiritual life. A wife will be my partner in spiritual living, Shira. It's hard to do this alone."

"But this is what sadhus do. Go off alone and be with God. Meditation and silence. Sadhus don't have wives. I don't know what a sadhu would do with a wife, even. How would he support a wife? How can you meditate all day and support a wife? This is what I do not understand."

"Shira, don't you know the Sikh tradition? Sikhs don't become sadhus. Sikhs are householders. We base our spiritual practice in a holy life, but an ordinary life. We do business, we have sex, have children, have homes, but also pray and pray and pray."

"Yes, it's true."

"And a wife will enable me to be respected as a spiritual teacher, also. You see, when a spiritual teacher is a single man—well, it's just unseemly. It's natural for devotees and followers to love their teacher. If a teacher is good at all, that is going to happen. If he's married, then okay, he's off limits, but if he's single, then that love can take on a more earthly dimension, which is unhealthy and misplaced. That's why I need a wife. As a spiritual teacher, I fear I really won't be able to resist the draw of my female followers! You see, Yogi Bhajan had all these beautiful secretaries, but he never touched them. He was on a higher plane than that, but he was also married. He had a good woman in his life and didn't need to go out searching for more. That's the point I want to reach. "

Shira looks down. He folds and eats his chapatti. "Okay, Guru *Sant* Singh." Then, almost in a whisper, he adds, "Do you want to be a guru?" He doesn't look up from his plate.

"Not a guru, a spiritual teacher."

"And you want to teach people this Yogi Bhajan yoga?" He plays with his food.

"Well, yes, I will teach yoga, but there are many people teaching yoga today, you know. I want to teach people about the Sikh spiritual path. Vegetarian diet, chanting the Lord's name, meditation. People need a leader to live this way."

"But Guru *Sant* Singh?"

"Yes," I answer impatiently, gesturing to a waiter for the bill.

"Sikhs, we are not vegetarians. Whenever I can get meat, boy oh boy, I eat it!" He finally stuffs the last of his chapatti in his mouth.

"But Shira, Gursikhs follow the vegetarian diet, the warrior's diet. Ordinary Sikhs don't do it, sure. It's not for everyone."

"Okay, Guru *Sant* Singh," he says with a shrug. "I will put in the ad. We will try to find a lady that is good enough for you." And with that, I hold my breath to walk out the glass front doors and through the colony of flies. I keep my head down until my eyes adjust to the sunshine and my body submits to the heat.

chapter 36

Over the course of the next week, Shira begins to field calls for me. I call him daily to find out how it is progressing. He says there are many calls, but none are good. Most of the would-be candidates can't speak English. For instance, a relative will call and claim the lady speaks English, but the lady won't get on the phone with him.

"I am not Dadaji," says Shira. "I am not that stupid! If she won't talk to me, then forget it!"

I am intrigued by this process all over again, and by the fact that Shira is being so conscientious about his role in it. My days of thrilling to meet all the random women in India are gone. This time, I'm serious. I thank Shira frequently for his work, but he always shakes his head, clucks at me, and says, "Why didn't you come to me in the first place?"

"Come to you? How could I have come to you?"

Nevertheless, "Tsk, tsk, tsk, you should have come to me before," says the kid. It's an Indian thing. They have to berate you for your stupidity. I think it's a way of showing they like you.

Shira has made some significant money from me by now and I guess he doesn't give it all to his mom, because he has taken to wearing a wide silver chain around his neck. He looks like an American gangster posing for an album cover, but acts like a mother hen.

The applicants that pass the screening send me photos of themselves dressed up and posed, stiff and unsmiling, in front of Shangri-La backdrops—waterfalls, virgin forests, green meadows. Mug shots from faerie land. Sometimes they send emails, like this one:

NAME: HARCHARAN KAUR
DATE OF BIRTH: 1984
QUALIFICATION : B.SC IT
YOUNGER BROTHER: (SYPRUS)
LAND : 5 ACRE
In reference to ur matrimonial add
I m sendng my Bio data along with my latest pictures
Name Neetu khokhar
Dob = 3rd dec 1978
Height= 5'4'
Complexion = Weaitish fair
Qualification = M.A economics, M.A English, PGDCA
Occupation = teacher in a public school
Caste= ramgarhia khokhar
martial status= never married
father=- retd bank manager persently roads contractor
Mother= house wife
Brother= one elder finance professional
sister= none
Contact No....... +91xxxxxxxxxx
+91xxxxxxxxxx fathers
Awaiting ur response

Notice the inconsistencies. At the top she is born in 1984, then later lists her date of birth as December 3, 1978. At the top she has a younger brother listed, but later states her only brother is an elder brother. Even her name is listed twice—two different names. First, she lists her "qualification" as a bachelor of science in information technology (IT), then she states she has master's degrees in both English *and* economics, although she only works as a school teacher. I never know if it's a translation problem, sloppy lies, multiple personality disorder, or what, but I meet with this woman and many more like her, anyway. They turn out to be the same type of women I met through Dadaji—too young, too old, uneducated, toothless, and so forth. All are desperate, for one reason or another, and all are lying about something. But they are such bad liars, such basically good people at heart, that the truth comes out immediately.

I meet the candidates at Virsa restaurant, the place I have come to consider my own little dark oasis. The sparse dining room has a pillar in the center, which divides the side lit by the daylight coming through the glass front door from the side shrouded in cool darkness. It has a disgusting, spider-filled bathroom, but at least it has one, and is centrally located, near the Golden Temple. On lucky days I can grab a seat in front of a little plastic fan. Here in India, these tiny luxuries are few and far between. I have met the owner of the restaurant, and he is a nice guy, likes having me around, probably thinks my white mug draws business. If so, I'm glad to help.

I meet with a woman in her thirties. She has an intelligent face and is well dressed.

She speaks English and says she is a nurse. Strangely, though, she has come alone. I talk to her for quite a while, until finally she comes out with it:

"I want to go to America, why won't anybody help me?" she answers, stars in her eyes. I see visions of Beverly Hills mansions and Broadway musicals dancing around her head like the proverbial sugar plum fairies.

"And once we are living there," she says, "nicely, comfortably, and all, we can bring over my family."

This same scenario actually plays out, with different women, at least three times over the course of these meetings.

chapter 37

A couple of weeks before my hearing, I pay another visit to the police station, to see S.H.O. Mohander Singh; this time, with Shira in tow. While Mohander Singh digs through the storage closet for the chess board, I tell him about my latest conversation with Puneet, and how the advocate told me everything seems to be going well.

Mohander Singh doesn't answer me, but he and Shira get to talking in Punjabi. Soon they are laughing up a storm.

"What? What's so funny?" I inquire.

"Oh, nothing," says Shira. "Just advocates."

"What about them?"

"Oh, you know, how they are."

"What do you mean, how they are? How are they?"

"You know," says Shira, shaking his head. "One minute they say 'not guilty,' the next minute . . . who knows?"

Mohander Singh sets up the chess pieces. *Plonk . . . plonk . . . plonk . . .*

"What are you talking about, Shira?"

"You know how it is. You can never trust these guys."

"Yes," adds Mohander Singh. "Advocates, men like Puneet . . . I don't know."

"Why can't you trust them?"

"They're advocates!" adds Shira, grinning, while Mohander Singh sets up the other side of the board. *Plonk . . . plonk . . . plonk . . .*

"What the hell are you guys talking about?"

"You know . . ." says Mohander Singh, finally. "Guru *Sant* Singh, you know Varanasi?"

"Where the Hindus burn the bodies?"

"Those untouchables men? That are to be carting away the ashes of dead bodies? I think they are better than advocates."

Shira laughs.

"What are you laughing at?" I ask.

"It's true, that's all. Advocates, they are scum."

"Do you trust this Puneet?" asks Mohander Singh.

"Yes, I trust him. I guess. I don't have any reason not to trust him."

"Yes, you should not trust him," says Mohander Singh.

"Why not?"

Mohander Singh shrugs, and Shira answers. "I guess it's just a feeling. He told me he had a bad feeling about Puneet."

Mohander Singh advances a pawn and invites me to join the game.

"Wait a minute. Puneet said I was going to be pardoned at this hearing. He said it was all set up. Everything was fine! Everything is going to be fine!"

"Yes," says Mohander Singh. "But I would not to trust this man, Puneet."

I am standing now. I do not know what I am doing; my arms are flapping or something. I begin to pace the room, trying to formulate words. "Well . . . Mohander Singh . . . what am I going to do? What should I do? Tell me what to do! I've bought a plane ticket! I'm expecting to go back to America! What can I do?"

"It's okay, Guru *Sant* Singh. Why don't you have some juice?"

Some police lieutenant appears and pours me a glass of warm fruit juice.

"I have to go home! I must get cleared of these charges! You told me I was going to be cleared! Listen, tell me the truth, okay? What's going on? Why would Puneet screw me like that? Why?"

"I don't know. I don't know what Puneet will do, but you should have a re-investigation to be done."

"A re-investigation?"

"You can apply for one re-investigation of this case."

"How do I do it? Come on, tell me what I have to do, my friend, Mohander Singhji."

Mohander Singh gets laboriously up out of his chair, groaning, as if he had *just* settled in for a nice game of chess and now I am causing all this trouble over nothing. He goes to the filing cabinet and rustles through it for a while. He can't find whatever it is, so he sends the juice lieutenant away with some curt words in Punjabi.

"Just you wait small small time, Guru *Sant* Singh. My man will get this form for you." The lieutenant leaves the building, and Mohander Singh returns to his chair. "Now, let's have our game!"

I submit to the will of God. I submit, I submit, I submit. But no amount of submitting will allow me to win or even enjoy this chess game. Finally, the sun goes down, and the lieutenant returns with a fistful of papers. Mohander Singh tells me to fill the forms out, not to miss a single dotted i or crossed t, and then to take it over to Pratap, his commanding officer, at the police administrative office.

Shira and I work on this thing nonstop for three days. It has all got to be written in Hindi, of course, or Punjabi, I guess. I don't even know what language the kid is writing in. I have to compose a formal statement, then Shira has to write it in triplicate, which he does, sitting comfortably cross-legged, on the floor of my room in the Nivas.

He laughs. "Just like in school! We used to have to sit like this and write, write, write until the hand hurt!"

Heaven forbid they should waste good carbon paper on a bum like me. The kid is sure earning his four dollars a day, now! I have to give character references, too. I give Dr. Jagdesh, my atheistic, whore-mongering physiotherapist and new best friend. That is all I've got.

The form asks for my plea and reasons why the case should be listed for re-investigation. I submit the fact that I have no motivation to commit this crime, since the amount of rupees Dadaji earned from the women would be practically worthless to me in America. In the statement, I also emphasize my thirty-year commitment to being a Gursikh and my sincere desire to find a Gursikh wife.

The form asks for the conditions of my arrest. It also wants my father's name and occupation (of course). It is a very thorough thing and by the time I am done, I wish I had known about this form long ago. I have been wanting to write all this stuff down and explain it once and for all. Now I am finally getting that chance. Of course, I have no idea what Shira is really writing, but I have to hope for the best. At the end of it all, I have a brainwave. I tell Shira to go back to the references section and add Bibiji, Yogi Bhajan's widow. Anyone who respects Yogi Bhajan's memory will really be impressed by that, and I feel sure she will back me up.

When we are finished, I'm quite proud of the thing and entirely sure it is going to get my case thrown out of court.

"Here goes nothing," I say, as Shira and I jump in the yellow tuk-tuk that takes us to the police administrative office. The officer in the front office tells me he will take my forms to Officer Pratap, but I hold on to them for dear life.

"No. I must submit these in person," I insist, and Shira translates.

The guy looks at me funny and wiggles his mustache. He tells us to wait, which we do, sitting on the floor for an hour or so, in a big, empty hallway. Men in uniforms with matching olive-green turbans walk back and forth and, of course, stare at me. Finally, the officer comes back and ushers us up a stairwell to a large, but sparsely furnished office. Pratap stands up from behind his desk and offers his hand. It is warm and plump, but when I shake it, it doesn't shake back.

"I am commanding officer Pratap, what can I do for you, sir?"

Pratap, with his slicked-back Hindu hair. Immediately I decide my first impression of him was dead on. He thinks he is a regular Sherlock Holmes, what with his televised press conference calling me an international criminal. And now he acts like he doesn't even know who I am.

"Sir, I was arrested on January 12th at the Dadaji marriage bureau, on the GT (Grand Trunk) Road, on suspicion of marriage fraud. I am innocent of any wrongdoing and there is no evidence that can convict me. I believe this case is a simple matter of a misunderstanding. I have a hearing on April 14th and expect to be cleared of all charges, but just to be sure, I have come here, with respect, to submit these forms to you, in person, for re-investigation of my case. I think you will find that I am completely innocent of all charges."

"I see. But, to my knowledge, you have not been charged with any crime yet."

"That's right. I don't expect to be charged. I would like this case reinvestigated, please, to ensure confirmation of my innocence. This is upon the recommendation of my arresting officer, S.H.O. Mohander Singh."

Pratap takes the forms. He looks at them, at all the painstaking writing Shira did, at all the lengthy explanations. He turns them over— front, back, front, back—like he has never seen a piece of paper before in his life. He opens a desk drawer and pulls out a rubber date stamp. He adjusts the date a few clicks, and stamps the document. "Okay," he says, and sits down and ignores me.

An officer ushers Shira and I back down the stairs and out to the street. In the tuk-tuk going home, I look at Shira's face and he seems as exhausted as me, which is rare. The kid is less than half my age and usually full of verve, but I think Pratap has that effect on people. He psychically sucks your energy. I hope I never have to see him again.

chapter 38

I don't expect Shira to understand why I need a wife for my spiritual ambition. He did not know Yogi Bhajan, so his experience of Sikhi is pretty traditional. I don't spend a lot more time trying to explain my need for a wife to him, and luckily he doesn't pry. No one who has never been exposed to Bhajan's system of secretaries could ever really comprehend the importance of women to a true spiritual teacher. They are so crucial, because they are so very powerful. Having one woman as a legitimate wife and a bunch more, preferably twelve or so, to work as your managers, virtually ensures success.

I remember Dadaji's words: "Maybe soon a queen will come along!"

Finally, Shira fields a call that interests me.

Shira almost does not set up the interview because the girl is only nineteen, but when he tells me about her father, I say, "Do it! Do it!" I really want to meet him.

"You just want to meet the father?" Shira asks.

"Yes, it's just for that. I don't want to really marry a young girl like that."

"Alright," Shira replies, ever vigilant. "If it is just for the chance to meet the father, I'll set it up."

Throughout the meeting, the girl sits there staring at her hands. She is cute, no doubt, but her father is more interesting. He is a *ragi*, a spiritual musician, who sings kirtan, like me, and tours all over India, like a rock star.

The idea of being related to a real Sikh *ragi* fascinates me. So, a few days after the initial meeting, and after meditating on the subject, I call and offer to buy him lunch. He arrives at Virsa, as I had hoped and suspected, without his daughter. I tell him about my years of singing kirtan, then pull out my computer and play him my stuff.

"Yes," he says. "This is very good. Your Gurbani pronunciation is excellent. You are a real Gursikh, are you not?"

"Yes! Yes!" Finally, someone recognizes the real me. I feel so bonded with this man. He has his own devotional songs on an MP3, and lets me have a listen. Yes, indeed, he is very good. Far, far better than me. I would have so much to learn from a man like this. I imagine going on tour with him, singing my kirtan on stages all over the world. They would call me "The White Sikh," and I would be a phenomenon! I wonder if perhaps that is how I am meant to lead: through song.

"But Guru *Sant* Singh, are you drinking the wine? I am not to let my daughter marry a man who is drinking the wine. We are one devout Sikh family."

Oh I love him more and more every minute. I assure the *ragi* that I am a complete Gursikh; that I abhor alcohol and meat; that I chant, meditate, and do yoga for hours every morning; and that I wake during the ambrosial hours of three to four a.m.

"I aspire to live a holy life," I tell him. "On an ashram or in some holy place. I do not seek this business success and this type of life. I am a holy man seeking for a holy wife. This desire has brought me to India."

"And what is this yoga?" asks the ragi. "Meditation yoga?"

"Yoga? It's yoga . . ." How can an Indian ask an American what yoga is? I don't know what he is getting at. "Yoga . . . yes, meditation and yoga. Morning sadhana: meditation and yoga." I have always assumed that Gursikhs the world over practiced the same sadhana we do in 3HO. I am puzzled.

"Yoga . . . this is a Hindu practice, this yoga. How can one Gursikh be practicing the yoga?" he asks.

Now I am even more perplexed. "No, it is sacred yoga. Sikh yoga for enlightenment. Taught by Siri Singh Sahib Bhai Sahib Harbhajan Singh Khalsa Yogiji, my spiritual teacher, the leader of Sikhi in the Western Hemisphere."

Now he looks as confused as I am. The only solution is to let the subject go, and he does. "My daughter, Balwant Kaur, she is a good girl," he says.

"Yes. She is very beautiful. But she is very young also. Are you sure she would like to marry me? Because I think I would like to marry her."

"She will marry if I say so," says the ragi, adding, "I have many relatives in America."

"Oh?"

"Yes. They have private homes and such. They are, you know, very success. Very rich."

"That's nice."

"When you marry with Balwant Kaur, you will bring us both to America, yes? I would like very much to show these cousins that I am a proud man also. I am also with success in America."

So the truth is out. I have something to offer him, and he has something to offer me—both his daughter and the chance to have a *ragi* for a father-in-law. I feel like we are friends already, and this deal is a good one. The match will surely catapult me toward success as a spiritual teacher.

I had not planned on marrying a teenage girl. God knows she probably does not want a fifty-year-old man, but I will be good to her. Her family would benefit immeasurably from the chance to go to the U.S., so I think she would see it as a sacrifice worth making.

Back at the Nivas that night, I meditate on the situation for hours. The next morning, I call the *ragi* and tell him, "Yes, I'll do it!" To celebrate, I grab a tuk-tuk, swing by the internet café, pick up Shira, and take him out to Dr. Jagdesh's office. I buy chai from a wallah on the street and bring it in.

"Oh, chai!" says Dr. Jagdesh. "Why chai, Guru *Sant* Singh?"

"We're celebrating! I'm getting married!" When I describe the man and his daughter, Dr. Jagdesh gets excited.

"Does she have light skin?" he asks.

"Yes, it's pretty light. But I don't care about that."

"I do!" says Dr. Jagdesh. "How old is she, my friend?"

Shira is sitting still as a statue, and I suddenly don't feel like answering the question. "Oh, about twenty five."

"Oh, twenty five. Well, that is okay. That is not too old, eh?" says Dr. Jagdesh with a sneer. "She is going to be really good!" I smile awkwardly, trying to pretend not to know what he means.

I try to steer the conversation back to the ragi, but being an atheist, Dr. Jagdesh doesn't care about devotional music. He just wants to talk about the girl, and suddenly I am very embarrassed to have brought Shira. I didn't want him to see this side of my friend. Quickly, I lie and tell Dr. Jagdesh that we really just came out there to visit Puneet at the courthouse across the street and only stopped in briefly to tell him the good news. Shira and I escape the office with Dr. Jagdesh's heartfelt congratulations ringing in my ears.

On the street again, we cross over to the courthouse and wander silently past the typewriter men and through the arrangement of offices, goats, mango trees, and cows. I visit Puneet's office, which is locked tight, and put on a show of waiting ten minutes for him to show, then cursing him for missing "our appointment." Shira just follows along silently. As we are about to get in a tuk-tuk, he finally asks me, "You are talking about the *ragi*? The meeting that I set up for you at Virsa? At ten o'clock? Last Tuesday?"

"Oh no! Not that one . . . well, yes, I guess, yes it was Tuesday. Maybe that's the one." God, I'm a terrible liar. But anyway, Shira has caught me. There is just no way out of this one.

"That girl is twenty five?"

"Sure. Yes, she looks twenty five."

"Because the ragi said she was nineteen."

"Oh. Did he?"

"And I don't even think she's nineteen," adds Shira. "He sent over the information, and it says 'birth year: 1991.' That girl is actually seventeen."

"Oh. Really? I don't think so. No, no, she couldn't be!"

"I wasn't even going to set up the meeting, but you said yes, to meet the father only, so I set up the meeting, but just to meet the *ragi* only. Not for marriage."

I don't know what to say. I had come out here to celebrate, and now Shira is judging me. I can't tell him not to, though. I don't feel prideful enough about this to start a confrontation. Also, I still desperately need him. I can't afford to lose him, now. Caught red-handed, I just laugh.

"If a fifty years old man tried to marry my sister, a seventeen years old girl, I would not allow that. Never. I would kill him first, if this was my sister. My father would never give her away like that. Not for anything," says Shira. "That is not a good father, to do that." Shira does not look me in the eye when he says it. He looks at the ground and shuffles his sandals, then climbs in the tuk-tuk and sits stony-faced the whole ride back. I just laugh it off. I can't think about Shira and his moralizing right now. The *ragi* and his daughter want to go through with it, after all. Nobody is forcing them! What's the big deal?

A couple of days later, I am on the phone with the *ragi*. "I am looking for a wedding palace," he says. "We must get the place for three days at least. This will be a big, big wedding with so many peoples!"

A wedding palace is a uniquely Indian institution. As you drive through the Punjab you see them, garishly—and generally tastelessly—built along the roadside near any sizeable town. Sikh weddings *(Anand Karaj)* are held in Gurdwaras where meat and alcohol are prohibited. So, after the *Anand Karaj*, most wedding parties repair to a nearby wedding palace for meat, alcohol and general debauchery as part of the wedding reception.

I don't think the *ragi* wants to have meat and alcohol at his parties; he has a reputation to uphold. But there is still a certain amount of prestige to be gained from holding these events at a gaudy wedding palace.

Great. I tell him to just go for it. Whatever he wants, I'll pay for.

"But first, we have the engagement parties. We will have one just in one week."

Wow. Well, why not? Let's get the show on the road!

"That parties will be at my house. Three parties altogether. There are many peoples to invite. But you should only come to one, the first one."

"What do you mean?"

"You should come to this party! Yes! But not all the parties. Grooms not having to come to all the parties."

"But I don't want to miss a thing!"

"You will not miss. But only one party attending. And Guru *Sant* Singh, when you come at the party, you must be in fashion."

"In fashion? What's this fashion?"

"You must paint your beard, that is all."

"Paint my beard? Dye my beard! You must be mad! I would never dye my sacred beard!"

"Yes, yes, yes. It is very much in fashion, Guru *Sant* Singh. And my daughter, she is so young. Peoples cannot be seeing her with a gray-beard man."

I do not agree to dye my beard. I would never ever dye my 30-years growth of holy beard. Not in a million years. Imagine what Yogiji would say! I hang up with the ragi, feeling furious. Then I stay up all night, meditating on the situation. The next morning, I walk the marble *parikarma* around the Golden Temple, praying for an answer from God. I can barely eat, I am so depressed. Finally, the *ragi* calls me again to make further arrangements and give me cost estimates for a growing number of parties I am not going to be allowed to attend.

Finally, I can read the writing on the wall. He is ashamed of me, and of himself, for what he is doing to his daughter. There is to be no pride in this match. He is going to do his utmost to keep my age, and, if possible, my entire identity secret. Shira's words sink in, then.

This is not the Sikh way. It is merely one man trying to use his daughter as currency. The chance to go to America is not even necessarily something she wants. It is something for him, a way for him to prove his worth to his relatives. This is not right by Indian cultural standards or anyone's. I can see that now. I had wanted to trust the *ragi*, to follow his lead, but it is a bad idea.

The *ragi* has made no secret of the fact that he wants to come to America. And where there is one Indian, there is an entire extended family. How can I bring an entire family over to America and support them? I don't have that kind of cash. I will have to go back to work full time, probably doing something illegal, immoral, or both. Then again, there is the thought of having such a beautiful looking young woman for a wife . . . it is almost worth it.

But no.

I call the *ragi* and cancel the whole thing.

Luckily, he doesn't press charges.

chapter 39

I give Shira the news, and his relief is palpable, even over the phone. He renews the newspaper ad for another week. Pretty soon, I meet Wadha Kaur.

She arrives to our meeting at Virsa Restaurant with just a servant. She is in her mid-twenties and a big "healthy" girl. Her English is not very good, so Shira translates as Wadha Kaur tells me that her parents live in a village near Chandigarh, a two hour bus ride away. She happens to be in town with her servant, praying at the Golden Temple, and she chanced upon my advertisement.

"You probably want to go to America, I guess. That's why you answered the ad. No?"

She says no and claims she is merely interested in meeting me to see what kind of man I am.

Shira shrugs, "She says she would never want to live too far from the Golden Temple."

Also, as part of the conversation, Wadha Kaur lets it slip that her parents are quite elderly and cannot travel as far as Amritsar. That is great news for me. If they can't make it to Amritsar, they certainly won't have any desire to come to America.

Wadha Kaur comes across as a meek, unassuming girl. She is plain looking, but has a very mild quality, a nice shy smile, and a lack of specific demands. We meet several times, and she never seems to grow impatient with what I have come to realize is a distinctly American get-to-know-you process. I try our third meeting in a public park, without Shira.

"I hope we marry, Guru *Sant* Singh," she says. "I love you!"

She is so sweet, so innocent to think that she loves me already. I start to be able to imagine a future with her. I speak of my ambition to be a spiritual teacher. I tell her how I want to live a life in service to God, perhaps in an ashram.

She smiles and says, "I will like to be a good wife to one great, holy man. I am praying always."

"You know, Wadha Kaur," I continue, "No one has heard of me yet. I'm just a humble Sikh, serving God. But one day I will teach many people. I will be a great teacher, like Yogi Bhajan. I feel this in my heart."

At this point, Wadha Kaur sinks to her knees, touches my feet, and then returns to the park bench. She does it with amazing grace and subtlety, especially for such a big girl. "Praise God! I would like to be a wife of one great Sikh. This is one honor so great for me."

I don't propose marriage this meeting, or the next. After all, I am not physically attracted to her, but in every other way she seems perfect. Over time, she tells me that she has had many marriage proposals from Indian men, but that she turned them down. She says she does not trust them. "I am not want to marry a crime man. A man who is doing these bad cheatings and things. Many Indian men are like this."

I doubt she is telling the truth about these proposals, but that is okay. A girl has to have her pride, after all.

At another meeting, with Shira's help, I explain my legal predicament to her and emphasize how it is all just a big misunderstanding.

"Oh, the Punjabi Police are very bad! Everyone knows this!" she tells me.

I explain that it all came about because I was looking so hard for a good wife. "I'm going to be pardoned on April fourteenth," I tell her. "Assuredly!"

"That is good, Guru *Sant* Singh," she says. "Praise God! I love you! I really do!"

Finally, I decide to go through with it. Sure, there are cuter women I could marry, like the *ragi's* daughter. I mean, I could have married that little girl and just made love to her until I was dead. I wouldn't care if she could cook or anything. But I have my feet back on the ground, now, and I realize that was not the point of my quest. Maybe the *ragi's* daughter was a vain little beauty queen anyway. I want a different kind of wife. I have a vision to follow, and that entails finding a humble, devout woman like Wadha Kaur, even if she's not a looker.

I hadn't been physically attracted to my second wife, Sat Siri Kaur, either. I had thought our intellectual attraction would be enough. She was such a brain. In the beginning, we used to stay up all night just talking about everything: politics, Shakespeare, Emerson, Plato. Spirituality, too: Sikhi, Christianity, yoga, Sufism, tantra. Nothing was off limits. She was ten years older than me, but as soon as I met her, I wanted to spend all my time with her. It was not a sexual attraction, but what happened was one of Yogi Bhajan's secretaries, Surya Kaur, had observed our friendship. She approached me one day, in front of the Gurdwara.

"You know, Guru *Sant* Singh, men and women can't be friends in 3HO. That never works," she said.

I asked Yogi Bhajan about it, and he agreed. He said I really ought to marry her, so I went ahead and did it. My first wife Prem Kaur had recently left me and I did not want to be alone. What kind of man remains single, if he can help it? We Sikhs do not believe in sex outside of marriage. In 3HO, it just does not exist. (That's not really true; let's just say that everyone *pretends* it doesn't) So I jumped right back into marriage. Also, on a practical level, Sat Siri Kaur was in the real estate business. She taught me how to buy these huge tracts of desert, divide them into lots, and sell the pieces for a tidy profit—a perfectly legit business! I guess Indian-style practicality comes naturally to me, where marriage is concerned.

chapter 40

Finally, Shira and I go out to Chandigarh to meet Wadha Kaur's parents. We take a bus, and Wadha Kaur and her sister pick us up at the bus station in a little, beat-up car. As we head down a highway, then a country lane, Wadha Kaur drives faster and faster. She laughs and shouts back over her shoulder something about how she wants to be like a famous racecar driver. In the back of the car, with Shira, I am so terrified, I clutch his arm.

"Guru *Sant* Singh? It seems you have your balls in your mouth!" he says. "It's just an expression," he adds when I look at him strangely.

"My God, Shira, tell her to slow down. Oh, please tell her to slow down!"

Wadha Kaur and her sister are singing gaily along with the radio, driving faster and faster and giggling now and then about how much they want to have a Ferrari instead of this junky old car. I don't know what they are saying, but it sounds like they are debating the merits of a red one over a black one and selecting amenities like sun roofs and power windows and such. I have no idea how they have even heard of such things. Television, perhaps.

Even now, in a state of abject terror, I can see another side of Wadha Kaur: she is just a bored country girl doing what all country kids do—driving fast, singing along with the radio, waving out the window to passing friends and neighbors. She has no particular method for getting out of her small town. She has not received a good education, and doesn't have the brains to pursue one anyway, nor any savings, nor any special skills. She is surely expected to marry some village boy, have a passel of kids, and stick around forever. As we pass through the village, I see it is pretty primitive, with none but the most basic shops. I can imagine Wadha Kaur getting awfully bored out here.

I recognize something else in her, too. Wadha Kaur has that itch to be different, like I do. She will never be satisfied until she has shown she is not just another small-town girl going nowhere. As long as she lives in this village, she will always be driving too fast, laughing too loud, looking for some excitement or some opportunity that is just never ever going to come to this backwater. I see her youth now like a sloppy coat of paint on the surface of her. I know that even while she displays this thoughtless zest for life, she has some awareness of the fact that paint does peel. If she does not find a way out soon, Wadha Kaur will have to resign herself to typical village life, and she knows it well. This period—her mid to late twenties—is Wadha Kaur's only window of opportunity.

I know enough by now to understand that an Indian woman can sometimes postpone arranged marriage until her late twenties if she shows her parents she has something better going on—schooling, a business opportunity, or something else worthwhile. Wadha Kaur has not got anything like that, but now she has me. And her little country girl heart cannot really imagine anything more exciting than having a rich husband and a fast car. If I can give her that, well, she thinks she will be happy. But she won't.

To be happy, she needs the Guru. She needs to live in God. I can offer her that, but she doesn't fully understand it yet. Hopefully, one day she will.

Shira asks her to slow down. She makes a face like, *old people! What can you do?* and, thankfully, slows the car. Soon we arrive at a large but modest country home full of sunlight and space. There is even a garden with a protective wall. It is a sweet place, a fine example of typical Indian rural living. The living room is furnished with an actual couch—what a luxury! The walls are the same poured concrete as most Indian homes, but are prettily painted in bright pastels, and the floors are nicely tiled.

After we arrive, Wadha Kaur sends her servant away to prepare dinner and we sit down with her parents. A second servant brings us chai. I have no idea how many more servants could be lurking in the wings. It does not mean the family is rich. Labor is one of the cheapest things to come by in India. Sometimes, if you give a servant a concrete floor to sleep on and a few warm chapattis every day, that's all you have to pay.

My conversation with her parents is mostly polite and business-like, but I notice with relief that her parents do not talk as if they are eager to leave this little palace. No one speaks of going to America or sending relatives overseas or anything of that nature. Wonderful.

The next day, I visit Wadha Kaur in the nearby city of Chandigarh, where she has an apartment. This is very unusual, but I guess her parents are the permissive type. Chandigarh turns out to be a really nice city. It is actually a "planned city" and has named streets in a grid, trees growing in the medians, and all kinds of metropolitan amenities. I could live here if I stayed in India.

Over the course of the next two weeks, I visit her home twice more. She, her parents, and I mostly chat about the weather and such things.

On my next visit, I hire a taxi and we really tour the city, talking about areas where we might want to live and so forth. It is exciting, awkward, and surreal. I have not kissed her yet, and I am not sure how close I can sit to her in the back of the taxi, but when I finally put my arm over the back of her seat, she does not shrink from it. In fact, she smiles at me, then gives the driver some instructions.

We soon find ourselves in a posh housing development, what they call a "colony." Shira explains that these places are built for the "NRI's" or non-resident Indians who live and work abroad and just visit their Indian homes occasionally. Wadha Kaur has actually arranged for a real estate agent to meet us at one of the houses! As we remove our shoes, enter a big, two-story affair, and pad over the marble floor, I see the place has been tricked out, western-style, with a flat-screen television and plush, modern furniture. It must have cost a fortune to have all that stuff shipped over.

I tell her I am not interested in this type of home and try to explain that I actually came to India to get away from this kind of materialism.

"I love you! I really do!" she says, out of the blue, then a lot of stuff in rapid Punjabi.

"What did she say?" I ask Shira.

"I don't know. Something about houses and clothes and cars. It doesn't make a lot of sense, actually."

Once we are back in the taxi, heading someplace for lunch, a black SUV drives by, a really modern looking thing. It pulls into one of the posh homes, and Wadha Kaur follows it with her eyes. She speaks again, this time directly to Shira.

"Uh, she says that car is some kind of car. It is . . ."

Wadha Kaur speaks again, sounding impatient.

"She says it's called a Bolero, and that is the kind of car she wants."

"She said that?"

"Yes. For sure, she said that." While Shira translates, Wadha Kaur begins chattering away again, demanding Shira's attention. He tries to stop her in order to translate, but she won't stop talking, then she starts getting shrill.

At the restaurant, Shira continues trying to translate as we get out of the car. "Uh, she says she will show you the things she needs for a marriage. And she wants to have a home. She says it is important . . . uh . . ."

Wadha Kaur speaks again, shrill and angry.

"What was that? What did she say?" I ask Shira.

"Oh, she just said I'm an idiot and I should speak faster."

"She did?"

"Yeah," Shira says, and laughs. "I don't think she likes me too much."

I am half-starved and hope a little food will return Wadha Kaur's good humor as well as my own, so I lay on a big cheesy grin and say, "We eat!" Wadha Kaur smiles demurely back.

Over lunch, I talk about my ideals, my love for chanting and singing kirtan. I keep it simple, though, so Shira can translate. She answers with a lot of "Praise Gods!"

"What I really want, Wadha Kaur," I say, slowly and clearly, "Is to return to the days of communal living. To stay on an ashram and be a teacher. To live simply, you know?" I don't add in the rest of the fantasy: that I would be the head of the ashram and everyone there would look to me for psychic transmissions, intuitive knowledge, spiritual guidance, business acumen, words of wisdom, and transmissions from the Godhead.

"I know!" she answers.

"You are a spiritual woman. You understand this, do you not?"

"Praise God!" and "I love you! I really do!" are Wadha Kaur's best phrases in English, and she employs them now. She adds a lot of excited Punjabi to this, and Shira tells me it amounts to a lot of praising of the Guru. She continues and Shira tries to interrupt every few sentences to translate, but this seems to annoy her. She snaps at him in Punjabi. He snaps back.

"Shira, what's going on?"

"Okay, Guru *Sant* Singh. This woman is wearing me out. First, she said that she wants a house and a car. It is important because she wants to have that security, and to know that you are a man able to provide that sure-ness before she is to marry you."

"Oh. Wadha Kaur, you want me to buy you a house and car?"

She smiles demurely.

"Then," adds Shira, "She said she was going to slap me if I didn't translate faster."

I laugh. "That must have been a joke."

Shira shrugs and eats his meal.

Wadha Kaur's servant, who is always present, eats her own meal in silence.

The next day, the four of us meet up again. I have meditated on the subject, and I think Wadha Kaur's request is not unreasonable. After all, she does not really know me, does not know if I can really provide for her or if I am just full of hot air. A woman wants a house, wants to decorate it and stuff. Woman stuff. We can stay there when we are not touring ashrams. It's logical. I ask Shira to call a Chandigarh real estate agent, so he takes care of that.

Before you know it, we have all piled into an auto rickshaw and the agent is directing the driver to a house. At the house, we tumble out of the little vehicle and I pay the driver, but Wadha Kaur begins to talk to him. Her voice takes on that shrill tone and she rattles off something curt before tossing the end of a pink scarf over her shoulder and marching after me.

"Shira, what did she say?"

"She said to the tuk-tuk driver, 'Stick your ass here and stay here. We're coming back!'"

Immediately, Wadha Kaur informs me that the house is not to her liking. It is too small, too dull. She wants a garden, and bedrooms for children, and more for servants. She wants a large living room for entertaining. We are not even married, and trying to please her is already giving me a stomachache.

The agent likes what she is saying, of course. He offers to show us some more "personal luxury" style homes. I am sure he would love to, but I tell him no. We visit a couple more humble dwellings, the kind of thing I have in mind, and she is not happy. Finally, she asks to talk to me (with Shira along, of course) in "private." We excuse ourselves from the agent and go out behind the house.

"This house . . . how will I have my friends over? It is so small! I must have a nicer house. . . and a Bolero. It is only fair," she says, then adds, "*before* the wedding." She looks at me coquettishly, then. I am not sure, but I think she is dryly implying that getting her in the sack is going to blow my mind from here to Pondicherry.

Again, I meditate on the subject and decide that Wadha Kaur is a young woman, after all, and if she wants to have children, I am okay with that. If she wants to have friends over, I am okay with that. As long as she fulfills her role as a true Indian wife, as long as she is devout and I can say I am married to a real Indian Sikh, that is the main thing. Sure, she is not exactly the woman I first thought she was, but she will do, and I have put so much energy into this project so far. I want it to work out, so I come up with a compromise that might work for us both.

On my next visit to Chandigarh, I put Shira to work calling around town, and he finds what I am looking for. When we meet, I give Wadha Kaur a slip of paper. On it is the address of a local aerobics studio.

"I have signed you up for some exercise classes," I tell her. "I would like you to lose some weight before the wedding. If you can do this for me, then I will consider buying a good-sized home for us."

She smiles at this and shrugs. "Yes, Guru *Sant* Singhji! I will do this thing! I love you! Really I do!"

Over the course of the next couple of weeks we meet many more times, and she claims to be attending the aerobics class religiously, always adding a few "Praise Gods!" to the conversation for good measure.

Finally, one day, I go to the club to see if this is true. I peek in the window and, sure enough, there she is, eating an Indian sweet called "burfi" at the counter. And there is her servant, out on the exercise floor, huffing and puffing away!

Shira and I enter, laughing. Shira scolds her in Punjabi, jabbing his finger at the gyrating, sweating servant. Wadha Kaur looks at me wide-eyed, and says something like "What? Isn't this the way it's done?" Then she shoves Shira and tells him to get out of her face.

Finally, I have to face facts. Having Wadha Kaur for a wife is going to be just like bringing up a child of my own. I will be a single parent, trying to raise my wife. She will have kids, and they will grow up to want houses and cars too, not to mention servants to do their phys-ed classes for them.

With all this on my mind, I catch a bus back to Amritsar. It is April 13th. My hearing is tomorrow morning. I log zero sleep hours at the Nivas, then meet Shira at the courthouse. I am a lost and bewildered man, caught in his own net.

chapter 41

I go up before the judge—not smiling, not frowning, business-like. I expect this to be over quickly, and my mind is more on the Wadha Kaur problem than the legal entanglement. Puneet is here, by my side, distracted as usual.

"A *challan* has been filed," declares the judge.

"What? What is a *challan*?" I ask Puneet.

Puneet looks at me with his jaw hanging open. "Guru *Sant* Singh, a *challan* is a notice of formal charges!" Puneet approaches the bench, takes a paper from the judge, and shows it to me. The *challan* is in Punjabi, but I can see it is signed by both S.S.P. Pratap and S.H.O. Mohander Singh himself, that fink!

"The next hearing in this case will be three months' time," says the judge. He gives me my next court date and summarily dismisses me.

In a daze, I hit the streets. Shira finds us an auto rickshaw. I tell the driver to go straight to police headquarters, where I confront Mohander Singh.

"You said I was going to be cleared!"

"Yes! Yes!" he says, "I lied! We never did a re-inquiry into the case!"

"So all those papers I filed for a re-inquiry? What was that for?"

Mohander Singh shrugs and smiles, like he has heard a joke he doesn't get. "You are very innocent, Guru *Sant* Singh! I know this! The Guru will help you."

I sputter something about the formal charges and he just says Pratap, his superior, made him do it. What can I say to that?

I call Puneet, and he says, "Where did you go?"

"To police headquarters to give a piece of my mind to that son of a bitch Mohander Singh!"

"Do not waste your time with him," says Puneet. "Come back and see me in my office. We must talk about this."

So Shira and I return to the back of the courthouse and weave our way through the chickens, cows, goats, and fruit vendors until we get to Puneet's office.

"Guru *Sant* Singh, listen carefully to me! With this *challan* filed, I think there is no chance of getting a trial in less than seven or eight years' time."

Now it is time for my jaw to drop open. The only thing I can do, he says, is to get a lot of people on my side and have them write letters to the Sessions Judge, who has the power to order a speedy trial.

"Letters? Really? That would make a difference?"

"Oh, yes," answers Puneet. "Most assuredly. A prominent man will have his day in court very soon, but a nobody will have to wait for years and years. Oh, so many years you will have to wait."

"Even though I'm American? And they have taken my passport?"

"No matter what! But if you have friends in America, prominent people of any kind, or even just a lot of friends, many many many friends and relatives, then the judge will really consider your case."

By now I have spent almost all my money, but that is the least of my worries. The real problem is I haven't any American friends.

"Seven or eight *years*?" I ask Puneet, just to make sure I have got this right.

"Yes, Guru *Sant* Singh! Seven or eight years it will be!"

I really have to think about that. I mean, seriously, seven or eight years in this byzantine cesspool? That is like a lifetime. With the barrels of plastic garbage burning in the streets and everywhere the high-sulfur diesel fumes shooting right up my nose? Seven or eight years of these people, with their "Doooooooon't worry Guru *Sant* Singh" and "You must do this!" Seven or eight years of either having crap on my shoes from the filthy streets or crap in my pants from diarrhea. Seven or eight *years*? In India? Sure, it is my spiritual homeland, but enough is enough.

I desperately want to go home, right this minute.

But even if I could, what home would I go to? Sat Siri controls both our houses. If I flew home today I would end up staying in a Motel 6 on the industrial corridor by the Albuquerque airport. What kind of life would that be?

"Puneet, should I call the American embassy? They ought to help me, right?"

Puneet shrugs. "You can try." He calls his secretary, or his father, or someone, and after a few more telephone exchanges, I have got the number. I call, get a recording, and leave a brief message about my plight.

"We'll see what happens," says Puneet. "Maybe they will talk to the judge for you."

Shira and I leave the office, and I get to thinking that if I had eighty grand under my belt, I would feel a lot better right now. So I find an STD booth and call my stateside lawyer, John Aragon.

"Sant, I don't know what to tell you," he says.

"John, has she deposited the money, or hasn't she?"

"No, and she's not communicating with me. I don't know if the case has been settled or not. I don't know anything. I'm sorry."

There is nothing I can do from India, where every day I count out change for bottled water from my last handfuls of rupees. Eighty thousand bucks is slipping through my hands, and I am looking at an impoverished eternity in a third-world country. I cannot help but ask myself, *is this God's plan*?

I surrender, I surrender, I surrender.

No, actually I don't. Come on, why should I? I surrender to God, but I certainly do not surrender to Sat Siri Kaur! I was more than fair to her, and now she just cuts me out of the loop? But still, I have to marvel at this strange twist of fate. What happened to all those art deals? My baseball betting scheme? What about my Blackjack game? All that money is as gone as youth. Who knows where it all went.

Using the internet, it used to be such a cinch to make money gambling, especially on baseball games, as long as I had my system set up—four computer monitors doing ongoing calculations displayed upon color-coded spreadsheets, a rolling tally of astrological forecasts for specific hours of the day, and numerological analyses of the birthdays of key players. As long as I had my wife Sat Siri Kaur, crunching numbers for about six hours a day, internet, baseball betting was a pretty sure thing for me. At the end of the day I probably never made more than forty bucks an hour doing it, if you actually counted out all the time and prep work put into it, but who cares. Everyone has their scheme, and that was mine. Of course, I started it all back in the pre-internet days. Gambling was a lot harder then!

Back then, I had to find bookmakers to take my action. Trouble was, I was good. Too good. I made sure I always came out ahead. When I got good at counting cards at Blackjack, I learned the hard way that it doesn't pay to win every time. Pretty soon, none of the Indian casinos in northern New Mexico would take my action, so I went back to betting on baseball and found a new bookmaker in L.A.

A lawyer friend set up a meeting for me with this guy Lou at a pizza place on Melrose, so I flew in from New Mexico and found the place, which was papered with pictures of mobsters, really pushing the Goodfellas theme. I sat there and waited until a fat man came up to me—and this man looked exactly like an Italian mobster out of the movies—and he said, "You lookin' for Lou?"

I said yes, so he took me to an empty retail store next door. There were curtains covering the windows, and in the back was a couch and an easy chair covered in white sheets. Sitting on them were three more big guys and a big woman. One of the guys said, "I understand you want some action." That was Lou. I told him yes, and he asked me a little about where I lived and what kind of play I did.

"What kind of numbers are we talking here?" asked Lou.

"Why don't you give me a fifty thousand dollar line of credit?" I suggested. My friend, the lawyer, had told me these kind of bookmakers are the type that are reputed to break your legs if you don't pay, but in reality that is strictly old-time-movie stuff. Nowadays, nobody does that. It's too risky. My friend, the lawyer, told me he himself had stiffed plenty of bookmakers in his time and still had both legs intact. No problem. So I asked for a fifty thousand dollar line of credit and got it.

I bet with Lou for quite some time, but in the end he started to see my method. Most of his clients will sit down and bet the whole board in a day, then have to pay out at the end of the week. Me, I only bet one game a day. My action was a little bit up, a little bit down, but always up at the end of the season. That concerned him. Eventually Lou figured out he wasn't making any money on me.

For my last payout, I flew to L.A. Lou handed me ten thousand dollars in cash and told me flat-out he didn't want my action anymore. So it was back to the casinos for me, and I had to start traveling to Las Vegas, where they didn't know my face yet. At every new casino, I always stayed long enough to get kicked out for counting cards. I liked the notoriety.

Now, with the internet, it's a lot easier to place bets without leaving home, but I kind of miss old Lou and his "action." Either way, I can't place any bets from India. Now that is action no bookie in the world would take!

I can't gamble and, even if I wanted to, I'm starting to take my role as a Sikh much more seriously. Sikhs are flat out prohibited from gambling. Of course, that doesn't stop a lot of them including Yogiji, who used to like to go to the summer races at the racetrack in Santa Fe and place bets on the horses. It certainly didn't stop Hari Jiwan Singh who loved to play craps and invite all the ashram underlings along to shoot the dice with him at the Big Rock Casino. In fact, HJ's outings to the Casino with Yogiji's Beverly Hills jeweler, Jerry, inspired me to learn how to set the dice for the best advantage at the craps table.

Sikhi is a way of life that encourages independent mindedness amongst its adherents and Sikhs tend to be an independent and rather headstrong bunch. Sorry, a *very* headstrong bunch.

Over the centuries this led to many different interpretations of its tenets. In the first half of the 20th Century a number of attempts were made to bring together Sikh scholars and other respected elders in order to codify the tenets of belief and standards of behavior for all Sikhs. In 1950 these wise men finally succeeded in producing a document known as *Sikh Rehat Maryada.* This is considered to be the ultimate "rule book" for what it means to be a Sikh and how to live as such.

Yogiji had never mentioned this document during the 30 years I spent with him and I knew nothing about it until I came to India. When I read it there were many things that stood out to me but these particular lines reverberated in my mind:

The true Sikh of the Guru shall make an honest living by lawful work.

It is forbidden for Sikhs to practice: Influence of stars, Magic spells, incantations, omens, auspicious times, days & occasions, horoscopic dispositions.

And then this:

A Sikh should not steal, form dubious associations or engage in gambling.

It set me back on my heels. Certainly I had often wondered about the ethics and morality of how I had made my money over the previous years. But I always figured that Yogiji knew what he was doing. He was a spiritual teacher. So, if he said that my gambling using astrology was acceptable, if he said the boiler room operations were OK, if he said that there was "no karma over the phone", then all these things must have been OK. Right?

Well, maybe not. You can call it conscience, loss of innocence or just a wakeup call. When I saw those words in the *Rehat Maryada* I knew that I had to live my life differently. I couldn't go back to my old ways. Selling in the boiler room could not be described as an honest living, or lawful work. I don't think I had actually stolen but I *had* been a professional gambler and, by God, I had cultivated many—too many--dubious associations.

I am beginning to realize that maybe my idea of myself as a Gursikh—a true, devout Sikh—was, well, maybe a little over-optimistic. Certainly a real Gursikh would not be selling in a boiler room, using computers and astrology to bet on baseball games or dealing with dubious characters like Lou the bookie.

I am all too well aware that the American Sikh community, the support system I depended upon for thirty years, has abandoned me. This would never have happened if Yogiji were around. To him, family was family. But now that he is dead, I guess white Sikhs are picking and choosing their family members. The black sheep are out on their asses!

I hate to do it. My God, I am fifty years old. But there is no choice. I will have to call my dad and ask for money. I do it. He wires me plenty of cash with a minimum of questions, for which I am immeasurably grateful.

chapter 42

The good news is, this turn of events gives me an excellent excuse to break off with Wadha Kaur. I am in imminent danger of being thrown in jail again; I am under investigation by the police; and I now realize that no matter whether I win or lose the case I am liable to get deported. That means I would never be able to return to India. If she stayed with me, Wadha Kaur might never see her family again! Not only would she have to leave India, but we could even get separated in the deportation process, and who knew if she would ever get a visa to enter the States? Not to mention a green card! The marriage isn't fair to Wadha Kaur, truly. Thank God.

I meet Shira at the internet café and tell him my plan. He shrugs and books bus tickets to Chandigarh. As he types, he glances up at me from the keyboard and says, "Why like this, Guru *Sant* Singh? Why like this?"

"You've heard the girl, Shira. You of all people know she's a nut case! A lunatic! A . . . just a child, that's all. She's not devout, she's not . . ."

But then I see Shira's sly smile. He understands. He is teasing me. We break out in laughter and I feel suddenly, irrationally, like everything is going to be okay.

Shira and I meet Wadha Kaur at a restaurant in Chandigarh. I know I should meet her at her home, but I just can't. I don't want to face her parents.

We eat, and I try to stretch out the story about my hearing so that it finishes when she is done with her food. As a result, there are some long, awkward silences and I can tell she is growing suspicious. Finally, I explain how and why it is in her best interest to cut off with me. Wadha Kaur grows red-faced and slams both fists down on the table.

She does not want to hear my reasons or any talk of legal problems.

Shoulders scrunched up, brow wrinkled, she screams at Shira, "I don't like you!"

He takes the fall for me.

"Women!" he says, later, after he and I have put Wadha Kaur and her servant into an auto rickshaw and are rid of them forever. "What can you do?"

He and I celebrate with American-style chai lattes in the local Coffee Day, India's air-conditioned answer to Starbucks. That is to say, I have a chai latte; he just gets an iced tea. The kid never takes anything extra, nor can he seem to stand to see me waste money on luxuries, either. He certainly won't allow me to spend anything extra on him. He is like my depression-era grandmother—frugality at the core of his being.

I have never seen anything like it. All over India, everyone from lawyers to perfect strangers to little girls are trying to rip me off, but Shira, who hasn't got two rupees to rub together, and a bum leg on top of that, does not want anything except exactly what he is due. No more and no less.

I sip my chai and agree with Shira's assessment of the female mind. It is truly unfathomable. I expected Wadha Kaur to see the undeniable sense in this breakup, but no. She was all emotion and no logic. Exactly like Sat Siri Kaur.

Yogiji always said you have to watch out. Women will try to trick you and trap you in every way possible. They will take over everything in your life, if you let them. The only way a man can hold his own, he said, is to marry a woman and assert calm, loving, spiritual superiority to keep her wild, unfettered power in check. Then she will have someone to keep her calm during all those times when her emotions are flying off the handle. Because, Yogiji used to say, the other thing about women is that despite being living infinities, they are always insecure.

Yogiji taught us that a woman is an endless font of human potential. She can be so spiritual, she can be so powerful, all without saying a word. She can communicate a thousand ideas with a single look. But all of this should come across with "grace." If a woman ever raised her voice or acted angry or impatient, Yogiji said it was a source of shame for her. A woman who is fulfilling her true potential should be a quiet, smiling, all-knowing font of silent gracefulness.

Yogiji held special camps for women and gave them special exercises to increase their inner strength—spinal twists, toe-touching, arm circles, all done while sitting serenely on a fluffy white sheepskin. Bhajan's Sikh women all aspire to be these all-knowing, silent women who express their wise thoughts with just a smile and a look. Or, at least, they are supposed to.

Likewise, Bhajan taught that we men are meant to be powerful, opinionated, and successful. Not as smart as the women, admittedly, but more powerful in a worldly way. The women are supposed to be above business and things like that. Being so wise, they should be assisting us with their grace and trying to make sure we men don't screw everything up.

These teachings represent the way I truly want to live, but without Yogi Bhajan to teach her, I don't know if Wadha Kaur could have learned to live in her full grace. Apparently, it's pretty difficult. Neither of my wives ever really managed it.

chapter 43

At the Coffee Day, I indulge myself in a little self-pity, asking Shira, "Why can't I just find a woman like Bibiji? She let Yogi Bhajan shine, stood by his side, and was happy to be financially well-off and taken care of. Like my mom! She had that grace Yogiji always spoke of." That elusive grace.

"Oh Guru *Sant* Singh, what do you want a woman for anyway? If you want to be a guru, as you say, then just go to an ashram. You have so much experience with the meditation. You will gain many followers, I think."

"Not yet," I tell him. "I have got to have a wife first. Every great guru has a serviceful wife."

He shakes his head and looks out the window. "Guru *Sant* Singh?"

"Yes, Shira?"

"I've been thinking. You have some time now. Three months, I think it is."

"Yes. God! What am I going to do!"

"I think we should go to Rishikesh."

"What's that?"

"Ah ha!" says the kid, beaming in spite of himself. "It is the yoga place! It is where all the western peoples go for the yoga classes and yoga ashrams. There are so many ashrams there, I don't know how many, but there are so so so many!"

"I don't need anyone to teach me yoga."

"No, Guru *Sant* Singh, that is not my meaning. We go where

they have the yoga, because wherever there is the yoga, there is also . . . the women! Western girls!"

"I've had enough of western women!"

"Guru *Sant* Singh, you must listen! There are many white people in Rishikesh. So many, from many countries. You will see. You will like it. And you will meet many western people there and have a good time. You will have so many conversations with so many many western people. Americans, British people, Israeli people, Spain people. All kinds of girls!"

I am just adrift on the wind, so I say okay. Why not? I enjoy putting a smile on his face, and that is reason enough for me.

We board the train, stow our gear, and fall into silence as the train begins its journey. A chai wallah comes through and I buy us two of the worst-tasting cups of chai ever. After one sip, we both stare into our little plastic cups, trying to figure a way to dispose of them without drinking. I decide to throw them in the toilet, so Shira shrugs and hands me his cup. I make my way to the bathroom and discover it is just a room with a hole in the floor! The railroad ties pass beneath the hole one after another as I brace myself and stare down. I hate littering, even in India, where it is completely accepted, but there are no garbage receptacles, so down go the chai cups. I piss after them for good measure, imagining how crap-covered these old tracks must be—just one long exposed toilet across all of India. When I return, Shira is in a talking mood.

"You will really love Rishikesh," he says. "Maybe you will become a guru there! You will see."

I cannot imagine the Indian utopia he describes. Between Amritsar's swarming flies, its cloying heat, and its impenetrable, sweaty crowds with their ever-shouting vendors, I can barely cross the street without stopping to get my bearings. Who, in India, would follow me? I'm a fish out of water!

Anyway, I like the kid's enthusiasm.

More passengers get on at the next stop, and now we have company in our little compartment—a redhead from San Francisco with a million earrings in her head. She says she is going to a meditation retreat at Shiv-Shakti ashram, a place she found online. She suggests we come along and see if we like it there. Also, sharing a taxi from the train station will save her a load of dough. We decide to do it and soon find ourselves in a Jeep taxi, bouncing and jouncing seven kilometers into the heart of the jungle.

When I get to the ashram, I meet the swami's assistant, Stephanie, a black British lady. Everyone calls her "Stephanieji." She tells me about the retreat. It sounds great, but they never allow Indians into the program. Apparently, it is just for fat-wallet westerners. I tell her I will pay for Shira. I need him as my interpreter.

She laughs. "You won't need an interpreter, Guru *Sant* Singh Ji. You're meant to spend the entire two weeks in silence. You'll eat in silence at the appointed times in our dining hall, meditate and do yoga with the group, and go on silent meditation walks in the jungle. We have one dharma lecture each evening, and it is conducted in English, so don't worry. The retreat isn't so much about communicating. It's really about going within." She says it with an ultra-serene tone of voice and a condescending smile. Ah, just like home.

Shira is perfectly okay with being excluded, possibly even relieved. He says he would rather stay in a hotel on the main strip of Rishikesh while I do the retreat.

"Meditation, Guru *Sant* Singh . . . it is not for me. I will stay in the town and make some friends! It is a good arrangement. If you need anything, I will hire one taxi and bring things to you, like a courier."

So I check into the ashram and see Shira off with a roll of cash for food, entertainment, whatever. He looks at it and smiles broadly, infectiously. He is trying to turn the corners of his mouth down, trying to conceal his glee, but he can't. "This is a lot, Guru *Sant* Singh!"

It's nice to be able to make someone happy so easily. In America, I felt like the more cash I handed over to people, the more they wanted. A wad of cash never satisfied anyone—my wives, Yogi Bhajan, or anyone. There were always lingering questions: is it enough? When will I get more? Could the wad have been bigger?

"I'm sure you'll spend it wisely," I say.

"Money is honey!" Shira says, kissing the roll, pocketing it, and showing me his teeth.

It makes me feel a little like Yogi Bhajan to be handing out large sums of cash. I feel magnanimous, like he was. When I was at my lowest, Yogiji used to kick into action and really take care of me. For instance, during my first divorce, after the failure of my Warhol investments, I was very depressed and owed everyone money. I sold my art gallery for about thirty grand, but didn't know how to divide up the money. I owed seventy thousand to Jacqueline Forsythe, a lot more to my wife's sister, and smaller sums to a few other ashramites. Everyone wanted that money and there was not enough to pay off all the debts, so I got it all in a cashier's check and just handed it to Yogi Bhajan. I told him he could keep it or divide it up among my debtors as he saw fit. Well, he sat on it for a little while, then divided it in half and gave half back to me and half to my ex-wife. He didn't want my money when it was given that way—in sad, spiritual desperation.

Of course, another time he asked me for five grand for some Indian refugees he wanted to help. I just gave him the cash in an envelope without hesitation. As long as the money was passed around with conscious free will, that was the main thing.

chapter 44

The turban, the beard, the years of experience doing Kundalini yoga . . . my very presence fascinates everyone at the retreat. I make friends, talking (out in the orchard, where no one can nail us) with beauties from all over the globe. Other times, I try to relax into meditation, but I can't enjoy the experience like I should, because this business about the *challan* is heavy on my mind. I still don't even know exactly who is accusing me of what.

I can see and hear the rushing waters of the sacred Ganges from my simple room. Outside my window, a perfectly triangular mountain rises in the near distance. It comes right out of the earth like a knife point, as if angry sky gods had yanked it up by the spindly trees clinging to its pointy top. The sheer side facing me is decorated with serrated granite stripes, and at its base, tiny distant farmers plant fields so green I want to breathe them, eat them, disappear into them. Throughout the day, the farmers' wives seem to be perpetually hanging laundry and taking it down, wearing their saris of blue, pink, and yellow. Their children—miniscule in the distance—play at running and jumping in a riverside sand dune.

I walk local paths in silent thought, and the perfume of jungle flowers greets me on cow tracks, along hiking trails, and in boulder fields bordering the river. It permeates the ashram's rambling herb garden. At night, the clean air is still except for the constant singing of the sacred river and the bells, the bells, the bells. High ones, low ones, all different kinds—the swamis ring the hell out of them to awaken the Gods. It's a Hindu thing, but I don't mind. Pink and purple mums as big as babies' heads, petunias in every color of the rainbow, orange trumpet vines, and so many more flowers comprise an ever-expanding garden in the ashram's central patio. Outside the ashram walls, red-assed monkeys scamper through the undergrowth. You have to watch out for them, I am told. They will attack you for food. Only the smaller, black monkeys are cute and friendly.

One day, a ten-meter boa constrictor as thick as a man's leg slithers right through the ashram's central patio. An old swami laughs and says it is a former student's soul returning. The place is wild—a little habitation carved out of absolute wilderness—and if ever there is a paradise on this earth, as far as I'm concerned, Shiv-Shakti Ashram is it.

While Shira lives in a paradise of his own (lunching and strolling and riding around on rented motorbikes all day with giggling, international lady tourists) I learn a new style of yoga. Ashtanga. There is a lot more stretching and less of the vigorous undulating and repetition involved with the kundalini and tantric styles I learned from Yogiji. The yoga is fine. I enjoy the exercise. Pretty soon, I start to be able to surrender to God again. I actually think things might just work out, after all. Tucked away in the green mountains, beside the cool river, away from the smog and the noise of the city, I feel hidden and cared for and safe.

A fortyish woman named Lalamji runs the ashram, under the tutelage of her own swami, an old holy man who speaks no English and is seldom seen. The two of them are sanyasi, a Hindu term for celibate, dedicated to God—the monks and nuns of yoga. Lalamji's English is pretty halting, so Stephanieji leads the meditative hikes, helps during yoga class, and translates the dharma talks.

I am curious about their arrangement, and gradually find out Stephanieji is a volunteer here. She works as Lalamji's twenty-four-hour, seven-day-a-week personal assistant and manager. After sundown, talking is permitted, and Stephanieji sometimes draws small groups to listen to her expound upon the magical healing powers of Shiv-Shakti Ashram, and how happy the place has made her. I linger on the periphery of these sessions, listening in.

"The modern world is so toxic, you know. I used to get very depressed in that life. Once, I almost committed suicide. I told my mother I was going to do it. I *was* going to do it, but she had me committed. I lived for six months in a mental hospital, on all sorts of prescription drugs, like a zombie," she says.

Her talks are always about this type of thing—how she falls easily into deep depression, how she nearly committed suicide several times, how she used to hate herself but then came to Shiv-Shakti for a retreat and decided to stay. Here, she is able to commune with God and let the world go by. Here, she says, she is celibate and poor, but sane and happy for the first time. She worships Lalamji almost like a goddess. She constantly speaks of Lalamji's wisdom, of her bravery in taking on the life of a female swami—a very unusual thing in India, almost unheard of.

I do not like to participate in these talks, because I understand Stephanieji all too well. I sense she is still on the edge. One misstep could pull her down again, and if I get too close, I could fall with her. She is still new to the ecstasies of yoga and meditation, still having her honeymoon with it. But listening in on her talks brings back memories, both good and bad.

It must have been 1978 or 1979. Sat Kir*pal* Singh invited me to drive down from Oregon, with him and his family, to the Summer Solstice event Yogi Bhajan held every June in the Jemez Mountains of New Mexico. This was before I had ever met Yogi Bhajan, before I changed my name. I was still learning how to wrap my turban. Most days, it looked like a messy bed sheet balanced on my head. Like Stephanie, I was engrossed in the ecstasy of my new spiritual practice and fascinated by the altered states of mind I could achieve through the long meditation sessions, hours of chanting, and repetitive movements of Bhajan's special brand of yoga. Already, the spiritual discipline of Sikhi had rescued me from a lifetime of depression, nightmares, generalized hatred, and free-floating anxiety.

Summer Solstice was held at a forest campsite, where a giant, open-sided, white tent had been erected. Under it, white sheets were stretched out and tethered to the ground. All around this meeting space, people set up their tents, campers, hammocks, bedrolls, tarpaulins, or whatever they had. It was, essentially, a big hippy scene. We got fed twice a day. In the morning we had chili-hot potato soup, oranges and bananas; in the evening, spicy beans and rice with slabs of lettuce. No salad, no dressing; just large chunks of raw lettuce. After not eating since the early morning the lettuce tasted like the nectar of the gods.

For hours each day, we would concentrate on Bhajan's tantric yoga. Tantra is an offshoot of the kundalini yoga I was already doing daily, but this stuff is at a higher level. It is about balancing the crucial male and female energies, but on a spiritual level, without sex.

Long rows of men, dressed completely in white, sat facing long rows of women, dressed completely in white. Bhajan, as the world's only "Mahan Tantric," or tantric master, had the power to channel the sacred "Z" energy. This is a celestial energy he could send zipping, in a "z" formation, from male to female to male to female, all the way down the line. Sometimes the yoga required you to hold your arm up in the air until all the blood drained out of it, and then a while longer still. Sometimes Bhajan had the guys touch palms with their female partners, breathe deeply, and stare into their eyes for hours. Other exercises included touching the soles of your feet with your partner's, or standing back to back, buttocks touching, making certain patterns with your arms.

Despite the requirement of total celibacy and silence for seven days, a lot of people got very turned on by this stuff. I used to see guys in the line with no underwear under their kurtas and giant hard-ons. At night, I would see tents swaying from the orgies going on inside. On the outskirts of the camp, couples would lay down in the sandy arroyo and rut under the stars, making wild animal sounds and attracting coyotes. A lot of them were tripping on drugs, too. I do not know what kind.

True to my nature, I had studied up on tantric yoga before the Solstice. I understood the concept of Siddhi powers, the incredibly powerful energies we were dealing with. I knew it was completely disrespectful to exploit the energies in this way. Tantric energies are supposed to be channeled into the spiritual realm. They are supposed to enhance your ecstasy with God, not just give momentary physical pleasure. I could tell Yogiji was being very patient with these people. He was always lecturing, gently but firmly, and trying to guide their minds to higher consciousness. Most just blew it off, but there were some yogis who left because of this repeated emphasis on celibacy. They thought Bhajan was trying to turn them into squares.

I was naturally square, so what did I care? Spiritual communion was what I was after, and I was disgusted by the lack of discipline I saw. Maybe that was why, out of thousands of people, Yogi Bhajan noticed me. A Sikh I did not know approached me one day, out of the blue, and told me I had been granted a private audience. He gave me a penetrating look, raised one bushy eyebrow, and pointed at Yogi Bhajan's cabin.

I walked in. The great man sat there in his big chair, surrounded by massive handmade garlands, endless swaths of fine silken fabrics, and golden urns overflowing with fluffy ostrich feathers.

"Clark!" he said, "What took you so long?"

I touched his feet.

"I know you," he said, "You want it all. You'll be lucky if you're not crucified on the cross like Jesus Christ! You'll never be satisfied until you are ten times greater than me!"

Immediately I knew he was a genius, and clairvoyant.

That day, Yogiji insisted I get baptized as a Sikh. Nothing else mattered. I was one of his people, and he claimed me.

"But Yogiji," I said, "I've already been baptized in the name of Jesus Christ."

"No!" boomed Yogiji, "Guru Ram Das!"

Only a couple of years before, I had dropped out of Texas Christian University and renounced the Christian Church altogether. The threat of hellfire was still very real to me. Nevertheless, I decided Jesus would understand my need to switch allegiances. He had to! He was Jesus! So I did it. I got officially re-baptized as a Sikh.

There was a ceremony: sacred chanting and five Sikhs dressed in orange kurtas stirring a bowl of sugar water around and around with an iron *Khanda (*double edged sword*)*. After many hours, the sound vibrations were imbued into the nectar and they sprinkled it into my eyes, on my hair and into my cupped hands for me to drink.

The baptism was very moving, but my meeting with Yogi Bhajan affected me more deeply than anything. The way he compared me to Jesus, the way he already knew about my intense ambitions, and the way he said, "What took you so long!" as if he had known me since before I was born . . . I just knew this was a leader I could trust with my very soul. After that, I got serious and started to exclusively wear the white, knee-length *kurta* and pajama pants that constituted the uniform of a Yogi Bhajan devotee and member of the "Happy Healthy Holy Organization." I learned to wrap my turban correctly.

I was feeling so good I decided to write to my mother:

Dear Mother,

I enjoyed your letter. I feel very blessed by God to have you as my mother and blessed that you could bring me into this beautiful life to be happy, healthy & holy. God has given me many wonderful gifts, for which I cannot even begin to sing and worship His name enough.

God has given me another gift recently. The people that I live with here in Eugene have been wonderful sources of God's love. I want to serve God and be a light to elevate others in their love. Mother, your love and trust, Jesus Christ's infinite love and guidance in values and actions, and other friends who speak God's truth, have had such an impact on me to reach for the highest divinity and truth. I have made a decision to become a minister. God's love has inspired me to live as a true saint, exalt the Lord and live a humble life. Health, happiness, and holiness are my natural way. Becoming a minister of God is a pleasant and natural step for me, I will show dignity, divinity, and grace in business, marriage, or counseling and in whatever God's will is. How did all this come about? Well it hasn't been a snap decision, as you know I evaluate and consider decisions and actions to reach the best outcomes. I have been living with Sikhs (Searchers of truth) here in Eugene. I have learned many things about living a spiritual life and feeling this happiness that comes from directed efforts and working through negativity in myself and the people around me that we may live to the full potential of love that God wants for us. Because Sikhism originated in India and seemed very strange and different from Christianity, I tended to stay clear of any commitment when I first moved into the Ashram a year ago. In this year I have explored and prayed to God. From this feeling and faith in the one true lord God, I have decided that commitment for myself to the Sikh way of life is the will of God. Becoming a Sikh is my best way of serving God, it's not the only way to serve or worship God. Christianity, and other religions that worship the one true lord are beautiful, I respect and love anyone who holds the lord in their heart. For me it's not so much the label of Catholic, Sikh, Baptist or whatever- it's the grace and courage you bring to the commitment we make to God. So I have chosen the life and people that I feel comfortable living with.

We all have different creative ways of worshiping God and God loves the true people who sing his praises and worship his name in the conscious way that we choose. What is really important for me is that we not be attached to any particular rituals of religion, holding love for the different ways of singing God's hymns and speaking about his love are endless and most beautiful.

I have made some important decisions when I decided to take Sikh vows. One, I have been given a new spiritual name—Guru Sant Singh Khalsa. I use this new name to acknowledge and allow God to add his love which will remind me that I am his saint. I still love you just as much mother. I will also wear a white turban on my head. The turban is a reminder and symbol of my commitment to God. God wants us to enjoy life and be happy—this commitment makes me very happy.

P.S. Guru Sant means Saint of God.

Love,

Guru Sant Singh Khalsa

P.P.S. I'll send a legal certificate of name change in case you need to change any documents.

Mom was real sweet—if somewhat predictable—in her response. She said: "You'll always be my son but I think you're still a Christian no matter what you say."

Back in Eugene, in our community, I finally looked like I belonged, but out in society at large, I stood out like a sore thumb. People pestered me, teased me, even threatened me. I loved it! I felt like a celebrity. But more important was my dedication to the Sikh path. After baptism, my meditations became deeper and my yoga, more strenuous. I liked having a code to live by again, and I liked my new relationship with God. I was as zealous as they come, just like Stephanieji. I still am, but after all my ups and downs with the 3HO community, it is different now. Not as innocent.

chapter 45

At Shiv-Shakti, there is a fire pit in the middle of a three-sided, roofed concrete patio, and every night we sit around it while Lalamji leads us in shaking bells and chanting prayers. The experience is hypnotic, really. You can see her going into a trance in the firelight while the smoke goes up and forms fascinating Rorschach patterns on the ceiling. This is her whole life, this constant prayer, and she does not hold back.

In many ways, for me, this retreat is just like the old days in Eugene—the simple living and plain food, the hours to meditate. Just chanting the evenings away with so many enthusiastic young people. Shaking the tambourine. That feeling of changing the world on a psychic level, of doing your part to fill the world with peace and clarity. Such a high we all got from it.

And the night air off the mountains, cooling the skin just enough.

Lalamji directs us in chants that praise the Hindu god Shiva. Stephanieji says the program is "non-denominational," but I know better. Regardless, I enjoy it. In fact, I want to stay forever. This is such an innocent place, really. I start to wonder if seven or eight years of this wouldn't be a bad idea after all. I could wait out my trial in this hidden paradise. Sure beats a Motel Six in the Albuquerque industrial corridor.

Two weeks after it all began, the kids on the retreat hug one another and cry and leave to go do a rave in Goa or a trek in Darjeeling or white-water rafting on the Ganges. Many are on their "year out" after college, and now they each head off to find a new thrill, but I sign up for another couple of weeks of ashram life.

One day, I take a hike, and suddenly butterflies are everywhere! The huge, colorful things brush right by me like I am not even there. One sits on a branch and seems to watch me. It is green and looks just like a leaf. Later, I sit and meditate on the flat roof of my dormitory, and a trio of multi-colored parrots swoops past, buoyed by air currents, or perhaps just by spirit. Wonders never end at Shiv-Shakti. They just never do.

One day, as I meditate in my room, there is a knock on my door. It is Stephanieji.

"So sorry to disturb you, Guru *Sant* Singh Ji!"

"Not at all, Stephanieji, what can I do for you?"

"Lalamji asked me to invite you to the patio for chai. She'd like you to join her, privately, for chai." Like that nameless Sikh at my first Solstice, she gives me a grave, perhaps even melodramatic, look and a little knowing smile.

Over chai, Lalamji asks me about myself. Her English is not great, but she is very interested in my turban, my faith, and my obvious experience with meditation, yoga, and chanting. She has never met a white Sikh, and knows nothing about Yogi Bhajan, so she is curious to know how I came to be the man I am today. I try not to gush, but it is hard to talk about Yogi Bhajan without flying off into worshipful ecstasies. She replies by nodding sagely and looking off into the distance.

Over time, meeting for tea becomes a habit, and Lalamji and I become friends, of a sort. Eventually she shares her story with me.

"I was sixteen," she says. "I came from one family that was a little bit devout only. Not so much. Not so much devout Hindus. But I felt one call to the devotion. To do yoga, to do ashram living.

And not to marry. Being as close with God. To do this life, like this, Shiv-Shakti Ashram."

She came out to Shiv-Shakti when there was nothing here. No electricity, no bathrooms, no running water. There was just one swami, who became her teacher, and a couple of rude huts. She had to wash everything in the river, cook everything over a fire. It was terribly hard.

"Why did you do it?" I ask her. To worship God is one thing, but to be so alone, at such a young age, is quite another, especially for Indians, with their communal ways.

"I made this decision," she says. "Not to marry. I made this decision to become swami and celibate sanyasi. Okay, my parents are finished, then. My family is finished." She makes the characteristic Indian gesture that starts with both hands upturned, fingers spread as if holding a pancake, then they flip, as if dashing the pancake to the ground. It means "finished" or "no more." In this case, it means they disowned her.

Just like my father had disowned me. Fortunately he and I made up; I got the impression that Lalamji's family never did. Some people can be so heartless.

Regardless, she took her vows, came to Shiv-Shakti, and has now spent more than thirty years dedicated to Shiva.

She does not get paid, just gets her needs taken care of. Her teacher, her swami, owns the ashram, and when he dies, his nephews will inherit it. For all she knows, they may sell it for condominiums. So, with each new gray hair on the old swami's head, her lifestyle here, and her very livelihood, become more and more tenuous.

Eventually, however, I learn that Lalamji does own one thing of value: a car, a brand new black Mercedes the ashram bought her for emergencies and grocery runs. After all, she was the one who built the ashram up from two primitive huts to the assortment of three-story dormitories, teaching facilities, yoga rooms, temples, flower gardens, and orchards that it is today. She was the one who developed the meditation-retreat program, bringing in westerners, with their money. Shiv-Shakti Ashram has become a very successful endeavor, and she has made her old swami a pretty wealthy hermit. All the profits go into his *dhoti.*

All Lalamji does with her magnificent car is to drive it a few miles, once every couple of weeks, into Rishikesh and back. She keeps it in a garage and keeps it shined up. It is blacker and shinier than her own rope of jet black hair. It gleams like the sun, this dark beautiful thing stuck away in the gloom all day and night.

Lalamji is a recluse by social standards, but by the standards of the sanyasi, she is practically a socialite. She enjoys the influx of new blood that comes with each scheduled yoga retreat, even though she is seldom able to communicate with the English-speaking spiritual tourists. Over time, through our halting, and very polite, conversations, I sense she has grown a bit bored with her life here. Not that she would ever willingly leave the ashram. This is her home. It is like a marriage. But I sense she needs something. Maybe just a friend.

I grow comfortable at Shiv-Shakti. I follow my own meditation schedule now, as do a few others who have decided to stay on after the retreat. There are a few British girls that seem to be friends; a boyfriend/girlfriend couple that, of course, does not share a room; and two single European men. I chat with all of them, just in passing, but the communal meals are silent, by requirement, and I have a lot to work out on the psychic level.

Like Stephanieji said, this is a place where people come to go inward, not to make friends, so solitude suits us all. I reach new heights of meditative ecstasy, either strolling beside the Ganges, or sitting on the roof that overlooks the neighboring farms. The sweet breezes here, the beauty of the jungle, and a sense of overwhelming peace fill me up every day. But then, in the middle of my fourth week at the ashram, something happens that changes everything.

The boyfriend comes to the office, saying his girlfriend had gone hiking to a waterfall by herself the night before, but this morning she is nowhere to be seen. Lalamji and Stephanieji call a meeting and they tell all the residents something disturbing. This remote area is no stranger to rape and murder. Only a few weeks previous, a tourist was stabbed, at night, on the streets of Rishikesh.

Then there are the jungle animals.

Last year, a swami was crushed by an elephant. It sauntered out of the jungle, wrapped its trunk around the man's neck, picked him up, threw him down, and stood on his head until it popped.

Nobody knew why.

The baffling thing was, the man had spent his life as a vigorous devotee of Ganesha, the elephant-head god.

"Ever notice the iron fence around the ashram, with the spikes pointing out?" asks Stephanieji. That, apparently, is to keep out the leopards.

Lalamji announces that the police will be coming to look for the girl. I can picture it now, a real Agatha Christie affair: *Murder at Shiv-Shakti Ashram*. Some detective will walk in with a magnifying glass in one hand and a revolver in the other. He will close the double iron doors with a clang and announce, "No one leaves this ashram until the mystery is solved!" Something like that.

Maybe I am letting my imagination run away with me, but, looking ahead, what I see is that the cops are going to ask all the guests for their passports and go over them with a fine-toothed comb. When I fail to produce one, I will get to see how the Rishikesh jail compares to the Amritsar one. When they learn I am awaiting trial in a case of marriage fraud, they will think me a sexual predator. It will be an easy-out for the cops to blame me for the girl's disappearance. They will put my mug on TV again, saying I am now suspected of two different crimes against women in the space of six months. Then won't I be "in the soup," as the Indians say.

I take Stephanieji aside and confide in her. I tell her about my legal situation and my confiscated passport. She shakes her head, sighs, and says I had better tell Lalamji. I do this, but what with the language barrier, I can only get across that I am in trouble with the police, not the full story of my innocence.

Lalamji isn't happy. "You put this ashram in a danger. We are not to be a place for the crime hiding!" Her eyes shoot white hot flame at me the way only a swami's eyes can. I understand. The last thing she needs is for Shiv-Shakti to get a bad reputation as a shelter for ne'er-do-wells. She is holding onto the place by the skin of her teeth as it is.

Lalamji tells me to pack up and get lost before the police arrive, and adds a few choice words in Hindi that I will be happy to never have translated. Then, while I am throwing my things in my bag, the missing girl shows up, skipping down the lane, completely fine and unharmed. She had merely gone out for an early morning hike, by herself, without telling anyone. Lalamji calls off the investigation, but the damage has been done.

Head hanging, beard grazing my thighs, I spend the day walking along the roadside, back to Rishikesh. I try to flag down passing cars, but no one stops. I nearly get sideswiped several times. I could call Shira, but I do not. Maybe I want to punish myself. Maybe I just need to think. For seven kilometers, I warily eye the gathering crowds of monkeys, who seem to delight in showing me their red asses.

chapter 46

When I find Shira at his hang-out, the Little Buddha restaurant, I tell him my tale and, lacking any better idea, suggest we return to stinky, hot, dirty Amritsar. Shira just laughs. A month in Rishikesh, eating his favorite western food (toast with Nutella) at his favorite restaurant, while flirting with western girls and living worry-free off that roll of cash I gave him, has loosened him up completely. The kid does not take anything seriously anymore, if he ever did.

"Don't be stupid, old man! Let's just go to Dharamsala! The weather is shifting anyway. It's the perfect time to go." Shira is full of ideas. Nothing fazes him at all.

"Really?" I ask. "Dharamsala? Where's that?" I am not in the mood for taking chances.

"It's up in the mountains, and very cool!"

That sounds nice. I will do anything to keep from returning to Amritsar's oppressive heat, so I let his enthusiasm sweep me away.

We drag my two rolling suitcases into a bus depot. All he carries is a small blue backpack, like a schoolboy's book bag. It looks about ten years old and is not even half full. It occurs to me Shira is the ultimate dharma bum. We hop on a nondescript, unmarked bus, standing among many others. How anyone is supposed to know what bus goes where and when is a complete mystery to me, but Shira somehow intuits these things.

We head to Dharamsala, but technically we wind up in McLeod Ganj, an unlikely name for a Himalayan settlement. Seems it was named after Sir Donald Friell McLeod, a Lieutenant Governor of

Punjab during the British *raj*; the suffix *ganj* is a common Hindi word for "neighborhood." McLeod Ganj is a suburb of Dharamsala and turns out to be a small town, far smaller than Rishikesh, bustling with western tourists and fresh-faced, yoga-loving youth. It is the headquarters of the Dalai Lama and his Tibetan Government in Exile. I must admit I am a bit suspicious of the place, suspicious of Buddhists and their carefree lifestyles, but also curious. The town is in the heart of the mountains, amid a ponderosa pine forest. The mountain breezes are refreshing, and the weather is like springtime every day. I go around in my shirtsleeves, but Shira says the air is "very cold!" and buys a fleece pullover.

At night, the young backpackers turn Dharamsala into a crazy international playground. One evening, a fire juggler performs in the central square. Another night, a kind of impromptu parade seems to be winding its way through town. Handmade signs announce, "Intuitive painting class, with Catherine," and "Tibetan art school." There are far fewer yoga schools here than in Rishikesh, and a lot more restaurants. Roving bands of young tourists seem to be just hanging out, enjoying the weather, buying trinkets, flirting with each other, and going on hikes in the forest. No plans for the future. A lot of people literally sit around and do nothing all day—some are tourists, others are Tibetan refugees, monks with their begging bowls. Everyone sits around like this for days, even weeks, on end. With a regular stream of cash, a man could spend his whole life here, doing nothing. People do. Is that the Buddhist influence? I wonder.

I call Shira when I need him, but mostly I do not need him. Like in Rishikesh, I give him a roll of bills and let him do his own thing. Periodically, we run into each other in restaurants or on the street. He is always talking to someone. Sometimes they are young ladies, but other times old ladies, old men, Tibetans, street vendors, even local children. I have no idea what he is always talking about, but still, it is amazing. Talk about "the art of conversation"—Shira could teach classes in it. I am a little envious, wondering what my life would have been like if I had had that kind of savoir faire in my twenties. No matter, I do my *Nitnem* and daily meditation, and stay busy with my inner work.

In Dharamsala, I keep going to internet cafes, checking the chat rooms, and posting my situation all over the web. Finally, New Mexico's *Albuquerque Journal* picks up the story. A reporter actually calls S.H.O. Mohander Singh and then interviews me online about it.

I'm shocked when the reporter tells me that Mohander Singh stated I'm "a good man, but a little bit guilty" and I "cheated one woman out of fifteen thousand rupees."

Now I am even more confused. I call Mohander Singh and ask him about this interview.

"Am I really accused of cheating one woman out of 15 thousand rupees? That's absurd! Who is accusing me of this?"

"No, Guru *Sant* Singh. I don't think so. I had to tell that reporter something, so I told her that."

"Mohander Singh, what am I actually accused of? What does this challan say about me?"

"Oh, it says only that you are accused of marriage fraud, that is all. Many women have signed this thing, saying you are a cheat and you promised them marriage."

"But I didn't!"

"I am sorry, Guru *Sant* Singh. This is what the challan says."

I get out my copy of the challan and ask Shira to tell me what it says, exactly. It is sloppily handwritten on ten pages of forms. He studies the first few pages carefully, then becomes impatient. He quickly rifles through the rest of the papers and says, "It is just a lot of women saying, 'yes, he is guilty, he cheated me,' chiefly a bunch of garbage. Don't pay any attention to this."

"Is Sukhvinder Kaur one of the women?"

"Who? Oh, Sukhvinder Kaur, I don't know . . ." he is getting impatient now, turning pages and scanning them lazily. "I don't think so, Guru *Sant* Singh. I don't see the name." He puts down the papers and picks up his backpack. He has places to go and people to see, and leaves me alone in the hotel room.

Shira is no lawyer, but I like his laid-back analysis, so I try not to pay any more attention to it. Nothing I can do anyway.

Internet cafes in most parts of India are dirty places. You don't want to touch the walls. You wonder what happened in there. A chai thermos exploded? Buffalo sleep there at night? It doubles as an auto rickshaw garage? You cannot explain the filth. You pay for your time there, then the electricity goes out while you are online. You are expected to sit and wait for it to come back on. Ten minutes. An hour. Nobody comes around saying, "We're terribly sorry for the inconvenience." They don't care.

But in Dharamsala it is different. This is paradise. Many internet cafes, as well as restaurants (which are called hotels) and hotels (which are also called hotels) are run by American, European, and especially Tibetan expats. Their pleasant little parlors dot the cityscape, and each one serves better chai than the next.

One restaurant is owned by some American hippies that got out of the rat race decades ago. They are happy people, and very relaxed, you can tell. The place serves Mexican food and something called "the Santa Fe omelet" and even fresh-baked bread! It's crazy, Dharamsala. You can get anything you want!

I make friends with a bunch of tourists that like to go to a certain Japanese restaurant every night, where they have an open-mic. Everyone participates. People go up on stage and play an instrument or tell a story. Some people even sing songs or do little skits!

In addition to tourists, some Tibetan refugees come to open-mic night, too. They seem to be going crazy in this limbo land. One guy likes to get drunk and get up there on the stage and just basically strip. He takes his clothes off down to his underwear, singing terribly the whole time. Then he tries to get women up there to dance with him. But somehow he is actually funny, just being so ridiculous and lost.

With the Tibetans, I see a lot of drinking. They are big meat eaters, too, these people. I can't understand their religion; it seems pretty loose. A lot of the Tibetan kids here are monks, but you see them coming down from the mountain with beers in their hands. I don't think they are pious. In fact, I suspect they just do the monk thing for room and board. Everyone has got to make it one way or another, I guess.

One night I go up on the mic and tell all these western kids about the elevator at the Golden Temple. They love it.

You see, most Indians have never seen an elevator, so a lot of people don't know what it is. Once, I opened it and there were some kids in there naked! They thought it was a changing room!

Of course, most Indians know nothing about elevator etiquette either, so whenever the doors open, all the people inside start shoving to get out at the same time all the people outside start shoving to get in. Meanwhile, the doors are trying to close and they just bounce in and out on the masses of bodies, going *ding! ding! ding!*

It's just like the way Indians stand in line for train tickets or anything else. Everything is a shoving match. At the restaurant, everyone gets a kick out of that story. I am having fun here, definitely.

chapter 47

In a restaurant in Dharamsala, I meet another Sikh. We get to talking and I tell him my situation, more or less. The man's bushy eyebrows shoot up and he grins, shakes my hand, hugs me, and calls me brother. Eyebrows says he used to work at Miri Piri Academy and knew Yogi Bhajan very well. In fact, Yogiji had treated him like a son! The fellow's own mother used to fry paranthas for Yogiji. The great teacher used to ask young Eyebrows to slather them with butter behind the backs of his secretaries, who were concerned about his weight.

Eyebrows shares the story of this butter conspiracy with me and we have a good laugh. It is good to find someone who really knows my people, and I sense a special bond here.

We talk more, mostly about the corruption and brutality of the Punjabi Police. I am not sure why, but he brags that he and his brothers once beat and nearly killed a man, then paid off the police and stayed out of jail. Then he says he knows people in the Akali Dal, a powerful political party, that could help me. He seems eager to help, so I say, "Sure, have them call me." Why not?

He calls me alright.

A week goes by and Eyebrows rings my mobile phone with his uncle, or whoever it is, standing by.

He says, "Doooooooon't worry, Guru *Sant* Singh. My man will straighten everything out for you. Of course he wants to help you! You are his Sikh brother! My brother! Of course arrangements must be made . . . My uncle is an old man, you know. Very ill health. He needs many things. He is all the time paining. So much paining he has . . . He needs many things, Guru *Sant* Singh! Medicines! But my uncle will help you most surely. He is very powerful in the Akali Dal Party. Yes. Yes! There are so many powerful men that he knows. He wants to help you, but there are many doctors he must see. He is all the time paining . . ."

Exasperated, I finally ask, "Does this guy expect me to pay him?"

"Of course!" says Eyebrows.

"I'm not paying him one red cent!" I holler back down the line. "How can you call yourselves Sikhs of the Guru?"

"Don't you know that's how things are done here? You're in India! Don't you know how it works?"

"I'm not giving one dime to you greedy sons of bitches!"

"You'll be sorry for this! You'll be really sorry! My uncle can get your charges dropped for you, you stupid American. You are turning down a very good offer!"

I tell him to take a hike.

He says he will make me sorry, but I never see Eyebrows again.

Shira and I stay in Dharamsala for months. Neither of us has any reason not to, frankly. I spend a lot of time online, seeking attention for my case, and seeking individuals willing to write letters on my behalf. Eventually I receive an email from a man named J.S. Bedi. He is the Punjabi-born editor of a Los Angeles broadsheet called Indiapost. It is published for the non-resident Indians living all over Los Angeles. Apparently he has been following my case and thinks he has the whole thing pinned down. In fact, he goes ahead and calls me on an expensive mobile-to-mobile overseas connection. His dime!

"Indian women will screw you!" he says. "Men have no rights! They're going to extort all you have! Everything!"

Bedi tells me if I am not willing or able to bribe officials, I need to sneak out of India and quick. Otherwise I will get thrown in a terrible jail—a real pit of hell.

Yeah, yeah, I think, *and I'll lose my soul.* I have heard it all before.

What a typical Punjabi: "You must do this! You must do that! You must do what I say if you know what's good for you!"

I just can't say anything to the guy, he is so damnably confident. I am not going to follow his bossy advice. He is probably working some angle of his own in the whole thing. Has a bet riding on me or something.

But J.S. Bedi gives me a great gift. His personality is so forceful, so much like Yogi Bhajan's, that I realize, listening to him, how very unoriginal Yogiji actually was. I used to think the man was chosen. With that incredible confidence he had, I was sure he had to be in touch with the divine. But now I realize this is a trait common to nearly all Punjabi men, and it is not exactly the same thing as confidence. It's more like just plain bossiness. Now that I am used to being surrounded by ten-thousand Yogi Bhajans at every turn, the memory of my teacher is starting to lose its magic. It sounds like blasphemy, and I would not utter this aloud, but in a way, I am realizing now that Yogiji was just another one of *them.*

I tell J.S. Bedi I don't plan to bribe anyone and I am not going to leave India either. I am going to stay and clear my name. I am not guilty of anything, and I'll prove it.

He calls me simple-minded. Says he is afraid for me.

Then the *Santa Fe, New Mexican* gets hold of my story. They hit the front page with *Desire for Mate Becomes Legal Affair.* The reporter calls me for an interview and quotes me saying, "God gives us these tests." I like how it sounds. Of course, everyone at the 3HO ashram, back in New Mexico, reads the thing. Oh God! Online, a dam bursts.

Their vitriol against me is passionate, a little surprising, and very, very public. American Sikhs let me have it in online discussion forums across the virtual world:

"This guy is just a deluded, lonely old man. He is an embarrassment to 3HO and all of us."

"What an egomaniac. He's not a true Sikh, obviously."

"It's important to note that this man is not one of us. He's a sad, pathetic man who thrives on public attention and scandal."

Actually, they make me laugh, and I admit I get a little bit of a charge from the attention. I don't know why this is. I guess sometimes a sound whipping is better than a hot, wet kiss.

After all, all I did was try to pursue the arranged-marriage lifestyle Yogi Bhajan had celebrated for more than thirty years. 3HO members are just embarrassed that the world now knows what we are about. I am not embarrassed. Why would I be? But as soon as the details of my lifestyle hits the news, white Sikhs start vehemently denying sharing any of my values—like a pack of Judases.

Then there are my supporters. I guess you could call them supporters. They write articles on how I am being victimized by horrible Indian women who love to accuse men in "false dowry" cases. What happens, supposedly, is that the men are tossed into jail along with their mothers, fathers, sisters, and brothers. The family is ruined. The man's sisters can never marry. Some commit suicide. These people say I am lucky my family is in the U.S. or they all would have been arrested—my elderly mother and father included. They see me as just another example of man-abuse and are furious on my behalf. Furious!

The law against predatory men is created to help women, of course, but apparently a lot of women try to use it for profit. Just like the beer-drinking monks, I guess. Everyone has got some scam, and whether it is to make a million or just to get by, it doesn't matter if you offend a stranger, a friend, or God. Cash is king.

I thought Yogiji had taught me that already, but no. I realize now I am only beginning to get schooled.

Next, a reporter calls and tells me that he called the embassy asking for a comment on the case. Despite my initial phone call and the letter (supposedly) sent by the Punjabi Police department, the embassy claims to have no knowledge of the case. The reporter tells me the embassy now wants me to give them a call. I do it.

After five minutes on hold, I finally speak to an Indian lady, and for God's sakes, here we go again. She knows a guy who she thinks can help me. Supposedly he is very influential, an S.S.P., which is equivalent to a Chief of Police. She tells me the fellow has written four books, has a Ph.D. in criminology, and has studied in New York with the FBI. This guy is not the S.S.P. of the district where I was arrested, of course—that is Pratap, the lizard who initiated the *Challan* against me to begin with. Pratap is S.S.P. for Amritsar city; the new S.S.P.'s bailiwick is Amritsar R*ural.* Interestingly, their respective offices are only a couple of miles apart.

I am not sure what good she thinks another S.S.P., from a different district, could do me, but at least she does not ask me for thousands of dollars and tell me about her "incredibly influential uncle." She just gives me the fellow's contact information and says good luck.

His name is Amandeep Singh.

chapter 48

I ring S.S.P. Amandeep Singh from a shady patio table at Dharamsala's "Café India Abroad," with a copy of the Punjab Tribune on my lap, a "California Quesadilla" on my plate, and a fit 30-year-old blonde in my line of sight. He sounds educated, well-spoken, and smart and urges me to come back to the Punjab.

I don't want to.

I really don't want to!

But I can't back out now.

Amandeep Singh calls me several times over the next few days, just to make sure I am coming.

I give Shira another roll of bills and tell him he might as well stay in Dharamsala. He smiles from ear to ear, and I am glad to see the kid happy. I take a bus down to Amritsar to meet this Amandeep Singh. Meanwhile, I contemplate his resume—the Ph.D., the four books. He must really be something!

Of course, Yogi Bhajan had a Ph.D. too (psychology), but I know now that he got it from a diploma-mill type institution that is no longer in business and made his secretaries do all the work.

I arrive with a folder stuffed full of legal documents—all handwritten in Punjabi, of course. He gives it to some clerks and they go off. Like any good Indian, the first thing he does is ask me about my family, my father, my schooling. He wants to get a sense of my social standing, so I lay it on him. Why not? More than ever I have the distinct feeling of having nothing at all to lose and everything to gain.

At the age of 17, my father got thrown in jail for some typical teenage shenanigans. The judge gave him the choice of jail or the U.S. Marine Corps. He took the Marine Corps and stayed for 14 years. Dad learned a lot about life aboard the U.S.S. Nevada, which was at Pearl Harbor during the Japanese bombing. He was even among the brave American soldiers to storm the beach on the island of Saipan in the Pacific during World War II. With heavy Japanese fire coming in all around the Marines, Dad jumped into a bomb shell crater on the beach with his Captain. "Man this is rough," my Dad shouted as the bullets buzzed over their heads, to which the Captain replied, "Bill, when you make it through these rough times those are the ones you'll remember and learn from!"

Later, Dad married, and I was born, the eldest son out of two. Dad was dead set to give me the best education money could buy. He was very proud of that, so he sent me to Harding Military Academy.

By the age of 12, I was second in command at my school and a first Lieutenant in the California Cadet Corps. At the Corps' summer Camp in San Luis Obispo, the directors used to scream in our faces, put us through drills, then send us out in the California hills at night with no food. Grown men dressed like Viet Cong would come after us shooting blanks from M16s. I loved it! The kids they caught, they would strip naked, drop off five miles from camp, and make them walk back. I never got caught, and no one in my unit got caught either. I was a damn good officer. Clear headed.

I would find a ravine and hide my whole platoon in there, spaced three meters apart. We had secret bird calls for communication. We moved in the dark like ninjas. We were good. Very good. War! So exhilarating!

Nevertheless, there were still kids in my unit that used to crawl up to me in the ravine, in the moonlight, and whine, "Clark! We have to go out there and get them! We have to get them!"

"With what?" I would answer. "They have the guns. We have nothing. Don't be an idiot."

S.S.P. Amandeep Singh smiles as I gesture grandly. I thought he would. It's in every Sikh's blood to love a good conflict. I want him to understand I was destined to be a Sikh.

Dad's personality revolved around sales, the Marine Corps and Christian Church. The Power of Positive Thinking by Dr. Norman Vincent Peale was Dad's favorite book. This book was Dad's second religion; in fact, when he finally couldn't convince me to do it any other way, he paid me to read all of Peale's books. Dad loved me for sure but his way of expressing love was through discipline; his disciplinary style consisted of beating me (occasionally), threatening me with God's wrath (frequently), and exhorting me to repeat: "Every day in every way, I'm getting better and better!" (almost daily).

Most of the other kids in military school were real bad eggs. Some of their parents had just dropped them off at the gate and burned rubber getting away. But I was a day student and lived with my folks. I wasn't trash. At the time, I was no rebel either; I even received the Good Citizenship Medal from the Daughters of the American Revolution. I actually liked it there, and liked my life. For me, school was not about making friends. I just wanted to achieve my full potential in life; maybe as a soldier or maybe as a businessman. Of course, in those days, I had no thoughts of being a spiritual teacher, but Dad believed in me and I believed in myself.

When I finally met Yogi Bhajan, all those dreams started to become clear to me. It was like wiping a steamed mirror with a washcloth and seeing your reflection—*Oh! There I am!*

I pause so Amandeep Singh can take it all in. He asks some questions about my case, then nods and smiles mysteriously. "Very interesting, Guru *Sant* Singh. What I am going to do is have a private detective look into your case. He will talk to the women—the alleged victims of your crime—and get to the bottom of it." He goes on to say I did the right thing by alerting the online media, then he scribbles out the phone number for the Editor in Chief of the local office of one of the national Indian newspapers, a personal friend of his. I stick it in my pocket, and that is that. We do not discuss the case again.

Now that he knows I am a true Gursikh, Amandeep Singh wants to talk about Sikhi all night. I play him my kirtan on the laptop, like I did with S.H.O. Mohander Singh.

"Your pronunciation is wonderful!" he exclaims. "Now tell me, why is it, do you think, that Sikhi isn't spreading more rapidly across the world?"

He is a real zealot and goes on and on about his many strategies for spreading Sikhi across the globe. He is absolutely fascinated that I converted to Sikhi from Christianity. Whenever someone wanders through the office he tells them the story—how he was born a Sikh but I converted out of my own free will. He finds that just amazing and wants to pick my brain about how to bring about more of these conversions. He even started this group—a networking thing, where Sikh scholars are supposed to support one another.

"Maybe some of these people can help you," he suggests, handing me a flyer entitled, *A Group of Sikh Intellectuals in Search of a Viable Solution*. It outlines the points of their mission:

1.Create a unique institute of international level with distinctive features of a classless society.

2.Spread message of Sikhism by remembering Gurbani (the prayers) and helping others in this regard.

3.Sikhism doesn't need preachers, but missionaries, those who have changed their lives according to the Sikh tenets (of abstention from alcohol, drugs, and extra-marital sex, refraining from cutting the hair, and dedication to chanting the lord's name). For this we look for committed, devoted, selfless intellectuals of spirituality, active in life physically, action oriented persons, who can contribute time and other resources, support in our holy and selfless cause, without expectations for the cause of Mission of Guru Nanak.

. . . It goes on like that. Idealistic. He keeps me here until the wee hours of the morning, talking about Sikhi. His is what Indians proudly call "a government job" which means he makes his own hours and takes lots of holidays. Does whatever he wants, and what he wants to do is worship! We talk well into the night. In addition to discussing Sikhi, he gives me some other useful info.

"Indian prison," he says, "It is not like in America. I know this from my studies with the F.B.I.—in America, one must investigate thoroughly before making an arrest. But in India it is the opposite. If anyone is under suspicion, we just arrest first and investigate later."

Apparently people are always getting thrown in jail on trumped up charges and they are seldom convicted. "In India, the conviction rate is very low," he says. "Very very very low!"

But apparently the authorities have the power to keep you in jail for years and years while the investigation continues. That is the trouble. But he is eager to get off the subject of work, so Amandeep Singh brings the conversation back to Sikhism.

I tell him about kundalini, tantra, and my interest in yoga. He crumples his fleshy brow.

"Yoga?" Says Amandeep Singh. "This Harbhajan Singh taught yoga?" He calls my teacher by his proper name, Harbhajan Singh, rather than any of the affectionate nicknames I use, like Yogi Bhajan, or Yogiji.

I give him details: how many hours we used to practice. The power it gave us. My practice is still my life, and I am very proud of it.

"Sounds like the yoga they teach up in Rishikesh."

"No, no, no. You don't understand. Yogi Bhajan was the only

Mahan Tantric in the world!" I say. "Nobody taught it but him. He channeled it. He had an incredible divine connection. . . ." Suddenly I feel an energy of exasperation from my listener.

Amandeep Singh strokes his mustache and twirls little strings of his grey, cotton-candy beard. "A Mahan Tantric?" he says, with an uncharacteristically cynical tone in his voice.

"A Mahan Tantric! Of course! A living master. The only man that could ever channel the sacred Z energy from man to woman and back again."

He looks at me like he has just noticed I am white.

"Well that's just Hindu stuff. It's the yoga they teach all over Rishikesh. That's Swami Shivananda's stuff. It's been around forever."

"No, no, you're not getting it. That can't be."

"Ah, but it is, Guru *Sant* Singh."

I shake my head. He is so smart, yet so ignorant.

"Tell me about it again?" he asks, so I do. All the details.

"And how long have you been practicing this?"

"Thirty years."

"What else?"

I explain the extra exercises Yogi Bhajan gave me for gaining the ability to see auras: spinal twists, deep knee bends, shoulder circles with flexed hands. I have been doing them for twenty years now, but I still can't see auras. I don't tell him that, though. I tell Amandeep Singh about the different diets: only white food, only fruit with large seeds, only vegetables longer than your hand . . .

Amandeep Singh looks down at his lap for a little while.

Then he looks up, smiles broadly, pats my shoulder patronizingly, and changes the subject. He says he will get me a great lawyer named Randhawa, a very high profile guy. Usually he just handles murder cases, but Amandeep Singh says he will get Randhawa to represent me if the thing actually goes to trial.

That sounds good!

Amandeep Singh says he will help me as much as he can. "Clearly," he says with a small smile, "You are going to need it."

chapter 49

A couple of days later, I have another hearing in Amritsar. I think, *yeah this is going to do the trick*. Amandeep Singh is going to work his magic. This is where the judge will finally say I am pardoned and hand me back my passport.

He will say, "Please forgive the imposition."

And if he doesn't, the judge will have to deal with *Randhawa*. His very name sounds sexy, swashbuckling, like some romance novel hero. I picture Randhawa as a real killer. He will carry a bull whip. When he snaps his fingers, the world will fall into place. That S.S.P. Pratap is going to be sorry he ever got mixed up with me. Me and Randhawa.

Next thing I know I am at the courthouse, sitting on a bench in the back of a sweaty, overcrowded courtroom. Dadaji is there, too. We sit side by side. Puneet (who I now view as my weak, ineffectual, non-Randhawa attorney) is there too—running around as usual, doing who knows what.

"Where's your attorney?" I ask Dadaji.

"Oh! Same! Same!" he answers.

I think he means he has the same attorney as before—that sleazy guy Rajeev. But the sleazy guy never shows up. A few hours later, I ask Dadaji again where his attorney is.

"Same! Same!"

Finally I figure it out: Dadaji has contracted with the same attorney as me. Puneet! Considering my primary defense is that Dadaji duped me and used me as a cash cow, I don't see how he and I could both have the same attorney.

I confront Puneet about it.

"Oh, I'm going to get you both off! Doooooon't worry, Guru *Sant* Singh!" Puneet answers.

The term "conflict of interest" is apparently unknown to him.

It doesn't matter.

Nothing matters. Nothing makes sense and nothing matters. People just do whatever they want, I guess. My case does not matter to anyone but me. My life does not matter, either. My ability to get my passport and return to America—what does it matter? The thought of me getting thrown in an Indian prison for years on end just apparently does not matter—not to Puneet, not to Dadaji, not to the judge, not to anyone in 3HO. Nothing matters to anyone.

This whole thing is a great big joke to everyone but me.

Dadaji and I sit on the bench all day, waiting.

Eventually the hearing is declared postponed for three more months.

This type of stuff didn't used to happen to me. I used to have powers. Where did they all go? I have been doing my exercises, my meditations, and yet that certain vibration is gone. I wonder if it was Bhajan's death, if somehow he took some of the magic out of the world when he left. There used to be a certain buzzing, a certain reverberation inside when my siddhi powers are building. It felt like my blood was boiling. At one point, this power was so strong in me I couldn't control it. I mean I wasn't even myself. I was absolutely out of control.

In the early days, in Los Angeles, 3HO was its own little financial planet. As soon as I moved there from Eugene, I met this guy Guru Sikh Shakti Singh, who asked me if I wanted to go into business with him. His business was selling baby palm trees on street corners. Why not, right?

We had such charisma, Guru Sikh Shakti Singh and I. We would hit the streets right after morning sadhana, and man, our blood would be boiling. All those hours of chanting and flexing the spine, and our heads were just buzzing with spiritual fire. The washed-out, polluted, workaday people trudging along the street, with their little dreams about bigger televisions and prettier wives—they were our customers.

I would look into people's eyes and instantly have them. At ten bucks a pop, the trees went like hotcakes. People pictured their little tract homes surrounded with the beauty and majesty of Rodeo Drive. I later learned the cheap little trees would be dead in a week.

But we had such intensity. People just kept on buying and buying. And now? I can't even get a judge to hear my case.

Three months later, I drag my ass back into the courthouse.

Rhandawa never materializes.

Puneet, as usual, runs around dealing with every case but mine. So, this time, I stand up—just as the judge is about to pound his gavel and declare the thing delayed again.

"May I speak in my own defense, your honor?" I ask boldly. A hush falls over the crowd.

The judge does a double take. I may actually be the first defendant to have ever tried this tactic.

He shrugs and says okay.

"Your honor, I want a trial right away and I cannot just keep living without a passport. Without it, I am not safe from police persecution! I cannot be expected to be a law abiding citizen, or tourist, or whatever I am. I am not convicted of a crime, yet I have to walk around like a criminal in hiding!"

"Oh," he says. "Well, I can't do anything about a trial for you right now but concerning your passport, just apply to the Director General of Police for the State of Punjab. He'll give your passport back to you. Doooooon't worry."

Bang. The gavel comes down.

"Next!"

Now at least I have something to do for the next three months! So I call Shira and tell him to get his ass back to Amritsar. He must find out who this Director General is and where to find him. This alone takes days of exhausting work. Endless rupees go into tuk-tuks zipping this way and that across town, going to wrong offices and getting wrong advice and following it. Shira and I suck in leaded exhaust all day, every day, in those damn tuk-tuks. But we are dedicated to this horror. We embrace it like flesh-eating zombies.

By now I think we must have visited every government building in the Punjab. Some look like the Taj Mahal; some, like abandoned carnival grounds. Some are surrounded by typists in their makeshift booths. Some are surrounded by cows and goats. You have to watch out for the goats. Turn your back and they will eat your papers—staples, paper-clips, and all; then you're right back where you started!

Eventually we find this Director General. I make an appointment, wait a week, then meet with him.

He smiles broadly beneath his gold-spangled turban and tells me: "But my good man! This is actually a matter for the Director *Inspector* General, not the Director *General* General!"

I slump in my seat and hold my turban in my hands, shaking from head to toe with a combination of anger, fatigue, self-loathing, pure hate, and also the tiniest bit of laughter.

"But cheer up!" says Spangly Turban. "I'll order an investigation!"

I don't know if he suddenly feels sorry for me or if he has just been taunting me all along. Either way, I have no choice. I have to fill out an application for re-investigation. Shira is not with me today, so the Director General General, who turns out to be kind of nice, helps me pencil in the cumbersome pages in triplicate.

"It's the law! The Director Inspector General must look into it and report back to me within fifteen days!" he says.

Fifteen days later, I go back.

"Who? What? What case?" He literally says this to me.

Eventually, the Director General General remembers who I am. He dials the Director Inspector General on his rotary phone:

Zip! tata tata tata tata. Zip! tata tata tata tata. Zip! tata tata tata tata . . .

Turns out the guy lost my application.

Gritting my teeth, probably destroying the crowns I came to India to get in the first place, I fill out another application for re-investigation. In triplicate. With significantly less help.

Fifteen days later, I return, but the Director General General with the gold-spangled turban has been transferred to another district. The new Director General General informs me I will have to start the process all over again.

I tell him forget it. I'll just take it up with the judge.

At my next hearing, my judge is gone, too. The new judge does not want to hear anything about a re-investigation. He declares my hearing postponed . . . yet again. Down comes the gavel.

Bang.

A month later, S.S.P. Amandeep Singh calls to tell me he has gotten in touch with advocate Rhandawa, and the legal hero has decided to take my case! I don't meet Rhandawa until the next hearing, three months later. Alas, he does not carry a bullwhip. He does, however, agree that Puneet representing Dadaji is a conflict of interest. He seems quite intelligent. Nevertheless, when we get before the judge, the hearing is yet again postponed another three months.

I have no passport, no rights, nothing. I am just stuck in India.

But I am starting to see the up side.

At this point, I have overstayed my visa by several months already and do not have to renew it. I am on an extended stay in India until they either pardon or deport me. It is actually an incredible privilege, in a way. I can enjoy the easy living in Dharamsala. I can study Sikhi, go to sacred sites to pray, and pursue my purpose as a spiritual teacher—all until I run out of money.

chapter 50

My phone rings. It is Dr. Sobha Singh, from prison! He and Amrik Singh are out of jail and he wants us all to meet up for dinner. We meet at a restaurant that evening with lots of back-patting and congratulations all around. I tell them how complicated things have become with my case.

"I sympathize, my friend!" booms Sobha Singh. "The red tape is endless! Endless for an innocent man! In fact, I have a great idea . . . you must come live at my home while you go through this hell with the Punjabi Police. I insist!"

Why not? I grab my stuff the next day and move in. The Nivas manager is thrilled, naturally.

Dr. Sobha Singh's wife does not seem to have any opinion about her husband being framed for murder, or about his having an affair, if she even knows about it. Their marriage is strictly business. As far as she is concerned, the ordeal is over and that is that. But I soon learn that she has tricks up her sleeve as well. Ever since I crossed the threshold, she has been playing with an idea that is actually a more outrageous marriage fraud than any I have heard so far.

It goes like this: the family has two problems. The first is their son, who is a good boy with excellent marks in school, and he wants to make it big in business in America. He just needs a way to get there and get a green card. The second is Sobha Singh's wife's sister, who is 28. Her husband divorced her because she could not have children. The plan is that Sobha Singh would actually divorce his wife and trade her to me. I would marry her and take her and their son (now my adopted son) to America, once I get my passport back. Meanwhile, Sobha Singh would marry the barren sister and take care of her. That way it's all in the family! I do not know if he is actually hot for the sister, or what.

This ridiculous scheme is bandied around the dinner table every night, new improvements and details being added each time. At first I think it's all a joke and I play along, but eventually I realize they are dead serious. I reduce my participation in these conversations to vague smiles and nods. I am a guest here, after all. I'd like to bang my fist down with a resounding "no!" but I can't. To launch the scheme, they declare me the head of their family! They are ready to do my bidding if only I will play along.

These people are like worms. Oozing and squirming and slithering past each other, getting tangled up in great gooey masses of intertwined humanity. Trying to pull me into it. Meanwhile, Sobha Singh keeps on "borrowing" money from me. How can I say no? Over the course of a month I lose five hundred bucks to the guy.

Then S.S.P. Amandeep Singh calls me back for another visit. He crams me into the back of an old Ambassador with white curtains in the windows and we take off for a sacred place called Baba Bakala. Amandeep Singh is a high ranking officer, so we actually have a police escort! Two jeeps in front, two in back, and all the uniformed cops along the road salute as we go by. This Amandeep Singh, he is like some kind of maharaja in his little kingdom of cows. Meanwhile, in the car, he grills me about my personal life.

"Guru *Sant* Singh, after two marriages, you must have many children, no?"

"No," I tell him. "None. I had a stepson once. I tried to be a father to him . . . but that's over now."

"Can it be? How can it be that you have no sons of your own?"

"I don't know. Slow sperm? I don't know, Amandeep Singh. It is my fate, I guess. I think I am meant for a spiritual life instead."

"And no daughters? No beautiful little girls? I have two!"

"No. No sons, no daughters, and now . . . no wife!"

He contemplates this disturbing fact as we ride.

Soon we get to Baba Bakala, a cave-temple where the ninth Sikh Guru meditated for 27 years—a very sacred place. The chief minister of the Punjab is coming to visit in a few days, so Amandeep Singh is involved with getting everything ready for a grand ceremony: outdoor amphitheater, signs pointing this way and that, and a helicopter pad. He strides across the grounds, telling workers to put things here and take things there, and I just follow him around. Eventually, the guards let us into the temple's sacred inner sanctum, which is completely off limits to tourists. It's just a very plain, five-by-five-foot underground chamber.

We enter the tiny space and breathe its sacred air. The spiritual energy in this place is palpable and other American friends have told me how much they wanted to be allowed in here to meditate when they visited the shrine. Yet here I am without even trying. I can't believe it! In the middle of all the hubbub, Amandeep Singh and I go underground and stop to pray. He is definitely devout. My kind of guy. I admire him.

I really feel like God is saying something to me today, letting me into a sacred place like this. It feels like an omen—a sign that I will get out of this mess and reach my spiritual goals. Truly, I feel myself growing closer and closer to it each day. The extended stay in India, the time at the ashram, now this. It means something. It has to.

Of course, nothing is working out the way I had planned, but this is India. Why plan? God has his plans. That is all that matters here.

On the way back, the grilling starts again about the family and the kids and the divorce until Amandeep Singh finally says, "Listen, Guru *Sant* Singh, you don't have any reason to go back to America. You don't have anything tying you down. By the grace of Waheguru, my brother, why not stay in India?"

He says he will find me a nice bride. He will help me get married. And then he says he is building a sort of Sikh community center near Anandpur Sahib in the Punjab where I could live and teach. That's right! He is going to get me a woman and a place to keep her in and make me part of his community of intellectuals—suck me into his world. Relentlessly. Until I am one of the worms. Squiggling and wiggling, deep down in the cold cold earth.

As cautiously as possible, I turn him down.

At this point, the last thing I want is a wife. I have just got free of Wadha Kaur and am glad of it. What a relief! I have learned my lesson. Forget about sex, forget about the piping hot paranthas I envisioned, forget about female companionship, about making Bhajan's "ideal marriage" come to life. I intend to forget about it all and simply be a holy man. I tell him so.

Amandeep Singh is disappointed. Angry too. Dangerously angry. The way Punjabis always seem to get when you don't do whatever they say. The way Yogi Bhajan used to get.

The worst I ever saw Yogi Bhajan was when he was furious at me over a bad real estate deal. I thought he might kick me out of 3HO at the time. I really did. And it was so weird because Yogiji defined my ethics and my moral stance—all my beliefs, in a way. He was my spiritual guide. But at the same time, I was not prepared to let go of my own personality, my own morals, when I saw that he was in the wrong. He fought me tooth and nail over that.

What happened was, Yogiji had a Punjabi follower named Swaran Singh—some kind of timber tycoon from Vancouver—and he came down to New Mexico for a visit. The guy was a multi-multi millionaire, a real big shot, and he decided to buy a house near the ashram. I was in real estate at the time, so Yogiji told me to show the guy some places. One of those places belonged to a family called Montoya—a typical Hispanic family of the area. They were nice, humble people.

Swaran Singh acted like he was not at all interested in the Montoya place, then later he went back there and tried to make a deal with them behind my back. Not only that, he intimidated and browbeat these people and, according to what Mr. Montoya told me later, refused to leave their home until they had signed an agreement for a really low price. I was furious, both for my own sake and the Montoyas'.

I went to Yogiji, up in arms, and told him there was no way I was going to let Swaran Singh get away with this. Yogiji didn't give a damn for the Montoyas. In fact, he had his 3HO lawyer, GTS (Guru Terath Singh) Khalsa, represent his buddy against me and the Montoyas both. Yogiji kept asking me, "Why are you fighting this? We would have paid you off!" But that was not the point. It was the wrong thing to do, intimidating those people like that. Swaran Singh was a bully, plain and simple, and I would not be a party to it. Yogiji kept telling me, "Don't you know who this guy is? He is very rich and powerful!"

I told him I didn't care! Swaran Singh eventually dropped the lawsuit, but his parting words to me were, "We are enemies for life!"

Shortly afterward, Mrs. Montoya died. Apparently she had been very ill the whole time. I'm glad I stuck up for them against Yogiji, but I have never seen him angrier. He called me and roared, "Don't try and teach me!" That Punjabi pride came out and I had to face his steely eyes, his booming insults, and his threats that I would "lose my soul."

So when S.S.P. Amandeep Singh starts to stare straight ahead with slitted eyes, starts to seethe because I won't follow his directives, I know what I might be in for. But I have to stand up for myself. You cannot just let these Punjabis run right over you. I learned that long ago. So I hold my ground in my new anti-wife stance, and the moment passes without incident.

chapter 51

Back at Sobha Singh's place, I realize I still haven't called S.S.P. Amandeep Singh's contact, the chief editor of the local office of one of the national Indian newspapers, Jagjit Singh. I have been afraid of angering the Punjabi Police with local media exposure. After all, it could make things worse for me, although I suppose it could also make things better. What a crap shoot. But my last so-called "hearing" gave me another three months to think about it, and nothing much else to do. Eventually, in a state of desperation and boredom, I call the guy. He speaks perfect English and is definitely interested in the story. I bring my file to his office.

Jagjit Singh's office is a jungle of papers and clippings stacked up and balanced here and there, coming at you from every angle. I fill him in on the details of my case. He looks at the file and takes a great deal of time with the affidavits—those pages I tried to get Shira to read for me. He turns the pages very carefully, like it is ancient papyrus, and he, an archaeologist. Then he turns them back, and reads them again! Finally, he puts on a pair of magnifying glasses and does this a third time. Afterwards, he takes them off and looks at me.

"They all say the same thing, these affidavits. They all say that you met with a woman, promised to marry her, asked for a dowry of fifty thousand rupees, took it, then told her the marriage was off."

"What? How . . . But that's ridiculous!"

"That's what they say. Same thing for fifteen different women. And it's almost as if each woman were speaking with the same voice. Same words exactly."

"I swear those are complete lies!"

"I know," he says. "I'm quite sure they are lies. Probably the police said, 'Is this what happened?' and laid out the charge and told the girls to say yes. They might have even paid them to say yes and sign the thing. Clearly these charges were concocted by the police. There's no question about it, in my mind."

Then Jagjit Singh actually picks up the phone and calls the man who ordered my arrest, S.S.P. Pratap. He starts speaking in Punjabi, very quietly and calmly, but I can tell he is asking a lot of questions. He seems to ask the same things again and again. Then, after a long period of quiet listening, he hangs up.

"My, my," he says, leaning back in his swivel chair and tenting his fingers. He taps two fingertips together, then rubs them, as if activating magic.

"Well, Guru *Sant* Singh, Pratap actually warned me against publicizing your case."

"You mean . . . did he threaten you?"

"What he said, actually . . ." Jagjit Singh looks up at the ceiling and taps his fingertips together, seeming to be fitting the words together very precisely in his head. " . . . was that he had reason to believe you might be a spy."

I can only laugh. "Why?" I ask. "A spy for whom? For what? Not for the U.S. government? Not for George Bush!"

"I don't know. He wouldn't say," says Jagjit Singh, clearly perplexed. "But he did say this: if I publicize this case, if I bring this out into the media, it won't be good for you. In fact . . . he said he could make you disappear."

"Disappear?"

"I'm trying to translate the Punjabi word he used. It means to be invisible, to disappear, or to cease to exist in any way that's . . . you know, physically perceivable."

I rise from my chair and begin to pace. I feel, for the first time in a long time, genuinely frightened.

Then I get angry.

"I'm going to nail that bastard's balls to the wall," I tell the editor. "I'm going to burn him if it's the last thing I do."

chapter 52

I sulk at Sobha Singh's house for a couple more days—too angry to meditate, too confused to form a plan, and too scared to go out into the street. Then a miracle happens. My mobile rings, and it is Lalamji, from Shiv-Shakti Ashram.

"Guru *Sant* Singh Ji! How wonderful to hear your voice!"

"Sat Siri Akal, Lalamji!" I gush, forgetting she is Hindu and should have said "*Namaste.*" "I've missed you!"

Soon I learn that Stephanieji, the black Brit with the suicidal thoughts, has had some family emergency and gone suddenly back to England; meanwhile, the ashram is in the middle of a retreat. Having no choice, Lalamji has taken over teaching both Hatha yoga in the morning and Ashtanga yoga in the evening, plus morning and evening meditations, but it is too much work. She can't do the spiritual discussion forum; her English isn't good enough. She hasn't got the energy for the meditative walks, either. She is desperate to find a fluent English speaker with some spiritual street cred to pick up where Stephanieji left off, so she has forgiven me for everything and wants me to come back to paradise!

"God has sent you, Guru *Sant* Singh Ji!" she says.

Lalamji does not have to ask twice. I get on the midnight train and escape, again, into oblivion.

At Shiv-Shakti, I lead the campfire chants, the discussions, the walks. I greet students and make them feel as if they are being sagely guided on a spiritual path. Hopefully, this is true.

The path they are on is not mine, it is a Hindu path, but what the hell. These young kids see the white turban and my long beard and they just do whatever I say. Best of all, at Shiv-Shakti, I have a safe hideaway where I can go for hikes, breathe the fresh air, and have some time to think without worrying about getting politically disappeared.

I am respected here.

I am an actual spiritual teacher.

When ashramites start greeting me by kneeling, touching my feet, and calling me Guruji, I begin to think, *hey, I could get used to this.*

I can't believe it, but I am actually doing it: what Yogiji kept me from doing all those years. Being a leader in my own right.

First, he denied my dream to become a psychologist.

"Go work at GRD!" he said.

And I did it: I went from wanting to help people to taking them for all they had, in a split second. Then there had been my notion to become an actor—admittedly, a little farfetched but after all Yogiji's oldest son Ranbir Singh had a bit part in a blockbuster film, "Down and Out in Beverly Hills", as the family yoga guru for Nick Nolte, Richard Dreyfuss and Bette Midler, so why couldn't I do that too? It was my idea, my aspiration. How did Bhajan have the power to deny it? How did I give him that power? He just took it—and I let him; that's all. Then my desire to become a freedom fighter in Bhindranwale's army. He said, 'No,' and I just said 'Okay,' as if I were a child. As if the man were my father. I gave him that power, and he readily took it. So many dreams he took from me. So many dreams I handed over to him. I don't know why.

Candy from a baby, that was all it was for him.

My first wife, Prem Kaur, and I had a vision. A vision of a perfect life together that could have come true, would have come true, if it hadn't been for Yogiji. Yes, if it weren't for my complete surety that Yogi Bhajan was clairvoyant and had a direct line to the infinite,

I could be making love to Prem Kaur in the dappled shade of an aromatic orchard, right this minute.

Prem Kaur was the very embodiment of mystery and beauty and depth. Her grandfather was the chief economic minister of Mexico. Her mother had been some Swedish beauty. She grew up in Greece and studied Indian classical dance in India. Then she moved to L.A. and joined 3HO. I began courting her at the Gurdwara, day after day. She went for it.

"Marry her!" Yogiji said, adding, "She'll never divorce you!" I thought this was some kind of psychic premonition. I did not realize then that this is what everyone says in India. "She'll never divorce you!" It is like saying, "Good luck and happy days ahead!"

So we married, and the first thing we did was start visiting her rich relatives in Mexico. We found a cozy home down there, on twenty acres of avocado groves somewhere in the middle of nowhere. We planned to buy it and get away from L.A. and all the conniving and scheming; the law suits and mail frauds and telephone sales; all the thousand dollar lunches and white Mercedes' convoys and the material ambition that had replaced spiritual fervor.

Somewhere along the way, 3HO had become a cesspool of materialism. The communal ashram life was gone. Nobody did that anymore. Now everyone just tithed 10% to Yogiji's "GRD Enterprises." That was it. That was our sense of community. Ashramites were becoming society people: living in big houses, having families, keeping up with the Joneses. Meanwhile Yogiji sat around getting richer and fatter. It was all about who had the most palatial home, who drove the shiniest car. It was exactly what I had grown up with: utter crap.

I had done my share of money-grabbing as well, and did not like the taste it left in my mouth. I wanted out. Not out of 3HO, the only community I knew, but out of the cesspool; out of Los Angeles.

With Prem Kaur, I could be honest and say I hated it. Instead of reprimanding me for disloyalty, she agreed. She definitely loved Yogi Bhajan; that was beyond dispute. If she hadn't, I could not have married her. But she seemed to have a little perspective on it, something I lacked. And she could understand my disenchantment.

Prem Kaur and I envisioned becoming peaceful, honest people—selling avocados and meditating and giggling our days away swinging in hammocks under the palms. We had it all figured out. We were in love and this was it; what we really wanted: a new lease on life. I would learn a little Spanish, maybe restore a wooden boat. Work with my hands. 3HO did not have much of a presence in Mexico, but that was okay with us. Solitude was what we were after.

Prem Kaur was so beautiful. Oh my God. What a life!

We still believed in the yoga, the meditation, the chanting. We still believed in 3HO and Yogi Bhajan. We thought the materialistic trend was just a phase, that it would blow over in time.

Yogiji must have got wind of our plan, because one day he appointed Prem Kaur and me to attend an interfaith conference at this incredible retreat in the Malibu hills. It was to be just my wife and me and Yogi Bhajan, and we would represent Sikhi to all these Catholics and Methodists and Jews. It was a great honor. And this was Malibu! The beach, the sky, the perfection of nature, the balmy weather, the luxury of the place. Out there, surrounded by green rolling hills and the gentle surf, we had inspiring views of paradise. Just an unfathomable paradise. You had to be high on Malibu. There was no other way to experience it.

One morning, as the three of us strolled through the flower-dotted campus, my wife and I told Yogiji our plan. She and I held hands like a couple of lovebirds. So excited.

Yogiji stopped in his tracks.

"Mexico?" he said. "I wouldn't do that."

He looked out into the distance and stroked his beard, as if receiving a delicate psychic transmission.

"I see you two getting lost out there, losing the path. You'll leave the dharma." He shook his head sadly, "You'll lose your soul."

We assured him that was not the case at all. We saw ourselves as 3HO's ambassadors to Mexico. But he was not listening. He never listened. He just talked at you. The force of his words pinned you to the wall like knives. He was never unsure. Never lacked a single iota of confidence. His voice was resonant and all encompassing. It wrapped you in a warm, smothering blanket of rapture and promises.

"I see you getting divorced. Great tragedy will befall you. Great tragedy." Tears sprang to Yogiji's eyes. "There will be a massive disturbance on the psychic level." He sat down on a bench and rested his hands on his round belly. "Financial ruin. All I see for you is financial ruin in Mexico. I'm sorry."

He shook his head, so disappointed. He sighed a sigh of deep despair and disillusionment—a tragic, deeply hurt sigh that made us want to make it all better for him. Anything for him.

Anything for him!

"But if you stay in L.A," added Yogiji, brightening, "Oh boy! I see great wealth there. Fame, wealth, everything you want is right there in L.A. No need to go anywhere at all. You are already on the road to greatness," he said. But he was still shaking his head, convinced we would do the wrong thing.

Then Yogiji stood and continued walking as if none of it mattered. We followed like puppies. "It is as if everything you touch will turn to gold in L.A. Especially you, Guru *Sant* Singh. You will be like a man who has been touched by God!" Then he chuckled, a little sorrowfully, at our folly. He was so sure we would up and move to Mexico anyway.

Over the course of the week he continued to have these visions. He always said he saw great wealth, especially for me. I could not go wrong. I was destined to be a millionaire, a powerful man, a real mover and shaker. He would always look into the distance and ask me if I could see it too—my inevitable success. He said part of the vision was that I would help 3HO in many ways, and he never neglected to mention that I would be important to him, personally. Prem Kaur and I would be beyond happy in L.A., he promised.

All our dreams would come true.

He blew us over with this talk. Morning, noon, and night he would harp on about it. When he got started, there was no stopping him. He painted grandiose images of our success in L.A., of my inevitable wealth. Then he would paint equally horrifying pictures of Mexico: our falling into destitute poverty and divorce, losing the path and stopping our meditations, losing touch with God. Ill health would befall us, he said. We would each die hungry and alone, un-mourned. Our bodies, exposed to the harsh Mexican sun, would rot, and our bones slowly bleach, undiscovered, among rattlesnakes and scorpions until the end of time.

We would lose our souls, we would lose our souls—that was the refrain.

Oh, he went on and on. Days of this. When we got back to L.A., he sent me to this guy, Chakrapani, his personal psychic and astrologer, who confirmed it all with zeal and many colorful embellishments.

So, for Prem Kaur and I, the focus shifted from buying the Mexican property to getting into business in L.A. We did exactly as he said. It was impossible not to. He was such a force of nature. We so believed in his insight and we so feared his disapproval. We so feared it.

Prem Kaur and I never actually talked about the decision. It just happened. We never mentioned our disappointment. Never discussed that property again. Never in our lives.

The avocado groves. The walks on the beach. Making love in the dappled shade. It was all gone, like something shameful. That was when a massive silence—shaped like a ripe, green avocado—nestled between us, and stayed.

We could have lived the good life. It would have been so easy, with all her wealthy relatives down there. There wasn't any way we could have gone wrong. I really don't think there was. But Yogiji was psychic. He could see into the future, and besides, crossing his will would be dangerous; very, very dangerous. Foolish, too. If anything bad happened down in Mexico, it would be our own fault, wouldn't it? Yogi Bhajan would laugh in our faces. Our father. Our holy father. He would laugh in our faces, saying we should have listened. I simply did not have the guts to challenge him, even though a part of me knew he was dead wrong.

That was when something inside me broke.

I couldn't admit to being angry. Not at Yogiji. You might as well be angry at the wind.

"You must accept God's will," was what we 3HO Sikhs said to each other.

"You must submit."

chapter 53

After Yogi Bhajan denied my wife and me our Mexico fantasy, I did the only thing I could. I embraced everything he had said. I was to be great, was I? I was to become rich? Wealthy beyond imagining? I couldn't lose? I couldn't go wrong? Everything I touched was destined to turn to gold?

Okay. Let's just see.

It was suicide: emotional, social, spiritual, financial. Everything but physical. I extinguished whatever was left of me: my Christian values, my free will, my desire for peace, Emerson, Thoreau—their teachings. It all went away, like taking out some fishy old garbage.

I became a swindler, and Yogiji admired my initiative. For a while.

Sat Peter Singh, an ashramite fine art dealer I knew, introduced me to his source for Salvador Dali prints—a real fat cat with a Century City office and a Rolls Royce. He sold me all kinds of fine art prints dirt cheap. Everything from stupid stuff, like a sexy lady posing on a Corvette, to movie posters, to Cézanne's, Renoir's, all kinds of classics done up in cheap aluminum frames. Then I met this Arab with a gas station, so I paid him to let me sell the framed posters on his street corner. It was really lucrative, but after a while, the cops nailed me for illegal vending. That was bad, but what was worse was the fact that I had already written the Arab a check for the month's rent. I stopped payment on it, and the bastard sued me! It could have been a mess, but, just as Yogiji had predicted, it turned out great.

The People's Court saw our case on the docket—A Sikh, an

Arab, a street-corner art salesman. What drama! They asked us to go on TV, before Judge Wapner. We did it. What the hell.

Wapner was funny. During the proceedings, I kept objecting, saying the Arab was using hearsay evidence, and finally Wapner hollered, "What are you? A lawyer or something?" But in the end, the case was a slam dunk. You can't collect on an illegal deal. That's like suing someone for non-payment on a kilo of cocaine. It just is not going to fly.

I won and looked good doing it!

Everyone in 3HO watched the episode and I became a hero, yet again. They cheered me on and God showered me with gifts. I opened an art gallery and started making money hand over fist! It was like God was grabbing people by the collar and shoving them in there. The holiday season was unbelievable! I must have made ten thousand dollars the day before Christmas. Cash. All cash. I had cash in bags and boxes. I would come home and shower my wife with cash. We were lousy with it.

Yogiji got ten percent, of course.

Eventually I tired of the cheap poster art business. I was ready to move on, do something new. After all, I couldn't lose. Yogiji had said so.

It was at this point that I came across the deal with the Warhol silkscreen paintings. The deal that saw me lose most of my own money and hundreds of thousands of dollars of other people's.

Maybe I let Yogiji boss me too much. Then again, maybe a part of me had never wanted to be a psychologist, to act in films, to join Bhindranwale's army, to campaign for Sikh rights, or to pick avocados with a beautiful woman and make love under tropical palms until the day we died.

Maybe a part of me had thrived on being Yogi Bhajan's flunkey.

But now that I am teaching at Shiv-Shakti, I realize that part of me is dead. Sure, I still miss Yogi Bhajan. I miss being both berated and praised by him. I actually miss talking guns with him and fighting with him about real estate deals and being one of thousands sitting on stretched white sheets and listening with rapt attention to his every word.

But that life is behind me, now. At Shiv-Shakti Ashram, I have become a teacher in my own right. Others look up to me. I think I might just go along with what seems to be God's plan and stay in India.

Stay forever.

I am even considering not attending any more hearings. Of course, if the court convicts me, I will be a wanted man, but they will never find me on this mountaintop. At this holy place.

By the rushing of the sacred river, under the winds from the Himalayas, by the side of these stark cement buildings and their humble, cotton-batting beds, I feel like I am sitting in God's palm. Alone and safe.

Alone with God.

God . . . and some tourists.

Things pick up right where they left off with Lalamji. She showers me with attention, but she is sanyasi, so I know not to interpret it sexually. I try to be above that kind of thing.

I see this relationship as a great opportunity to try to emulate Yogiji's ability to be surrounded by women without seeing them as sexual beings. His secretaries would even give him foot and back massages, but he had such a high level of spiritual transcendence, he never fooled around with them. That is the mindset I want to develop here at Shiv-Shakti.

It's useless! After a couple of months, I think constantly about making Lalamji my wife. After all, it's natural. This is why the Sikh Gurus always recommended against going that sadhu route. Men are men. People have needs. Denying our basic human needs just isn't going to bring any of us closer to God. It is just going to drive us crazy, that's all.

Like any respectable Indian lady, she is always sure to meet me only in public places, never to sit too close, never to touch my hand, never to do or say anything unseemly. As much as she likes me—and it is clear that she does—I also know she would never consider marrying.

No, Lalamji does not want a husband, but I soon learn that, like so many others, she does want an opportunity.

"You and I," she says to me one day, "We will teach more than this ashram retreats. We can travel-teach the yoga. You talk to them, in the west, and make one voyage for us with the teaching."

She wants to go on tour—Europe, America, Asia, wherever I can get us gigs teaching yoga seminars and doing spiritual lectures. I get it. This would enable her to gain independence from Shiv-Shakti, just in case the entire ashram dissolves upon her swami's death and she suddenly finds herself out in the cold. A new career, basically. She wants to make a business partnership with me. Her spiritual cred as an Indian sanyasi, my English-speaking ability, our different yoga styles, the attraction of my being a white Sikh—it's not a bad idea. It could probably work, except for a couple of pesky little obstacles: the prohibition against my leaving India and the fact that my passport has been seized. Also, to be honest, I simply don't want to form this kind of semi-intimate partnership with a woman who is never going to be my wife.

But Lalamji never asks my opinion about the idea. She just decides it is going to happen.

"You make some calls," she demands.

Every time I meet her, she has more travel plans for the two of us.

If she would listen, I could explain I am simply not a man with connections.

After four months, Lalamji treats me exactly like I am her husband. She orders me here and there, gives me her personal errands to run, and assumes I am on board with her international yoga-touring scheme. At the ashram retreats, she still supervises my teaching of the yogic concepts and often gives me notes. I am to follow her instructions exactly.

I don't complain. I have plenty of time to meditate here and my own personal Shangri-La to explore. I never forget how bad things could get for me, quite quickly, if I leave this place. Meanwhile, I have achieved the status, as a spiritual teacher, that I always longed for. And, in Lalamji, I have a woman who likes me. She may even love me in her own way. I try to let it be enough. I tell myself that, having sworn off sex and marriage, this situation is pretty close to ideal.

chapter 54

One day, I meet Shira in Rishikesh for a cup of tea, longing to experience the refreshing hustle and bustle of civilization. At Little Buddha restaurant, where he constantly interrupts our conversation to greet his many new friends, I tell him my latest idea, which came to me during a deep meditation.

"I've been thinking about the sanyasi tradition, you know. And the sadhu tradition," I explain.

"After 50 years old a householder spends his old age seeking God which the Hindus call, *Vanaprastha*," Shira affirms, "After providing for his family. I know it, of course."

"It's a good tradition, I think."

"Yes, of course, Guru *Sant* Singh. This is the highest calling, to seek God in the old age."

"When I was a kid, I was Christian, you know, and I had Jesus. I tried to model my life after Jesus," I tell him. He nods. He knows nothing of Jesus. "Then I had Yogi Bhajan. He gave me a new model for my life."

"Your Yogiji, of course, your teacher."

"Now that he is gone, I don't have anyone. I don't know who to be. I am a spiritual teacher for many now, but who is my teacher? No one!"

"You can just be a good man, Guru *Sant* Singh. You can be a seeker, like any good Sikh."

"It's not enough. I need a guide, or at least a tradition to connect with. That's why I've decided to ask Sat Siri Kaur to remarry me!"

"Remarry your wife?"

"Ex-wife!"

Shira smiles half-way. He leans back in his chair, nods his head, strokes his goatee, and squints. "Excuse me, Guru *Sant* Singh, but I think maybe you have gone a little bit crazy."

I am surprised. I had thought this scheme was the obvious solution to every one of my problems. I had thought he would grin and say, "Of course, Guru *Sant* Singh, why didn't I think of that!"

So I explain. "A *Vanaprastha* has a wife, you see, but doesn't live with her! He sends her money when he has it. He supports her and cares for her from afar. That's the tradition! I could do that! I could have a wife that I don't live with!"

Shira nods and strokes the beard some more. "Why not just stay single, Guru *Sant* Singh? Be free, like me!"

"A spiritual teacher can't be single, Shira. It just doesn't look right."

Shira simply raises his eyebrows in response. The kid has no idea how complex the world really is. I am so wrapped up with the perfection of this idea, I can hardly sit still. I just want to do something righteous, something in keeping with the laws of nature and spirit. I think this might be it!

I dash to an internet café and email Sat Siri Kaur the offer of remarriage.

She writes back right away and tells me I am a rotten dog carcass that pollutes the planet with my gagging stench, and she hopes I fall into a bottomless Himalayan cave and drown in a puddle of yak piss.

So much for that idea.

After eight months at Shiv-Shakti Ashram I feel like I have arrived. I want to believe it, anyway. I want to forget about this ridiculous legal entanglement and my obsession with marriage and simply live, immersed in meditation and teaching. But in my head I keep looping back on that S.S.P. Pratap and what he said to the editor of the Amritsar Newspaper:

"We can make him disappear."

Who could forget a thing like that?

Plus, I am bored. I mean, sure, all this meditation and yoga is great. My head feels like a Disneyland inside. So much to explore. I get high from it daily. But the lack of schemes, of risks, of real estate deals, of law suits, of arguments with Yogiji . . . the stability, the placidity, the simplicity of it all . . . it's too much!

I need action.

Even a good bitch session would do. But these Hindus are so serene, you can't faze them. They forgive everything. They worship everything. They are compassionate to everyone. I think I will go crazy. Really crazy!

I try to stay focused on getting out of my legal predicament, try to work up some level of anxiety about it, just to keep me from turning into a complete amorphous blob of meditative love for all creatures. Eventually, I get so bored that I email Hari Jiwan Singh. Even if he cusses me up one side and down the other, I will welcome the jolt to my blood pressure.

To my surprise, he writes back right away:

Guru Sant Singh,

It's good to hear from you. I'm sorry to hear your case keeps being continued. Are you making money teaching? How is it living there? Do you have ample resources? The web site of the Ashram looks nice. Why not move back to Amritsar where Guru's hand can watch over you? Everything here is about the same; the winter has been mild—I've even got to play golf a few times. In fact, last weekend I went to Tucson with Daya and our wives to play golf over an extended weekend. We had a great time but I ate too much and now I'm watching my diet. Let me know what's going on with you.

Blessings,

HJ

Too friendly.

The man has hated me for years. This chatty missive about playing golf with Daya Singh, President of Akal Security, and overeating? It is strange, but I am encouraged. I have been in a spiritual underworld—a surreal limbo of compassionate detachment and eternal forgiveness—for the better part of a year. I don't know if my thinking is logical anymore, by American and 3HO standards, that is.

I can bounce ideas off my Indian friends, like S.S.P. Amandeep Singh, or Dr. Jagdesh, or Sobha Singh, but these guys are all nuts! Clearly! With their marriage schemes and sex obsessions, who could take any of them seriously? Besides, none of them knew Yogi Bhajan and his spiritual truth, not the way Hari Jiwan Singh and I knew it. None understand my culture as an American Sikh, nor my lifestyle. None of these Indians even comprehend the reality of money. The American reality, I mean.

I always want to tell them, "People do run out of money, you know!" But there would be no point. They seem to think I piss doubloons. These people do not really understand our system at all: how much money matters and how you have to always work, or scheme, to get it. They do not understand how, for Americans, independence is everything. With money, we have it, without money, we don't, and there is nothing to take the place of financial independence. No backup system. Just money.

Indians love money, no doubt, but they have their families too—their wormy, squirmy, ever-involved, stuffing-you-full-of-food, always-in-your-business families. So, in the end, money takes second place to that. In the end you always have your father's love, your mother's adoration, your wife's fealty, and that's your security. Here, a man lives with his parents all his life. It makes for a totally different way of viewing the world.

I write back to Hari Jiwan Singh and pour my heart out. I can't help it. The man suddenly seems like a friend. I tell him about Sobha Singh asking me to marry his wife, my chronic diarrhea, my offer to remarry Sat Siri Kaur, all the women trying to scam me for a green card, the ragi and his daughter, Wadha Kaur and her "exercise routine," all about being accused of being a spy, all about the Punjabi Police. Everything. I talk to him like some bosom buddy, tell him I am at my wit's end. Then I write:

When this is all over I have thought to move back to Española and live in one of the two houses Sat Siri Kaur and I own. I will always be an American Sikh and a student of Yogi Bhajan ji no matter what. I am wondering however at this point if I might be of more service by living elsewhere since it seems no one in Española thinks much of me. What do you think? I know you had problems with your image and I truly want to know your opinion on this subject.

After that, the electricity breaks down and the ashram computer crashes. I do not know if the message has been sent or not, and as I walk home in the starlight, listening to the myriad calls of mysterious night birds, I wonder why I even care. I even hope the email has not been sent. I pray that I can learn to adapt to all this peace and beauty and leave the rest of the world behind.

chapter 55

At Shiv-Shakti, it is time for the whole ashram to go on a break for a couple of weeks. I try to stick around and meditate on my own, but the solitude is killing me, so I take the train down to Amritsar to see S.S.P. Amandeep Singh.

"Now Guru *Sant* Singh, I have been thinking about this yoga that your teacher Harbhajan Singh taught you. I want you to tell me more about this strange thing."

"Kundalini and white tantric yoga! Yes! I would be happy to enlighten you!"

Finally, someone to really teach! I am so prepared to get across Yogiji's enlightened stuff, but I have never had a willing student! So I tell him about our exercises for transmuting sexual energy. I begin to blow his mind with one I particularly like: the man is on his hands and knees like a dog and the woman sits on his back, side-saddle, with her arms up at right angles. Then the guy arches and unarches his back, concentrating on the third eye. She is supposed to meditate on the third eye too, while she is riding him. It manifests the sacred "Z" energy.

I get on the floor and demonstrate the thing, lecturing while performing the asana. I get that kundalini flowing, get the blood boiling, arching and curling like a true yogi, completely dedicated to the work—talking the whole time, explaining every nuance of the thing, gesturing to indicate where chakras are opening as we speak, where energy is flowing into my various glands in a certain proscribed order.

Amandeep Singh watches me open-mouthed.

"It stimulates the pineal and pituitary glands," I explain, panting. "Which are the seats of, you know, spiritual power."

"Have a seat, Guru *Sant* Singh."

I stumble into the chair, dizzy. One of his assistants brings me water.

"That is very interesting. Very, how do you say? . . . energetic!" says Amandeep Singh, then he stares into space and drums his fingers on his desktop. I gulp down the water and ask for more.

I suggest that, as soon as I have caught my breath, he could get on the floor with me and we could practice it together.

"Better yet," I add, "maybe we could find a couple of women in your outer office to sit on our backs."

"That mantra . . . What is that mantra? Where is that from? A sacred text?"

"It's sacred. Yogiji said so. I don't know where it is from. Nobody knows."

"Hmm."

He does not practice the tantra with me, and he does not find a woman to receive my energy. He just orders us some chai. He changes the subject back to his *Group of Sikh Intellectuals in Search of a Viable Solution*.

I pretend to be interested.

It's just as well. Only Yogiji could really channel that energy anyway. His vibratory frequency kept our powerful auras from combining and bursting apart and creating lifetimes of psychic fragmentation. Who knows what would have happened if I had really practiced the tantra without Yogiji's presence?

Eventually Amandeep Singh changes the subject back to his old idea about getting me a wife. I tell him a little about Wadha Kaur, about what a child she had been. I tell him about my idea to remarry Sat Siri Kaur as long as I don't have to live with her, and how that fell through. I tell him how I have had enough of women and again plan to live as a sanyasi. I do not mention Lalamji; I would just come off sounding like a schoolboy with a crush on a teacher.

He shakes his head slowly, deliberately, then smiles in a way that seems to imply he has not given up pushing his agenda. Oh no, not at all.

These ever-patient Indians.

Amandeep Singh suggests he can find me a wife that would be neither too young nor too old; neither too pretty, nor too ugly.

"A very spiritual wife," he says, "who knows the *Banis* and would be willing to learn your tantric discipline."

"A wife who is learned, but not too learned," he adds. "A wife who is a great cook and very obedient."

He makes it sound pretty good. Pretty peaceful. But by now I know there is such a thing as too peaceful. Then again, Indian families are never peaceful. I have learned that too.

I wonder what I would owe him for that. I would owe him my very life for this ideal wife.

What does he want from me? I wonder. I simply cannot figure it out.

Exhausted from fending off Amandeep Singh's persistent pressure, I head to my hotel and stop to check my email at an internet café. Here is one from Hari Jiwan Singh.

Sat Nam Guru Sant Singh,

With regard to your question: Your image (right or wrong), as you have noted, has spread across the Dharma. Usually, when there's a unanimous opinion about someone or something, it's good to look at the opinion as if it were correct and then design a strategy to rectify it. It's a lifetime commitment and takes perpetual endurance.

As a sidebar, you should know this commitment has very little wiggle room for you. What does it mean: You will live your life for others and serve them as if your life depended upon it—as it does. Española is the only place which provides this great challenge continually.

Excuse me if I've gone too far; but, you asked for my opinion and I've done my duty. The way for anyone to change is to perform differently until the new action becomes who they are. Then, a new experience of reality is known. With you, giving, giving, giving is the way to liberation.

I pray that your current experience brings awareness and discipline to your future thoughts and actions which grows deeper each day in following His will. Please let me know how things are progressing.

Blessings,

HJ

Good advice. For a murderer or child rapist.

I am no angel, but I have done nothing as bad as that—I am just a garden variety adventurer and an incautious fool.

Hari Jiwan Singh's Yogi Bhajan impression is a good one—catch phrases like *humility*, *awareness*, and *discipline* show he is tuned in to the great man's frequency. But it is not good enough. It has no God-like authority, and it is too careful. Yogi Bhajan would have told me I was a bumbling shithead and an incurable retard before he went ahead and gave me his instructions. Also, he would have mentioned numbers, cash: how much I needed, how much he was willing to loan me, how much he expected to be paid back, and a time-table for payments. Interest. Percentages. So forth.

Bhajan would not have given vague reasons for returning home, such as, "*Española is the only place that provides this challenge continually.*" He would have just ordered me home. Would have said he needed me to earn money for the sangat (our community) and that was that. And if I did not, I would lose my soul and my bones would rot in a hell of my own devising. Nothing mysterious or moralistic. None of this *giving* and *liberation* and *perpetual endurance* bullshit. Bhajan knew when to talk mystical and when to get down to business. He never mixed the two, if he could help it.

Hari Jiwan, I think, *you bastard, you should see me in action at Shiv-Shakti*. I am a good teacher. I have authority. They touch my feet. No one touches Hari Jiwan's feet.

But there is one part of that letter that really kills me more than the rest:

You will live your life for others and serve them as if your life depended upon it—as it does.

As it does?

As it does?

chapter 56

Back at the ashram, I sneak into the office late at night and send a return email to Hari Jiwan Singh:

Dear Hari Jiwan Singh Ji,

I am writing to ask your help as a Khalsa brother. I have just learned the Judge in my case has framed the charges against me.

My attorney informs me there will not be a trial for 7 or 8 years!!

I asked him if there is any way to get a quicker trial. He said, "Yes, you can have anybody and everybody write the District and Sessions Judge, who can order a speedy trial in your case."

So there it is. I am asking quite clearly if he will help me with a letter-writing campaign. It would not cost more than the price of postage. All I need is his endorsement on the thing, his say-so, and hundreds, maybe thousands, of Sikhs will help me out.

Nobody will do it just for me, horrible old me—gambler, lawsuit maker, wife-leaver—but for Hari Jiwan Singh? Yogi Bhajan's right hand man? Yeah, they will do it; either to cull favor or just to stay in his good graces. They will do it. It could work!

I have formulated a new theory on what is really going on with this case. I suspect someone in the police force is trying to discredit American Sikhi through me. If this is the case, then to hell with them! I have to stand up for myself and all my people! So I add to the email:

I have been in India for almost one and half years without a trial. I am not going to sit in India for 7 or 8 years and let them disgrace Americans or Sikhs or make us look like wimps.

I have worked so hard, what with suing the Army and all. Yogiji worked even harder, teaching his yoga, wrangling so many Sikh converts, establishing the legitimacy of 3HO. He single-handedly taught us all a new lifestyle and a new form of worship, not to mention our yogic practice. For thirty years everyone from the U.S. media to the army and the government has been trying to discredit us. And here the Indians themselves are doing it, too. They want to show us American Sikhs we are nothing. The sons of bitches think they have a stranglehold on spirituality, arrogant as they are. I'll show them!

Since the electricity has not failed yet, I add more . . .

Let's show the world what Khalsa and Americans are made of! Personally, I plan to kick some ass and show these people over here that Americans and Khalsa stand for truth and justice. I want to face my accusers and the witnesses in a fair and speedy trial. I want to look the police and witnesses right in the eye and get the truth.

Hari Jiwan Singh Ji, You are the first person I am writing about this plan and I want to work with you on this. I think you are truly a Khalsa brother. Please let me know your position and thoughts as I want to write newspapers and media all over the world as soon as possible asking support in getting these letters written to the District and Sessions Judge ordering a speedy trial in my case.

I was expecting the power to fail. Did not expect to actually send the thing. Surely, either the computer would freeze up or the electrical system would black out the whole ashram. It usually did. But this time it did not. I hit send and it actually sent.

Surely, those letters would start pouring in, now.

Guru Sant Singh,

I may be able to help you, but not the way you suggest. You can't fight the Indian system the way you want. You must do what they require. You have stated in previous communications that you do not want to pay your way clear; you want to defend your innocence; you want to face your accusers; you want to stand for truth. With this attitude, I can't help you.

If you're willing to humble yourself; not fight the system; do what is customary; and pay the necessary people, I may be able to have someone broker a deal for you. This is the way things get done in India.

Before I contact my source, I want to know if you are willing to pay (maybe thousands of dollars), not "kick some ass," humble yourself and take direction without questioning, and be a contrite Sikh of the Guru who is willing to pay his karma gracefully. If you understand what I'm saying and are willing to follow this method, let me know and I will proceed accordingly.

It is my prayer that you find the grace within yourself to understand this problem is your making and nobody else's fault and take full responsibility for everything so you can move on unfettered by the past indiscretions.

Blessings,

Hari Jiwan

So here it is.

Just what I have been waiting for.

Hari Jiwan Singh's greedy hand won't come close to writing one simple letter on my behalf. All he wants is to get in the cookie jar and grab grab grab.

Proof.

It doesn't do me any good, except that it feels like sealing wax on the letter of his treachery. The thing is done. The truth is out. Hari Jiwan Singh, my last American contact, has been milked for all he is worth and turned up dry: spiritually, emotionally, and morally.

I particularly like the bit about *contacting his source*. Ha! I would bet anything he came to India ten years ago and met a guy that had a cousin whose friend knew a guy in a government office where the uncle of a sister of an old school chum of a high level worker supposedly had power over the decisions made at the highest level of the Punjabi Police force . . .

Or, more likely, Hari Jiwan Singh thinks he can call up Yogi-ji's contacts. For all I know, he has my teacher's rolodex. He thinks these Punjabis would treat him like the second coming of Bhajan, doesn't he? Oh God, it would be worth thousands just to see him laughed at by Bhajan's contacts; to see them take his money, then say, "Sorry, stupid American! There's nothing we can do for you! Take your backwards turban and run along back to your funny little commune!"

Thousands of dollars? Just to get cleared of marriage fraud? There is something written between the lines here, something he knows I know. There was an incident some years back with a white Sikh named Guru Shiva Mukta Singh. He had been running guns in the Punjab. I'm not sure why. Maybe personal profit, maybe something for Yogi Bhajan. Anyway, he was caught at the Indian border with several Glock 9mm pistols. They threw him in jail, but Yogi Bhajan got him out of there with a massive payoff. Maybe ten or twenty thousand dollars. And then there was another guy, Hari Gian Guru Singh, who was arrested for running drugs. Never mind the fact that Sikhi is completely against drugs, Yogi Bhajan was involved with this guy somehow and thanks to Yogi Bhajan and his connections, the guy got a slap on the wrist. Hari Jiwan Singh is reminding me that he knows how to get big-time criminals out of trouble. He worked close to Yogi Bhajan for a long time.

But he is blowing things way out of proportion! I am no drug smuggler, no gun runner. My case is nowhere near that bad. My attorney himself says all I would need is a hundred letters sent in, pleading my case. Maybe fifty would do it. Even ten would show that I am not completely unknown. But Hari Jiwan Singh has just decided, on his own, with no authority whatsoever, that it is not a matter of letters; it is a matter of thousands of dollars.

Fact of the matter is, if I wanted to spend thousands to bribe Pratap, I suppose I could do it myself, but the man is a liar. He has proved it already. He would take my money until I was empty as an old burlap sack, then laugh, re-issue charges, and throw me in the slammer.

More importantly, if I am caught trying to bribe officials, I could then be convicted of a real crime! Hari Jiwan Singh's scheme is a terrible idea. Worse than terrible! In fact, I suspect he may know it.

He may actually want it to backfire to keep me stuck in India.

Is there any good in him at all? I want to give him one more chance. I want to know for sure. If I have no money to offer, is he himself willing to "give give give" . . . or even give the price of postage?

Hari Jiwan,

Sat Nam, thank you for your mail and thoughts concerning my situation. I have given a lot of thought and meditated on what you said and proposed. But there is a major problem with this proposal as I see it:

I have no money!

As far as returning to the Española sangat, I think with the economy the way it is in the U.S., I am almost better off financially staying here at the ashram where at least my teaching is appreciated and I get a room and food provided.

He writes back, saying:

Maybe your parents can help you out financially so we can proceed as sug-

gested. If not, I see no other solution other than the one you propose. You are correct, prospects in the U.S. are not great.

The sun rises on a new day as I finish reading this last missive. I hike into the forest and sit on a rock overlooking the sacred, burbling Ganges. I meditate. After an hour, Lalamji comes dashing down the path. She appears out of the forest, in her orange robes, like the mystical swami that she is.

"Guru *Sant* Singh Ji! I've been looking for you everywhere! Don't you know it's shopping day?"

So I go into town with her in the big, black Mercedes. On a lark, I buy a phone card.

For the next few days, I meditate on that phone card, just looking at the thing. All week, its bright, promising color scheme glares like neon from where it sits on an apple crate cum bedside table in my cement hut. I could swear at night the phone card shines in the darkness. I dream it becomes an ember and burns a hot hole through space.

I have to wait another week for the next grocery run. Then, with an armful of produce and a twenty-pound sack of rice over my shoulder, I stop at the only STD in town: a corner storefront where an obese, balding woman in a dirty sari slouches beside a black rotary telephone, guarding it like Fort Knox.

She takes my phone card and inspects it for signs of forgery. I write down a number and she dials the thing slowly, deliberately, as if it is all she has to do all day.

She enters the phone card number, waits for the ring, waits for an answer, then speaks to the party on the other line, in Hindi. It is John Aragon, and I can hear him yelling at her to make sense.

She yells something back, and then hands the phone to me in a huff, as if she had expected something wonderful to come across from America. A singing telegram perhaps, or a Julia Roberts movie.

John Aragon is the best trial attorney I've ever met; in fact, he soundly defeated Yogi Bhajan in two lawsuits!

Yogi Bhajan had told one of his secretaries to get a hysterectomy and of course being an obedient disciple the secretary immediately went out and had her uterus removed. A few months later after the operation the woman sought professional medical advice and the doctor said she had never needed the hysterectomy at all! The secretary then sued Yogi Bhajan and Bhajan fought the case vigorously with the defense that his starry-eyed student shouldn't have listened to him in the first place. As the secretary's attorney, John took the case all the way to the New Mexico Supreme court where the justices ruled that the woman had the right to sue Yogi Bhajan for "outrageous conduct." After the ruling Yogiji settled for an undisclosed amount.

The second complaint was against Yogi Bhajan's Akal security. Akal security guards had attacked a race horse trainer at the New Mexico State Fairgrounds who fell and broke his hip climbing a fence to get away from the Akal rent-a-cops. Akal of course had hired a virtual bull pen of attorneys as hired guns to shoot down the complaint but John kicked their asses in a Perry Mason moment at trial and won a big judgment that almost bankrupted Akal.

Akal bounced back to later win billions of dollars in U.S. government contracts. Still, Bhajan's "Fake it and you'll make it" philosophy has been like a cancer eating away at his various enterprises. Akal for one has had to settle several cases for millions of dollars in which the U.S. government alleged Akal didn't train their officers properly and forced pregnant women from their jobs.

Looking back on my friendship with John, I must have really respected him for standing up against the great Yogi Bhajan and thrashing him in a court of law. John and I made a good team too as we won all my many lawsuits. I had full confidence that John would handle my affairs with Sat Siri Kaur, my ex, in a professional and competent manner.

I ask John about the latest news in the highway condemnation case. He groans. He does not want to tell me, but he does. The New Mexico State Highway Department deposited $168,000 with the District Court for John to collect on behalf of our limited partnership, but Sat Siri Kaur has fraudulently taken the money. She did not put the almost 200K in Aragon's trust account as promised but rather she diverted the cash to a secret account!

That means Sat Siri Kaur is managing over $80,000 of my money "unto infinity." I have also learned that Sat Siri Kaur inherited almost $400,000 so she doesn't need the money. Have Sat Siri Kaur and Hari Jiwan Singh been talking? I guess that was what Hari Jiwan Singh meant by giving.

Giving, he had said. *Giving, giving, giving.*

Unless you can get the money from your parents, Hari Jiwan Singh wrote, *You might as well stay in India.* So Sat Siri Kaur is not satisfied with eighty grand and almost half a million in cash she inherited. She wants to bleed my father dry as bones, too.

Bones bleached in the harsh desert sun, rotting alone and friendless in a hell of my own devising, to paraphrase Yogiji's elegant turn of phrase.

chapter 57

I have been trying to put the lost eighty grand out of my mind for weeks now. Meditation and yoga have helped, but still I feel the burn of Sat Siri Kaur's betrayal. I marvel at the strangeness of how the phone and internet keep me connected to that world of scheming, money-hungry bastards, even as I live this life of peaceful isolation. I think of Shiv-Shakti ashram now, more and more, as my home.

It is not a bad existence. Not at all. I do miss some American comforts: washing machines, for instance, and gleaming stainless steel sinks with clean hot running water on demand. But I do not think much about that anymore.

I stay entertained with deep meditation. Also, I have my scrapbook. I look through that sometimes, nights, when I am finished with my chanting and when a little moonlight creeps into my room. It is something to do. I look in the backgrounds of the pictures for subtle things I never noticed before. How the paint on my grandmother's house was peeling as she stood in front of it wearing a grim smile, a lacy dress, and pristine white gloves. I look at the shot of me at twelve, a happy Christian boy, holding my M1 Garand and grinning from ear to ear—my mother's rose garden in the background. Dad stands behind me with his mouth open, probably saying, "Now repeat after me! Every day in every way I'm getting better and better!"

There are a couple of photos of me in Oregon, at the ashram, mugging in my new white turban with Sat Kir*pal* Singh. The turban is badly wrapped. I was so proud of it at the time, but now I see it is sagging here and there, like a messy bandage. In the photo I grin and grin in blissful ignorance. Then there are the newspaper articles. Me suing the army. All those articles I sent to Bhindranwale.

Bhindranwale, the great martyr. The great man whom I had met. To whom I had written. To whom I had sent all those newspaper clippings about my activism. My activism. My international fame. Standing up for American Sikhi. Standing up for Sikh rights. Standing up for militancy. All those articles I sent to Bhindranwale.

All those articles.

He might have kept them after all, just as I had hoped.

Might have kept them.

All those quarter-page pictures of me with a benevolent smile and Yogiji's portrait in the background.

All those pictures of me.

All Bhindranwale's possessions are now in police custody, in an archive somewhere.

All those pictures of me.

And my name, bold as bad traffic: Guru Sant Singh Khalsa, the man with all the target shooting medals, the man who wanted to join the U.S. army, the man who wrote Bhindranwale in the heat of the Khalistan conflict.

And it suddenly occurs to me what S.S.P. Pratap might have meant when he said, *We have reason to believe he might be a spy*.

These days, the struggle for Khalistan is still going on, though mostly underground. There are still zealots. Outside of India, Sikh leaders still go on TV all the time, talking about the Operation Blue Star injustice and how NATO should have gotten involved. On the international stage, debates still rage as to whether or not the Khalsa will "rise again."

Young Sikhs do not remember the movement, nor the resulting civil war, and they are not taught it in schools. But those old enough to recall the gang rapes of Sikh women, the scalpings of Sikh men, the families torn apart and sent to internment camps . . . they will never forget.

The slaughter of six Sikhs at the Gurdwara in Oak Creek, Wisconsin, on August 5th 2012 may have been a shocking event to most Americans but, while Sikhs in general were shocked and hurt, to most of us it was small potatoes.

Sikhs quite blithely refer to the Chota Ghalughara and the Wadda Ghalughara—the "Little Holocaust" and the "Big Holocaust." Even today Sikh poets still compose proud poems about the ability of Sikhs to withstand such willful slaughter. The Little Holocaust took place in 1746 with the slaughter of seven thousand Sikhs over a two and a half month period; the big one happened on one day in February of 1762 with up to fifty thousand Sikhs being massacred.

Real Sikhs will always laugh when they look death in the face. They know that the possibility of being subject to genocide goes with the territory. Those who laugh at death will always be admired, even by their enemies; especially by their enemies.

In 1984, Indira Gandhi sent divisions of the Indian army with tanks and all to Amritsar in an action code named Operation Blue Star. Their primary objective was to root out Bhindranwale and his men who were holed up in the complex. In spite of putting up fierce resistance, the Bhindranwale group was eventually overcome and most of them were killed. Hundreds of innocent Sikh pilgrims—including women and small children—who had entered the shrine for a Sikh holy day were also slaughtered.

At the same time the army attacked many other Gurdwaras in the Punjab and met fierce resistance from the local Sikhs. Not necessarily militants but ordinary farmers and businessmen who resented their sacred shrines being attacked. The Sikh casualties were estimated as being in the tens of thousands.

On October 31st of the same year, Indira Gandhi was assassinated by two of her bodyguards--who happened to be Sikhs—in revenge for the attack on their most sacred shrine. In response, the Delhi central government inspired and organized "riots" in which tens of thousands of Sikhs were murdered all across India. Police stood idly by watching the attacks after having confiscated any weapons the Sikhs might have used to defend themselves. Although most of the casualties happened in the Sikh neighborhoods of Delhi, Kanpur and Indore, there were atrocities against the Sikhs in many other cities. Major Hindu government officials were observed leading and egging on these attacks; twenty-eight years later, none have been brought to trial.

Operation Blue Star and its aftermath was a holocaust, nothing less. But the Indian government wants to forget it. Sweep it under the rug. They do not want any Khalistan sympathizers in their midst.

Even with the conflict more than two decades past, the very idea of Khalistan is still dangerous in the Punjab. It is a threat to all that India has achieved on the world stage. All that commerce. All those awards for human rights. After all, the Dalai Lama has taken asylum from the sadistic Chinese right here in India. India is viewed as the "good guy" now, and wants it to stay that way.

Any remaining Khalistan sympathizers in India have long since been killed or run out of the country. They have changed their names and suppressed their pasts. If any are caught, even today, they get jail or worse.

For me, Bhindranwale's revolution is nothing but a memory. 1982 is ancient history—before I married my first wife, before I started gambling. I was just a kid, then. So easy to impress. So needful of spiritual guidance.

Even though I had thought about it, I had never picked up a gun for Bhindranwale. But what if the police held the letter I wrote the holy man? Sure, Bhindranwale would have kept it. Almost certainly I would have been the only white Sikh who wrote to him. Why wouldn't he keep it? And if the police found it among his personal effects, along with some newspaper clippings about me, why wouldn't they store it in a file somewhere?

Oh God! It was full of bravado about how the Khalsa would prevail. About how no amount of force was too much to defend our God and sacred Akal Takhat. I had made it clear I thought night and day of fighting for his cause, of grabbing a gun and finding a bad guy to shoot.

Sure the cops have not been actively looking for me, but they might have put me on some sort of list. For years, they probably thought nothing of it. I am American, after all, what could they do? Besides, I have never been convicted of a crime. They have nothing on me but a long-winded letter full of military-school platitudes.

But then I show up in Amritsar and make a fool of myself! One of the ladies— Sukhvinder Kaur, no doubt— probably got angry and suspicious about how Dadaji's marriage bureau was putting off our marriage, so she talked to the police, never dreaming what she was getting in the middle of.

I can picture it now: S.H.O. Mohander Singh hears her tale of woe and thinks, *Oh, it could be a marriage fraud, or it could be just some young girl that didn't get her way and wants to make an incident out of it*. But, because I am American, he passes the information on to his superior officer, S.S.P. Pratap.

Guru Sant Singh Khalsa? Pratap thinks to himself. *Why, I know that name! Now, where did I hear that name? Let's see. . . Let me go through my files . . .*

Pratap pulls out some yellowing old papers. He finds my name and—Oh God!—my picture!

Oh yeah! thinks Pratap, *That guy is a suspected terrorist. He's right here on the most-wanted list! Mohander Singh, you say he has committed a crime? Might have committed a crime? Made himself vulnerable to being framed for a crime? Good enough for me! Let's nail his ass!*

And what's in it for him? Nothing but fame, prestige, a promotion, perhaps international recognition. Any petty policeman's dream.

I walked right into the snare. In fact, I created the snare itself, set it up, and then jumped right into it and practically caught myself.

Arresting me must have gotten that skunk Pratap promoted beyond his wildest dreams! I picture him now in some marble mansion, being fanned by Nubian slaves with rubies in their navels. My arrest was his ticket to the top. No question.

chapter 58

Months go by, and, bored as usual, I am drawn to the bookshelves in the ashram office. Most of the books here are in Punjabi or Hindi, so it is somewhat of a hopeless mission, trying to find anything to read. But I have lived at the ashram close to a year and am, quite simply, desperate for entertainment. I will try anything, at this point. I will learn to read Hindi, one word at a time. I resolve to apply myself to it, doggedly learning the characters the way I learned to count cards—as if my livelihood depended on it. In truth, my livelihood does not, but my sanity might. After all, in the endless ashram lifetime I see before me, anything is possible . . . except escape.

The office is cramped—an assortment of desks arranged in no particular order. There is one ancient computer, on Lalamji's desk, that I am allowed to use, and a single metal storage cabinet in the back of the room. One of its doors is half hanging off. Inside, the top shelf holds neatly arranged books whose covers feature illustrations of meditating saints and Hindu goddesses. The second shelf holds a random jumble of papers and files and photocopied manuscripts. The third shelf is the same—just papers, unpublished papers. These are yellowed with age and nicely arranged by some long-ago hand into vertical stacks separated by bookends, sectioned off by colorful, cracked, plastic filing tabs written in Hindi. It is all crumbling quickly in the merciless humidity.

Some of these papers are in English and appear to be along the lines of college theses on yoga and Indian culture. Some are typed, some handwritten. Some seem simply to be the ramblings of swamis past—phrases about meditation, the glory of God, and then a page or two in Hindi, and then a page or two in English about meditative techniques—very technical stuff about using the forebrain and the back brain and the breath and the posture. Stuff about the perfect alignment of the spine . . . and then stuff written in dull pencil on unlined paper, all about ashram finances. There are a couple of charts and graphs and then the writing peters out into scratched calculations in margin notes.

I start at the top, peruse each book, take each one back to my room and meditate on it for a couple of days, trying to glean some knowledge, learn one word, find some entertainment there, somewhere. Then I move down into the manuscripts and notebooks and loose-leaf papers and finally on into some yellowed photocopies of long-lost books. That is when I find, to my surprise, a half-inch-thick photocopy of The Book: "Sikhism and Tantric Yoga: A Critical Evaluation of Yogi Bhajan's Tantric Yoga in the Light of Sikh Mystical Experiences and Doctrines." by Dr. Trilochan Singh. I am here in the night, squatting beneath a bare bulb. At first, I think it is a trick of the light, but no.

To have any of these works address Sikhi is beyond my wildest dreams; Shiv-Shakti Ashram is strictly Hindu. But to find this book—the very book that made Yogiji feel so threatened and inspired my suit against the army, so many decades ago—it is an impossible coincidence, and yet here it is. I look around, remembering the "Candid Camera!" show of my youth, wondering if I have somehow fallen into a practical joke. It simply could not be real. To find such a document . . . after all this time!

Outside the bulb's circle of light, the empty room shimmers with jungle heat, and the only sounds are the wind, the ever-rushing Ganges, and the leaves outside, slapping against the walls like applause. I wrap the stack of photocopies in the tail of my kurta—lest any leaves should drip water onto it, lest my clumsy boots should splash mud on its cover page—and I carry it back to my room.

I sit in my dark room, trying to feel Yogiji's spirit through the pages. I hold the thing like a telephone, a lifeline back to Eugene, back to Los Angeles, back to Española, and back to the world of Yogi Bhajan that I knew and loved once upon a time. I sleep with it under my pillow.

The next morning, at the crack of dawn, I begin reading how Trilochan Singh saw "false doctrines" in the teachings of Yogi Bhajan.

Oh? I wonder. What false doctrines are these?

Trilochan Singh was a Sikh scholar who went around the world giving lectures at Sikh Gurdwaras, universities, and so forth. He knew all about Sikhi and its history and how to worship the Lord in the traditional Sikh manner. He knew his chants, his prayers, his B*anis*, knew everything about Sikhism. He was a Sikh intellectual, like Amandeep Singh.

Then he came to America where Yogiji admits to Trilochan Singh that his basic faith is tantric yoga, not Sikhism!

The book is everything it was rumored to be: an indictment of Yogi Bhajan by a Sikh master. As I read, I begin to realize that although Yogiji told me and the other ashramites that we were Sikhs and that we had taken vows to become Sikhs . . . we were never Sikhs at all. It explains that the 3HO form of worship is something Yogiji made up. His rituals are made up, his chants are made up, even his prayers are made up. In the book, Trilochan Singh says that even some of his yoga is made up. Some of it came from Hindu ashrams, like S.S.P. Amandeep Singh said; some of it came from exalted teachers like Krishnamurti; and some of it was completely invented out of whole cloth by Bhajan . . . but none of it was from the Sikh tradition.

According to the book, what Bhajan taught us was some combination of Sikhism and tantric yoga, or his version of tantric yoga anyway, but Trilochan explains the Sikh religion is against tantra. He explains Sikhi is against seeking God-like power through Yogic exercises. In the book, Trilochan says Sikhi is focused solely on chanting God's name—worshipping God through sound—and that Tantra, and the exercise of Siddhi powers, is not about seeking God so much as about trying to become a God.

That sounds about right.

This yoga I love so much—in his book, Trilochan Singh says it is corrupt and will ruin me. He says that it will ruin all of us.

I have really been a cocky bastard, haven't I? So sure of myself as a Sikh, with such a strong sense of belonging to Yogiji's made-up world . . . and look at me now. Trapped. I realize that despite all the time I have spent at this ashram, I feel no special connection to God. None at all.

In the book, Trilochan Singh talks about his trip to America and all the Sikhs he met there, back in the sixties and seventies, including Black Krishna, Shakti Parwha Kaur, Guru Terath Singh and the highest ranking of Bhajan's secretaries, Premka Kaur. He wrote about the righteous arrogance of some of them, especially in the face of anything that contradicted Bhajan. In the book, he says these people were so full of themselves. It was arrogance for arrogance's sake, basically. It sounds about right. Bhajan taught us that. Taught us we were something special. We were kings.

Trilochan felt sorry for us.

Sorry for us! "Kings" that we were!

Did Bhajan think we were "Kings?" Hardly. There were many, many times when I was one of his bodyguards that he would be in a place—usually the house of some Punjabi in L.A.—where he would be sitting in a room with a bunch of Punjabi Sikhs as well as a group of his students. On these occasions he would hold forth in Punjabi, rarely speaking English. Slowly it began to filter back, through friendly Punjabis or American Sikhs who had learned Punjabi, that he would brag to the Punjabis that we were his "lap dogs" and he could do whatever he wanted with us. More often, though, he would refer to us by a common Punjabi epithet: "sisterfuckers."

Suddenly, crouched there in the morning light, listening to the day's first birdsong and the sounds of students shuffling by, sleepwalking their way to the first yoga class of the day, I feel distinctly that I do not know who I am. I do not know what I am. I do not know if the exercises and chants I have been doing for thirty years have any basis in ancient technique at all. Could it be I have been living a lifestyle made up entirely off of the top of Yogiji's head? Could it be that he was not a holy man at all?

All I have ever wanted is an authentic experience. To be a real Sikh. To be something better and deeper and more ancient. To belong to a better class of people. All our conflicts aside, I had thought we 3HO Sikhs were that—a better class of people.

So pure, in our white clothes.

In this moment, as the sunrise shadows climb the office walls, I doubt everything.

All the Sikhs I met in India would chant Sat Nam or (mostly) Waheguru. Yet I, in my white garb, gave myself a new vocabulary full of Himmee Hums and Tummee Tums, phrases that Yogiji taught us in his chants. According to Trilochan Singh, these words mean nothing in any language.

My mantras had been made up by a charlatan.

chapter 59

Without explanation, I ask Lalamji for a couple of days off from the ashram. She can see in my face that something is wrong, and nods her assent. I take the train down to see S.S.P. Amandeep Singh and show him the photocopy of Trilochan Singh's book. All I have are the first fifty pages of the manuscript, and I want to find the rest.

"Ah . . . " says Amandeep Singh, rocking back in his squeaky chair, tenting his fingers.

I can tell the message of this book comes as no surprise to him, and I am angry that he never told me before. Amandeep Singh flops his big hand at me back and forth, as if lazily conducting an orchestra. "Until now, you didn't want to know, my brother."

It is true.

So Amandeep Singh tells me what he knows.

"All his life," the man tells me, "Harbhajan Singh was a renowned fake. Sure, there are many who know nothing of him except his success in bringing Sikhi to the west. He is admired by them, surely. But among Sikh intellectuals and scholars, the followers of this Harbhajan Singh are truly pitied."

Amandeep Singh tells me true Sikhs understand that Bhajan's "tantric yoga" has no place in Sikhism, but the chanting, the *Banis*, and the sung prayers, those are real. They were the only real thing Bhajan taught me, and he did not even know what he was doing.

Amandeep Singh tells me about how, back in the sixties, Bhajan used to have a teacher in Delhi, named Virsa Singh. When he first came to the US, in 1969, Bhajan would speak about him in glowing terms and with the utmost respect bordering on adoration. In 1970, Bhajan returned to India with 84 followers and introduced them to the man. But Virsa Singh was disgusted that they worshipped Bhajan's picture, that they did Bhajan's strange yoga and that they went on Bhajan's strange diets. Things got ugly and Virsa Singh banished Yogi Bhajan.

Before leaving India to return to the U.S.A., Yogiji was arrested and released on bail. His crime? Marriage fraud--ironically, the same crime for which Dadaji and I were arrested. He was alleged to have promised that he would marry a Sikh man to one of his female American students and had taken 10,000 Rupees from the Sikh for the privilege. Yogiji had also promised this guy that he would get him a work permit in the U.S. Dr. Trilochan Singh, in his book, stated that he had seen a documentary movie made about the trip which showed Yogi Bhajan trying to arrange marriages with young American girls and Indian men.

The documentary—which was highly unflattering to Yogiji—was later purchased by him or his agents, probably for a large and undisclosed sum, and was never to be seen again.

Of the eighty-four people who made the journey, only a handful retained their white clothes and their loyalty to Bhajan.

Those were not the days of instant worldwide communication and very little of what happened on the trip was ever related to Bhajan's students back in the US and Europe. Virsa Singh was quickly written out of 3HO history. He went from being the teacher's teacher—a position so elevated that Yogiji kept Virsa Singh's shoes on his altar--to "someone that Yogiji might have helped out at some time," with a mere few typewriter keystrokes.

Yogiji had so much chutzpah that he took his banishment, arrest and the loss of a large chunk of his followers in stride. When he returned to the U.S. he gave himself the title Siri Singh Sahib and declared himself the Supreme Religious and Administrative Authority of the Sikh Religion in the Western Hemisphere. He continued doing his solstice camps and yoga lectures with new, eager students who knew nothing of his shame. At that time the Self Discovery movement was sweeping the U.S. and 3HO expanded hugely. Under his newly self-presented title Bhajan began to shift the emphasis of his teachings from yoga to his form of Sikhi.

In 1977, Trilochan Singh wrote his book, shaming him yet again. That also happened to be the year I joined 3HO and Bhajan used me to sue the army, establish legitimacy, and, once again, make a comeback!

Black Krishna stayed with him through it all, all the way up to his death, but Amandeep Singh tells me Premka Kaur, Bhajan's favourite secretary for decades, left 3HO and eventually filed sexual assault charges against him. I vaguely remember the incident, but barely. There were always naysayers—I and the other ashramites would just shake our heads when we heard of such things, call them traitors, say they had lost their souls, and forget about it.

Amandeep Singh says, "No one is trying to tell you what to believe. If you enjoy that yoga, then okay. Do that yoga. It is not a part of the Sikh practice, in fact the Sikh Gurus never taught tantric or kundalini yoga for a definite reason, it is against the Sikh way, but if you enjoy it, do it. Know that some of it is Hindu and some of it was entirely made up by Bhajan. Know these things and do as you like."

"Amandeep Singh, you don't understand! Yogiji's yoga changed my life. Starting to do kundalini yoga brought me out of a lifelong depression. It gave my body and mind strength. It made me into a man! Yogi Bhajan gave me everything. Without this practice, I would never have found my way in the world."

"Yes, Guru *Sant* Singh, I understand completely. It is good, this pranayama. The breathing, the yoga, I have heard it is very relaxing."

"It saved my life."

"It saved your life, yes."

"Yes, it really did. I owe him everything for that."

"Him?"

"My spiritual teacher, of course: Yogi Bhajan."

"Why?"

"I just said . . ."

"Yes, it saved your life, but why him?"

"He taught me all about chanting God's name. He taught me everything. How to live."

"So what? If not him, it could have been someone else."

"But it wasn't someone else."

"Listen Guru *Sant* Singh, if you need a good hammer, go to the hardware store. You buy the best hammer you see and take it home. It is a really great hammer, maybe even a magical hammer! Probably pixies come flying out of the handle or maybe later, to your horror, you see devils dancing in the air whenever you hit a nail on the head. So what? Do you worship the clerk who sold it to you?"

"The clerk?"

"Yes, yes, Guru *Sant* Singh, the salesman, the cash-register operator."

"I think you are calling Yogiji a clerk. How dare you!"

"I dare. I don't care. I will call him a clerk! He sold you yoga. He sold you meditation. And kirtan too, for that matter. How much did you pay him for that? Huh? How much?"

"I paid with my life!"

"And you made him a lot of money, besides, didn't you? Ripping people off!"

"He was a holy man!"

"He was a clerk! He sold you his yoga, as imperfect and discredited as it might be. You liked it. You bought it. Okay, great. But he wasn't yoga. He was just a man, a flawed Punjabi man. A yoga salesman. So what? Nobody's perfect."

I am still reeling from my master's betrayal. Not in my head, but in my heart. My heart is broken. No, not broken, shattered. With all this in mind, I take the overnight train to Haridwar and a bus to Rishikesh. The next night, after finally arriving back at the ashram completely exhausted, I unwrap my turban and sit there looking at it. White turban. White kurta. White everything. White walls. Suddenly it seems that white is not the color of purity at all. It is the color of an insane asylum. *Oh God*, I think. *If I never have to face another Punjabi again, it will be too soon*!

Do what I say!

Put ten lakh rupees in my bank account TODAY!

Doooooon't worry, Guru Sant Singh. My uncle will take care of everything.

. .

You must *do this. This is what you must do........*

I used to think it was Yogiji's direct line with God that gave him such balls. Brass balls, that was Yogi Bhajan's calling card. Innocent Protestants (and Jews –lots of Jews) from timid, perfectionistic families loved it. 3HO Sikhs like my second wife, who came from true blue-blood stock. No one had ever dared to scare her before, to tell her she was shit. Of course, it was true. We were shit, spiritually, before we met Yogi Bhajan. He was right. But it was just a coincidence. He would have told us we were shit anyway.

Over the next few weeks at the ashram, the Hindu nature of the things I am doing, starts to get to me. One evening I visit the Parmarth Niketan Ashram just down the road in Ram Jhula. I have heard that my old 3HO companions, Gurmukh Kaur and Snatam Kaur, are teaching yoga workshops and performing there. Gurmukh has become world famous with two large yoga studios both in Hollywood and New York. Gurmukh is known as the "Yoga Teacher to the Stars" while Snatam's "New Age" music has even received a Grammy nomination. But now when I see Gurmukh and Snatam waving the Hindu fire lamps around and worshipping Shiva, the destroyer, I realize all this *maya* isn't me. I want to be a Sikh. I want to discover Sikhi, real Sikhi, and make it my life's path. I do not want to play around with Hindu trappings.

On occasional trips into Rishikesh I start to do my own investigations into Yogi Bhajan's un-Sikh like practices and family history. I visit the Shivananda ashram in Rishikesh where an old swami / pundit tells me how Yogi Bhajan spent time there studying Shivananda's kundalini yoga. In fact the pundit says he was the "Puri family pundit" and describes how he had performed many Hindu pujas and given astrological forecasts for Yogi Bhajan and his family. The Swami also tells me that Yogi Bhajan's mother was a Hindu and how she influenced him in adopting some of the Vedic rituals.

I also start investigating the legal allegations I have heard against Yogiji. I discover that there were actually two lawsuits filed against Bhajan. The lawsuits were settled out of court for mid six-figure amounts of money and there was a gag order on all participants as part of the deal. The papers from the lawsuit disappeared into thin air. That is until some seeker of truth ferreted them out and posted them on the internet.

Premka's case was shocking enough but the other—from a very young lady named Katherine Felt, who had been a conspicuous favorite of Bhajan's --was mind numbing in the extent of the depraved behavior alleged on Yogiji's part. She accused him of—amongst other things--Fraud and Deceit; Assault and Battery; False Arrest and Imprisonment; Intentional Infliction of Severe Emotional Distress.

She claimed that he had lied to her by saying:

That the form of religious practice observed by Bhajan's followers was ancient in origin, and was followed worldwide by those professing to be Sikhs, including the Sikhs of India. In truth, Bhajan well knew the religious beliefs and practices espoused by Bhajan are not of ancient origin, are only superficially based upon the Sikh religion as it was practiced prior to the founding of Bhajan's organizations, and are very different from or contrary to the Sikh religion as it was practiced in India prior to the founding of Bhajan's organizations.

And:

That he was always faithful to his wife, and for a period of many years prior to meeting the plaintiff had been entirely celibate, when in fact he was at that time regularly engaging in sexual relations with various members of his staff.

The complaint went on to say that"

During the period between June, 1978 and February, 1985, the plaintiff was repeatedly struck or touched in a manner which any person of ordinary sensibilities would find to be highly offensive, and which caused the plaintiff pain and physical harm, as well as fear, apprehension and resulting mental and emotional harm. These incidents include, but are not limited to, beatings; involuntary sexual intercourse, sodomy and other sexual attacks; administration of ostensibly medical treatments; administration of bizarre rites; urination upon the plaintiff; and other particulars.

As a direct, proximate and foreseeable consequence of the defendants acts as set forth above, the plaintiff has suffered the physical, psychological and economic injury set forth above at paragraphs 62 and 63, above. In addition the plaintiff suffered severe infections of her bladder, kidneys and other internal organs; injury to her rectum and colon; loss of hair; bloody noses; split lips; bruising over her entire body; swollen tongue to the point where she could not take solid food for several days; soreness and misalignment of her jaw; contraction of herpes simplex and lesser venereal diseases; two abortions; permanent scarring of her internal sex organs and her back; and the tearing of a mole from her back.

We had been told that, while there had been previous allegations by some women of inappropriate behavior from Bhajan, these were without merit and the product of women who really did want to have sex with him but had been spurned. What is getting to me about these legal documents is the amount of detail. She was very specific. These didn't seem like some wild accusations that would not stand up under cross examination.

I want to know more and decide to call Peter Georgiades, the attorney for Katherine Felt and Premka Kaur, in Pittsburg. He is very cordial and tells me a lot about the case. He felt absolutely sure that Kate was telling the truth in her complaint or he would not have taken the case. He says that -- when she approached him—her whole body was covered with bruises; this was one of the main reasons why he decided to proceed with the case. He mentions that he had tried for several months to depose Yogi Bhajan—in other words, to ask him questions about the case under oath. He had been stymied by the fact that a doctor with the last name of Khalsa had insisted for that entire time that Yogiji was too sick to be deposed.

This strikes a chord in me as, during that entire time, I had been in Yogiji's security detail. He may have been too sick to be deposed but he sure as hell hadn't been too sick to go to La Scala for lunch, then to shop in Beverly Hills on an almost daily basis. There was no way to prove it but I felt like this had been a deliberate obfuscation to keep him from being deposed; hardly the kind of behavior from someone who has nothing to hide.

By this time I am in total shock. Had I been that much deceived for the last thirty years? I truly don't know what to do.

I consider S.S.P. Amandeep Singh's offer, again.

But the way he keeps on offering me a wife . . . and a place to live and teach? It seems fishy. I wonder what is behind this strange desire of his to pull me into his family and his group of friends? Such persistence! And why is Amandeep Singh so eager to set me up in India, to bring me under his wing? But what makes the whole thing really surreal to me is that Amandeep Singh was supposedly the best help the American embassy could get for me.

The American embassy itself, when one of its citizens, me, is clearly framed in a corrupt political scandal—involving jail time, the confiscation of an American passport, and completely false allegations—can do nothing for me except offer an introduction to a sympathetic police officer in an outlying district? Amandeep Singh has no power over my case at all. Something is fishy there, too.

I begin to wonder: Amandeep Singh's offer of a wife, and his exhortation to stay in India—are those sanctioned by the American Embassy? After all, he is my "embassy connection." At the core of my inquiry stands one nagging question that I am finally, after more than a year under country arrest, able to put into words for myself: is someone trying to keep me from going home? And if so, why?

chapter 60

I cannot help wondering, *what if the Punjabi Police told the American embassy about my involvement with Bhindranwale?* It is likely. I can see a meeting, or at least a conference call, taking place. Now, suppose the police had the letter I had written to Bhindranwale. Suppose they had found it among the holy man's possessions, and suppose once they found out I was in India, they scheduled a meeting with the Americans and said, "Hey, this guy is dangerous! Let's not put him back into circulation!"

I can see the American embassy agreeing with that scheme, what with terrorism being such a bugaboo these days. I know it sounds paranoid, but the fact of the matter is, the embassy has done nothing to help me. The American government has completely abandoned me. That is an unassailable truth. When I think about it, I can see them saying, "Okay, we don't want to be responsible for helping a potential terrorist escape."

At the same time, they have nothing on me. I am not a criminal.

"But we have this little marriage fraud racket," says some State Department Snidely Whiplash, " . . . and we can work with that."

So the Indians suggest, "Hey, what do you say we just keep the guy here? We know we have stamped out the Khalistan movement within India. Overseas, he could still be involved with these guys. Khalistani separatists are everywhere, still planning their overthrow of the Indian government, still planning their little bullshit independence movement. But Guru *Sant* Singh could stay here in India, you know, and have no means of support. He could just be living by hook or by crook, in and out of jail, with no passport or travel papers."

Eventually, the 3HO community would forget about me. My parents would accept that I was lost to them. Dad would accept that the devil had finally taken my soul. I would be living in limbo, indefinitely. And then boom, one day I would end up in a car "accident" or something!

After all, it happens every day. India is a world where people get killed by rogue elephants; they fall into ditches and disappear; busses tumble over cliff sides.

How convenient.

In my scenario, the Americans answer, "Okay, what the hell! It will get him out of our hair. We haven't received one single letter about him. Nothing from a human rights group, family, or anyone. This guy is a nobody. . . Leave him alone and he'll probably die of dysentery in a few years' time."

Okay, now maybe the embassy people are a little nervous. They do not want to get in trouble for sending a potential terrorist back to America, but then again, they do not want to get in trouble for denying me my rights as a citizen, either. So maybe, just maybe, someone in a back office at the embassy makes a call to 3HO. He just wants to find out if I will be missed. Wants to find out if I am maybe some big religious leader or something. Maybe this embassy guy asks to talk to someone in charge and he ends up talking to Hari Jiwan Singh himself.

Hari Jiwan Singh gets the picture. When it comes to intrigue and subversion, after all, he is your man and no mistake. So first he convinces Sat Siri Kaur to secure my eighty grand from the highway settlement, knowing I'm helpless to recover it, then he tries to extort more from me via email. When he sees that I am dry, he gives the embassy the go-ahead. "Do what you want with the guy. He is of no use to us."

Meanwhile, the embassy tells S.S.P. Amandeep Singh to "help me" without actually helping me. His role in the scheme is to encourage me to stay in India and keep tabs on me. He is to get me a wife, a place to live, whatever will keep me quiet. His instructions are to be civil, maintain contact, be my 'friend.'

The only fly in the ointment of this scheme turns out to be that Amandeep Singh actually grew to like me. He actually feels sympathy for me. Nevertheless, I suspect that he cooperates with the conspirators anyway. He is a government man, through and through. But in the meantime, he is trying to help me see the bright side of it all.

Sure, I am short on evidence, but I feel like I have put together the whole puzzle of this last year and a half. Maybe I am paranoid. Maybe not. But this scenario is the only thing that makes sense of all the loose ends in this story: the "spy" issue, Amandeep Singh's offer of a wife and a permanent residence in his community, my hearing getting postponed month after month, Hari Jiwan Singh's betrayal, Sat Siri Kaur's theft of my money, the trial that would take "seven or eight years," the embassy's hands-off attitude, and all the rest of it.

Finally, the peace has gone completely out of my life. The equanimity and the solitude and the forgiveness and the long hours meditating by the Ganges have a little edge to them. I begin, again, to grow a distinct fear of getting "disappeared" and I finally allow myself to get seriously angry about that stolen eighty thousand dollars.

It is time to go home.

chapter 61

There is nothing like sitting with prison bars in front of you to make a man realize—hey, I'm not in control here, and no amount of chanting is going to put me in control! God is in control. And now that I have given up Yogi Bhajan's tantric yoga, which was nothing but a quest for spiritual power and control over others, I have become closer to God.

Instead of gyrating and chanting to gain Siddhi powers, I have chosen to fully surrender to God's will.

Perhaps full surrender would be to stay in India and take whatever comes. But then again, perhaps the full surrender is my decision to escape—this acknowledgement that I can never clear my name here, that I can never get justice, and that I do not belong in this place. And maybe part of that is my return to New Mexico, where God has stacked up a whole mountain of legal battles that I must fight, and where I must make that decision time and time again: fight or surrender?

I am at once frightened and exhilarated by my decision to flee India. I might end up in jail again, but at least I will be back in the action. I haven't the faintest idea how to attempt this, but if I have to trek across the border, Sound-of-Music-style, I will.

In Rishikesh, I meet Shira at Little Buddha and tell him my decision. He nods and looks into the distance.

"What do you want me to do?" he asks, warily.

"I don't know yet."

He leans back in his chair, massages his bad leg, and sighs deeply. "I am not a tourist guide anymore, am I? Now I am getting into the soup with you."

I cannot do this without Shira. I take a stack of bills out of my wallet—I don't know how much—fold it discretely, and hand it to him. We lock eyes for a pregnant second, then he laughs and pushes it back.

"No, Guru *Sant* Singh. This is not about the money. You are in trouble. You are in need of help. Yes, I will help you. Surely, I will. I will not leave you now, my brother."

And so our quest begins.

To save my life, Shira uses the same method he uses for everything: he starts striking up friendships with tourists in and around the restaurant. I stand by his side as he works his magic, but even so, I can't figure out how he does it. He approaches complete strangers, smiles, and suddenly they are talking like old chums.

"What's our technique, here, exactly?" I ask, "Just to talk to everyone in the place? Shouldn't we be studying maps of the border or something?" I am finally bored of buying chai for every Tom, Dick and Harry.

"I am looking for travelers," he says. "You know, the dirty ones. The ones having the backpack on the back. Especially the big big backpacks as large as a man." I know the ones he means. I never stop marveling that these kids can carry so much weight. Or wondering why they would want to. "I am seeking for those men," he says, "that are ordering a big plate of food, looking as tired as one dog in the street. I am looking for these men. I think they have come from far away, perhaps across the border, Guru *Sant* Singh. They might know one border crossing that would be good for us. One out-of-the-way, small-town crossing place into Nepal, where you can go by just like that. No one noticing."

Indeed, we finally do meet one such man. I like Mike right

away—an Australian in his mid-thirties with sandy-blonde hair that looks like he cuts it himself with Swiss Army knife scissors. Skinny but fit, scruffy but bright-eyed, Mike is a spiritual wanderer with his feet on the ground. He has already been just about everywhere he ever wanted to go: South America, Asia, the Caribbean, Russia. Now he sits in Little Buddha doing the same as us, in a way—trying to get travel tips, destination ideas.

The three of us speak at length and trade war stories. For me, it is hard to keep the conversation away from my legal case, I am so eager to share with another "westerner," but whenever I open my mouth, Shira darts a glance my way, so I shut it.

Shira asks Mike about himself and his travels, especially in India and Nepal. "Have you been to Pokhara?" he asks. "How about Morawang?" Mike reels off a litany of Nepalese mountain towns and jungle treks he has done. Bharatpur, Gamauli, Ghiring Sundhara, Tamghas, the entire Annapurna Conservation Area, and of course, Kathmandu. He does not even hire a guide anymore. He just picks a mountain and starts hiking. Barely glances at his Lonely Planet. The kind of man who has reduced his needs to rock bottom. For him, the thought of a hot shower holds the same allure as Christmas morning to an American child, and sex? . . . surely, he catches it on the fly with the rare forbidden woman.

"So Mike, tell me, did you trek across the border?" asks Shira, casually. "Or cross at Mahendranagar like everyone else?" Mahendranagar is the typical border crossing from Nepal to India for those heading either north to Rishikesh or straight across to the international airport in Delhi. It is a big, bustling city with plenty of check points and border crossing guards. Strictly legit.

"Good God, Man!" cries Mike, "I wouldn't cross at Mahendranagar! It's like cattle being herded through a chute! And it's always tips here and bribes there. You can't just cross in a place like that. They stop you every step of the way, and pretty soon they want to inspect your jock strap for cocaine powder! No, no big border crossings for me, mate!" We soon learn that Mike, after some research of his own, chose to take the long way around and cross at a town called Sonauli.

Nepal is a finger-shaped country, the top of which is to the southeast of Rishikesh, about a five-hour bus ride away. Mike's border-crossing of choice, Sonauli, was another seven or eight hours south of that. The only people crossing there would be those coming from Kathmandu and heading south to see the burning Ghats at Varanasi—an uncommon tourist trajectory this time of year, as the heat in Varanasi is enough to give you the dry heaves, never mind the smell of burning bodies.

This past year I have learned that there is a kind of tourist triangle in India. It starts in Goa, a beach town in the south, in about January. Kids from Europe come to party and young Israelis congregate there as well, usually blowing off steam after their required stint in the army. As the weather turns and it gets too hot down there, about March or April, the kids grab a train and migrate a day and a half's journey north to Rishikesh and get their yoga on. Come June, Rishikesh itself is too hot, so they head up to Dharamsala for the refreshing mountain breezes and perhaps a glimpse of the Dalai Lama. That's when ashram business slows down and Lalamji and I get a break for the season. It's April now, high season for the ashram, but low season for the southern towns, so it makes sense that Sonauli would be low on security and reasonably tourist free this time of year.

"It's a dirty little border town," says Mike. "Nothing to see, nothing to do. No place you would want to stay any longer than you had to. But low key. Very low key, you know what I mean. You stroll down the central road, check into the border office, and update your visa. The guards are lazy and they'll stamp any old thing. They smile and wave you across!"

He winks, then pulls out his digital camera. He actually shows us pictures of the Sonauli border crossing. Indeed, the pictures show just a few guards lounging under the arch of a weather-beaten welcome sign written in a couple of languages, neither of which is English. "Oh, it's nothing for me, anyway," says Shira. "Indians don't have to show a passport to get into Nepal."

"Wait . . . what?" I ask, suddenly realizing Shira can actually come to Nepal with me.

"Oh yes, didn't you know, Guru *Sant* Singh?"

"I get it!" I reply, "Like America and Canada."

Shira shrugs.

Later that evening, the sun quietly sets over the Ganges footbridge, its cables dotted with brown monkeys snacking on filched popcorn and puris. Shira stands with me as I wait in a crowded lot for a jeep taxi to take me back to the ashram for the night. We talk of fleeing India through the Sonauli checkpoint, and he asks how soon I want to go.

I eye the taxi drivers as they negotiate fees with old sari-clad women and laugh at tourists trying to cram ten people into a jeep. I imagine any one of these drivers could be in the employ of the Punjabi Police, or even Hari Jiwan Singh, or even the American embassy. Any one of them could have instructions to quietly drop me off a cliff side on the road between here and there. I am also aware this could all be the product of my overactive imagination, but I can't forget all the evidence that has been stacking up. I consider the eighty thousand dollars Sat Siri has stolen from me and get mad all over again.

The rupees I currently possess are enough to either last another year at the ashram or, with luck, to cover the fees and bribes I will need for a border crossing, a new passport, fake entry and exit visas, and then airline tickets. I swallow hard and answer Shira's question.

"Tomorrow."

chapter 62

At the last minute, Shira could only get train tickets in a "second-class sleeper" car. Correction: he bought tickets for "second-class AC," an air-conditioned car, but got ripped off by the ticket agent and we ended up in "sleeper," which is basically a human cattle car. You can't learn to like it, but you can develop the grace to take your screwings in stride, so that's what I try to do. If I had bought the tickets myself, I would understand it more—rip off the white guy, and all that. But Shira is as Indian as they come. Even *he* got ripped off! I surrender!

The people in the sleeper car start pushing and shoving just as soon as we get on the train, and it does not end, ever. I feel my back and neck muscles clench in a visceral objection to everything about this environment. The sweat is pouring off my body, making a sticky glue between my fingers. I have to urinate all night but know if I move my ass even one inch off this bench, someone else will sidle into the spot and stick there like poured cement. The people standing in the aisles have to lean over. There is enough room for their feet, but not their shoulders. In the midst of this, those who have had the good fortune to find a place to lay down, on a bench or the floor, curl into human balls around their little sacks of belongings. They are so humble. I admire their willingness to lay right in harm's way and trust in God to protect them, but it makes it doubly impossible to get up and go to the bathroom, which I am increasingly tempted to do. My dysentery has improved but isn't cured, so I crouch on my wooden berth and try to meditate to calm my innards. Being suddenly thrust right back into the noise and crowd and stench and discomfort and total lack of privacy that is Indian everyday life, I realize, yet again, how good I had it at Shiv-Shakti.

Last night, when I told Lalamji I was leaving, she was furious, of course. I couldn't have picked a worse month to do it. The tourists are flowing into Shiv-Shakti like a river. I explained why I had to go, but as I was telling her my suspicions, I realized I sounded like a paranoid idiot, so I went ahead and embroidered a little. I said the police had approached me in Rishikesh. I told her I had been threatened directly, but kept it vague. She was still angry, but also accepting, and also a little sad. She put on a brave face. She is Indian, after all. She would never cry in front of me. I will miss her.

Twelve hours later, we arrive in Gorakhpur, India. My white kurta and white turban are filthy, my mind is fuzzy, and my body aches all over.

"Good morning Guru *Sant* Singh!" sings Shira, as he swings his head down from the berth above, big upside-down grin bobbing with the train's rhythmic movement. "Not far to go now!" Despite having slept sitting up, in his clothes, with nary a sheet or pillow for comfort, Shira appears reasonably fresh. But the kid is used to a mattress no thicker than a sandwich and, by his Indian nature, has no concept of privacy and a superhuman tolerance for chaos.

The train pulls in, and I carefully plant my feet in the tiny space between the head of one man and the feet of another. We disembark, and I manhandle my two large suitcases over to the bus stand. I am beginning to see the point of those enormous backpacks the kids carry. When the asphalt is always broken up like a bomb went off, there really is no point in having wheels on a suitcase. Shira and I climb aboard a "luxury tourist bus", which is the worst one I have seen yet. The headrests on each seat look as if they are in the process of exploding. The fabric is torn here and there and bits of foam stick out. The seat covers are filthy. I am in such a horrible mood, I want to shout at the bus driver, "There is such a thing as pride, you know!"

There is so little leg-room, that my knees are pressed hard into the aluminum chair-back in front of me. They go numb. Meanwhile, we ride past scenery so lovely it picks up my mood—green fields and farms and ladies walking around with bundles of sticks on their backs. I know I could not carry those bundles ten steps. Even so, I know it is not physical strength that keeps these women on their feet; rather, it is the sheer will to survive.

By the time we arrive in Sonauli, I feel as if I have been dragged behind a mule. I am covered with high-sulfur diesel exhaust and my leg cramps are starting to produce an occasional charlie-horse. I want a bath and bed worse than ever, but this town is no place to seek comfort. A wide avenue is filled with bicycle rickshaws and autos jostling for position. Roaming oxen eat garbage, which is plentiful in the street. Shira and I make our way through the rubbish and rubble, and my stomach clenches as the traffic swerves around us on both sides. Sometimes bicycle rickshaws go right up on the sidewalk and squeeze between us and the closest storefront. Construction materials lie in the way everywhere: steel rods, mounds of cement, tethered donkeys. Women pass by carrying big, overfull bags of sand on their heads. They are tall, proud, and unconcerned. A stooped woman covered by the Muslim's black purdah passes by, wraithlike.

The town is just as nondescript and ugly as Mike had suggested. It is the Tijuana of India. Dusty women's garments hang limply from ragged awnings outside shops, just as they do in shops all over India. Suddenly I wonder why. The Punjabi suits are all the same, all traditional. The saris are always the same as well—the same basic cotton swaths with simple, unadorned borders. Nothing unusual or fancy is ever put on display, though sometimes such things can be found inside. The message is: come and get your traditional stuff here. Plain, old boring stuff. Come on in and outfit yourself like Grandma. Innovation is taboo. This is why I love India and hate it all at once.

Shira pulls me into the entry alcove of a closed shop, and we watch the traffic. A couple of backpack-laden tourists head down the central road. A uniformed man steps out into traffic and waves at them. He ushers them into an office. They emerge ten minutes later with papers in hand, continue down the road, show their papers to the border guard, and hike under the arc of a concrete sign. Shira and I agree that if they had not looked like tourists—backpacks, white skin, too tall, hiking boots, bright eyes with a sense of amused detachment from their surroundings—they never would have been fingered by the officer at all. Never would have had to get papers or anything.

Shira and I huddle over the two suitcases and rearrange their contents. I take my briefcase with my computer in it. Nothing else. No identifying documents. I also change out of my hiking boots and into typical Indian cheap plastic sandals. I scuff my feet in the dust to cover their whiteness. We repack the suitcases with my personal effects on the bottom and clothes on top. Shira hails a bicycle rickshaw and loads my two suitcases and himself into it. I just sling my computer bag over my shoulder.

I am to appear as an ordinary Indian working man, walking across the border for his job in some Nepalese agency or store or business. As long as they do not stop and try to talk to me, I'm good, but if I have to speak a single word of Hindi, I'm screwed. At the last minute, Shira tries to teach me the Hindi for, "Good morning, officer!" I repeat after him, committing it to memory, but by the time we shake hands and wish each other luck, I have forgotten it.

Shira tells the confused rickshaw driver to just relax a while and hands him a few rupees for his time. Shira watches as I amble down the causeway, dodging potholes, beggars, and scampering children. I try to remember not to walk with my long, purposeful, American strides, but with the easygoing Indian gait that swings from the knee. Young women with parcels balanced on their heads waft past me as they conduct their daily comings and goings, the tails of their colorful scarves trailing after them like subtle perfumes. Indian businessmen—some beturbaned like me, some not—saunter down the road as well. We all follow the same general trajectory. Like me, they are all headed to work, innocently going about their daily routines, carrying briefcases.

Several guards mill around under the concrete arch. Many people cross back and forth without ceremony, but others are stopped for passport checks. I do not know how the guards are selecting their victims—perhaps by sheer whim. As I approach the arch, my head is spinning and I break out in a fresh sweat. One fellow to my right crosses and waves. A guard waves back. A fellow on my left crosses too, but the guard taps him on the arm. He produces a passport and the guard sends him on his way. A third and fourth man cross together, deep in conversation. The guards watch them go by. And here I go. I check my watch as I approach, like I am on an important errand. I pray that my exhaustion does not show. I want to look fresh, like I live around the corner.

And there I went!

The guard paid me no mind at all.

I am in Nepal! I can feel my heart beating, like a caged animal that wants out. I do not know where to go. I just keep walking down the sidewalk, trying to look like I am headed somewhere. Not too fast, not too slow. Every moment I expect a shout and the patter of running feet behind me, but nothing happens. Horns blare, a taxi nearly sideswipes me, and I fall into a bull. *This would be a perfect time to get gored by a bull,* I think. But the wall of flesh that is the bull does not even notice. I pass an open sewer and a pile of sand with a shovel in it. A child plays with a bright toy. A man is pissing on a telephone pole. Behind me, suddenly, there is a lot of honking. *This is it*, I think. *They're coming for me*. I pick up my pace—shoulders hunched now, head down. I pass a beauty parlor, a fruit stand, a dry goods store, a booth selling motor oil, a grungy tire repair booth, and a man with a bathroom scale who appears to be charging a rupee to weigh people. I consider stopping and getting weighed. It would give me a chance to casually glance back down the road and see what is going on. But I remember I am a businessman on an important errand. I keep walking, and eventually the honking dies down.

"Guru *Sant* Singh! Guru *Sant* Singh!" I hear a voice calling me and panic for a split second, then realize it is Shira.

He jumps off the bicycle rickshaw and unloads the suitcases, slamming them down on the sidewalk. He bickers with the rickshaw driver. Shira is really annoyed, which is rare. He shouts something at the driver and hands him some money. The driver counts it and starts to argue, but Shira shouts at him again, and the man rides off.

"What a motherfucking asshole!" he says. "Let's get out of this street, Guru *Sant* Singh. That was close, very close. Oh my God, that was so . . . what motherfuckers! Take one suitcase!" Shira doesn't curse often, at least not in English, but I have noticed he relishes calling someone a motherfucker when they really deserve it. Now he starts motherfuckering with abandon.

We look around for a chai shop, but there isn't one, so we just stand there on the street appearing exactly like the conspirators that we are, and Shira tells me what happened.

"One guard stopped the rickshaw. He asked me where I was going with so many suitcases. I told him I was going for one month holiday in Pokhara. 'Okay,' he said, 'but what about this red one? There are no red suitcases allowed!'"

"Red suitcases?"

"He was bullshitting, of course. Red suitcases! I told him 'that's not true and you know it!' He said, 'It is true. I think I should search that bag. Open it up.' I told him it was just my clothes, that is all, but he insisted."

The guard would have found my scrapbook, my personal effects, the photocopy of my passport, things that obviously do not belong to Shira. He would have known something fishy was up. *Oh God*, I think, *why did I have to keep all that stuff? Why did I risk my life for that stuff? What was I thinking!*

"Don't worry, Guru *Sant* Singh. I told him, 'I will give you fifty rupees. Don't search the bag.' And he said, 'Okay, but you have to unzip the bag anyway. You could be a terrorist.' So I unzipped the bag with all the turbans on the top, and he just saw the turbans and he said, 'Okay, okay, give me the fifty bucks.'"

"Thank God!"

"But that is not all! Up ahead was another guard, waiting his turn. He asked, 'Why are you going to Nepal with all these suitcases?' I said again I would have a holiday in Pokhara. 'Oh, a good time!' he said, smiling very big. You know what that means."

"What? What does that mean?"

"Oh, he means the only good time is sex. He said, 'Why don't you spend your money here with me, instead? I know some very nice girls.'"

"He *said* that?"

"Of course, Guru *Sant* Singh. What do you expect? He said he could show me a good time. All this kind of thing. I said no thanks, and luckily he let me go. But a third guard was waiting ahead! The rickshaw driver turned around and said, 'I'll drive right by him for 100 rupees, otherwise I'll stop dead in my tracks.' I told him, 'You are a real bastard, you know that?' but I gave him the money. So when we got close to the third guard, the driver shouted out, 'It's okay! It's okay! He already was searched! Ask that officer back there! He's cool! He's okay!' And, thank God, the third guard waved us by!"

It was my money he had spent, but he was upset about it. It was more, I think, about what this means about human nature, people taking advantage of other people, and the disgraceful opportunism of it all, rather than the loss of money. I replenished Shira's supply of cash, sure he would need to do more bribing for me before the day was through.

chapter 63

"But Guru *Sant* Singh," says Shira, "This money is no good; we have to change for Nepalese rupees, now."

I am desperate to get out of this town and further from the border, but he is right. We cannot get anywhere until I change my money. I look around and see nothing that looks even remotely like a money changing stand. Shira jerks his chin at a nearby travel agency and suggests we try it. When we enter, the man behind the formica counter changes our money at what is probably a terrible exchange rate, smiles broadly, and sends us on our way.

Outside again, I decide our first destination should be Kathmandu: a big city where surely someone can produce a fake U.S. passport.

Shira hails us a beat-up old taxi that charges me the equivalent of a hundred American dollars to get to Kathmandu. I could take a bus for about five dollars, but I want to get out of here on the double quick, so seven hours, fourteen piss stops, one flat tire, and three close calls with cement trucks on winding mountain passes later, we arrive in the fabled city of Kathmandu. It was a nasty ride. I get sick as soon as I step out of the car.

Shira knows a good guest house in the city, and soon I find myself in a clean bed. What a miracle! I bid him goodnight and hit the shower, but he heads outside, saying, "I will get something for you, Guru *Sant* Singh. Don't worry about tomorrow."

The next morning he shows me what he bought: a receipt for a bus ticket crossing the border from Tibet to Nepal. "You can tell the immigration authorities that you came in from Tibet and lost your passport," he suggests.

"Let me get this straight. You went out and bought this old, used bus ticket from someone on the street?"

"No Guru *Sant* Singh, it is not a bus ticket, just a receipt for a bus ticket. But it is proof that you did not come from India! Also, it is probably fake, but no one will know."

"You bought a fake receipt for a used bus ticket? People sell these?"

Shira laughs, "This is Kathmandu, Guru *Sant* Singh. You can buy anything!"

We find a travel agency, and I begin to converse with the man there, but I cannot pull off the weird lie about taking a bus from Tibet. He seems nice, so, foolishly, I tell him the whole story in a nutshell—how I was arrested in India, had my passport taken away, and escaped into Nepal. "I need a passport and a visa," I tell him. "Can you help me?"

He nods thoughtfully and takes me into a windowless back room, where an altar to Ganesha, the Hindu elephant-head God, is freshly adorned with marigolds. The light from its candle flame flickers eerily upon the walls. Another man meets me there—not a travel agent, but a lawyer. He faces the altar and does his puja, or prayer, to Ganesha, the God of new beginnings, before speaking to me. I tell him my story and suddenly realize he could go to the police and probably get a reward for turning me in. Damn. I should have stuck with the Tibetan bus ticket idea.

The lawyer says he can help me for the equivalent of $3,000. I don't have it. This isn't a matter of standing on principle, like with that first lawyer, Dadaji's lawyer. I still have to buy a plane ticket, after all. I can't spend that. I get up to walk out and he starts harassing me:

"You are going to get into trouble! They are going to throw you in jail!"

I have heard it all before—the threats, the warnings, the admonishments—and I just leave. I collapse into a bicycle rickshaw that Shira hails, and tell him I just want to go to the U.S. embassy now. I will tell them I am an ordinary tourist and I lost my passport. That is all. Very simple, very legit.

The U.S. embassy is impressive. A machine gives out numbers, and all the visa applicants wait in a tented outdoor area, approaching the windows only when their numbers are called. Brand new plasma screens display pertinent information. I take a number myself and eventually get the chance to explain to a bored-looking woman behind a window that I have lost my passport. That is all I say.

"Identification?" she asks.

I give her the photocopy of my confiscated passport. She admits me to a small, clean room, this time with no altar. Eventually, two men enter, a black and a white one, dressed in dark suits. I am such a bad liar; it does not take them long to get the full story out of me. In the end, the law prevails. They cannot turn down my request for a replacement passport, but they also cannot aid and abet anyone running from the law. So their bizarre solution is to give me a passport and tell me that I'll have to figure out for myself how to get a visa for Nepal. Through the course of the conversation, I learn these guys just got to the embassy. Apparently embassy workers are shifted around every two or three months. Nobody stays anywhere long. They are really unhappy with the situation and may only be helping me out of solidarity with a fellow sufferer. I don't know.

A day later, I have a blank passport in hand. Hooray! But getting the Nepalese visa is going to be another matter altogether. Shira and I put our heads together on it and eventually decide to place a call to Mike, the Australian, on his mobile. Miraculously, he answers. He listens intently to my story and is very excited that we have gotten into Nepal.

"Alright mate, here's my advice. Don't try to get that visa in Kathmandu. You are going to pay an arm and a leg and maybe come up against the police anyway. The police in Nepal are very strict. You really don't want to get involved with them. Just go back to the Sonauli border. There are plenty of people there willing to bend a few rules. No one is looking, after all! I have one name I can give you: a guy named Gagan Prashant. He helped me once when I crossed there. I don't know anything about him, though. I don't have his phone or anything. I don't even know what business he's in these days."

So, on the strength of the advice of an Australian vagabond, and with nothing in hand but a fake receipt for a Tibetan bus ticket and a passport as unmarked as a baby's bottom, I steel my nerves for another ride along the treacherous pass to Sonauli, this time by bus. I sit at the very front, hoping access to the big window will help me focus on the beauty of the terraced rice fields instead of the carcasses of wrecked busses and taxis that litter the ground at the bottom of the unguarded, thousand-foot drop-offs that border the road.

This time I do enjoy the scenery. The mountainsides are terraced with rice paddies so lovely, it is really picture-postcard stuff. Every single mountainside is transformed by these terraces. No inch of land is wasted. Even in the distance, where the mountains overlap and intersect each other in layers and layers disappearing into the mist, no hillside is naked. Each is farmed and green as eternal spring. An ox pulls a plow on one of the terraces. I want to shout, "Careful! Don't fall off!" The bus rolls on.

At one point, a big truck heads right for us—it is as gaily adorned as the rest of them, with spangles and dangling images of gods and goddesses and bright colors and metallic gewgaws. It is like heading for imminent death at the hands of the Ringling Brothers Barnum and Bailey Circus. At the last minute, the truck swerves around the bus, missing it by inches. Eventually, I have to shut the window when too many of these passing trucks expel their black exhaust my way.

We pass a village where I see a couple of grown women having a bath right under the town water pipe. They are fully clothed and just soaping themselves down through their clothes. Nearby, a woman in a red sari squats and washes clothes in a basin. She gazes off into the distance, perhaps at her kids, playing in the road. On the town's outskirts, tall cement houses, spaced acres apart, rise in profusion. Fourth and fifth stories are being added on to many of them—increasing the family stronghold while still preserving the farmland, I suppose.

Meanwhile, the bus driver is smoking, right under a big, red "No Smoking" sign. The smoke is choking me. It is so disgusting, and I cannot understand why the bastard needs to add this additional level of discomfort to the journey.

"Doesn't that say 'no smoking'?" I ask, pointing at the sign.

The driver muscles the enormous steering wheel to the right, leans into it, and inches us around another switchback in the road. "Listen," he says. "If you want to get to your destination, allow me to smoke, because I have been driving for three days straight."

After I apologize, we talk a bit more. His English is passable, and I learn that this is the way it always is. The companies push these drivers until their bodies are quaking wrecks. There is no regulation, the pay is rock bottom, and the buses are in bad repair, but the drivers have families to feed and very little choice in the matter. They are village dwellers, not Kathmandu guys. This driver is actually from Sonauli, so I ask him if he knows a guy named Gagan Prashant.

"Oh sure, sure!" he says. He tells me Gagan runs a travel agency near the border. I can't believe it. This could be our man, the money changer! God is really helping me now, I can feel it.

Shira and I finally disembark in Sonauli and find a grungy little hotel with cold running water and cleanish beds. My head is throbbing from all that cigarette smoke and my organs feel like they have been rearranged. I sleep badly, and the next morning we go looking for Gagan Prashant.

chapter 64

Shira and I enter the same dingy travel agency as before and ask the man if he is Gagan Prashant. He grins widely and nods. I tell him he was recommended by Mike, an Australian. Gagan laughs and raises his eyebrows, "Oh, yes!" he says. "I won't forget him!" He probably doesn't know the guy from Adam. I don't even care.

I don't like the look of him, but considering what I am in the market for, I guess I am destined to deal with shifty characters from here on out. Shira shows him my blank passport and points to the first unstamped page. They experiment with communicating in Hindi, which Gagan doesn't speak well, then Nepali, which Shira doesn't speak at all. Finally, they settle on English. Thank goodness. I can actually understand what is going on.

"This man needs a Nepalese entrance visa," says Shira, half-heartedly adding, "they forgot to stamp him at the border." Gagan smiles at this obvious lie, but Shira goes on. "Once he has the visa, he will be buying a ticket to America. He will buy this ticket from your agency!"

Gagan's eyebrows shoot up, and I wish Shira hadn't said that. Sure, it is obvious I am American from the passport, but did he actually have to voice the A-word? The one that means 'sucker' in every language?

Gagan leans back in his chair and shrugs. "Probably we will do something," he says. "I know many officers. We can find one man to work this. We meet at six tonight. We will go."

Shira and I leave and return at six, at which point we walk with

Gagan to the border. Every step of this short journey fills me with dread, and by the time we reach the Nepalese border guardhouse, I am breathing through my mouth, trying to fend off a panic attack. Gagan leaves Shira and me waiting while he heads into the guard office. He comes out a few minutes later.

"You have to leave."

"What?" Shira and I chorus.

"The guard, he says you must return to India to get this exit stamp, then get one Nepalese entry stamp."

Shira looks at me and shrugs. I shake my head with such force it makes me dizzy. "No way. No way, I am not going across that border. No way in hell!" As soon as I do, the guards in India could seize me and throw me in jail, legitimately.

Gagan goes back into the guard office and returns fifteen minutes later. "You can stay in Nepal one more night for one thousand rupees only." Gagan is holding my passport, and I am afraid if I don't pony up the money, he will hand it over to the authorities. I give him 1000 rupees in 100-rupee bills so he and the guard in the office can divide it up however they want. He goes back inside the office and comes out with a smile on his face. When he sees me, he quickly drops it to a sympathetic frown.

The three of us walk back to Gagan's office, where he settles into his chair and explains the problem: "This guard is not wanting to do it. You see, you could go to Kathmandu airport and the men there are wondering how you can have this Nepal entry visa. It is from Sonauli, but there is no exit visa from India."

"Oh, the visa states the entry point?"

"Yes, you see, it states the exact point of entry. If you came through Sonauli, you should also be having exit stamps on your Indian visa with your passport. This guard could get in very trouble. He could lose his job, even."

"Don't you know any Indian immigration officers who could give this Indian visa and exit stamp?"

"I don't know these fellows. I only know two Nepalese guards, you see."

"Listen, Gagan, you go to the immigration office on the Indian side, and you tell them whatever they want, I'll give it to them. I just need those stamps. Tell them to name their price."

I know I have really put my foot in the shitpile now. I have no idea what kind of outrageous price they will name, or even if they will cooperate. And there is always the chance someone will recognize my name and photo, confiscate the passport, and send the police after me. It's not like I am going to get any amnesty from the Nepalese. Dammit, I should have done this in Kathmandu after all! But Gagan says he will try it the next day and see what happens.

The next day, Gagan calls me at my guesthouse. "Okay, Guru *Sant* Singh, they might do it, but they want to meet you first. They want to make sure you are not some murderer or something. They do not want to get in such trouble."

"Where and when?"

"Meet them in the morning at the Arun Restaurant, on the main road."

I am at the restaurant before it opens. I pace in front of it, then try to go for a walk to calm my nerves, but there is so much construction all around, that proves impossible. I flatten myself against the side of the building as workers on scaffolding toss down chunks of concrete debris, willy-nilly. When I finally manage to get inside, I order chai after chai. I wait for the officers. One hour, two hours, three. . . Shira wanders in about noon, asking why I disappeared from the guesthouse.

"I didn't want to be late! Gagan said morning, meet them in the morning, I don't know what that means, what time. I just didn't want to miss them."

Shira laughs, and I buy him a meal. I keep watching the door, but he seems unconcerned.

"When do you think they'll come? It's afternoon now!"

He laughs again. "Oh," he says, "They'll come, but not in any hurry. These immigration officers, they are like advocates! You can never trust what they say."

"Oh God, don't say that!"

He laughs again. After he eats, he wanders outside to stretch his legs, and returns every hour or so to check on me. I am still here. I order food that I can't even think of eating, just so the waiter doesn't think I am a freeloader. Lunch patrons come and go, then the dinner patrons. I watch happy families pass by the window. Some stop in for chai.

I envy them.

Finally, about five p.m., two men who look like they could be plainclothes officers arrive: one fat, one skinny. Gagan is with them. They sit down and I order food all around.

"So what seems to be the problem, my friend?" says the fat one.

I start to explain and realize I should have rehearsed it. I do not want to tell them about my trouble with the Punjabi Police, but I can't figure how to explain the blank passport without it. I start by telling them I lost my passport and got a blank replacement, but that does not explain my hesitance to re-enter India.

"Just come across the border and get the Indian visa and exit stamp, the Nepalese visa and entry stamp, and then that is all. You can get on your airplane!" says the skinny one. "It is no problem for you at all."

"Anyway," adds the fat one, "it is many Americans coming to Nepal for the Nepal women. This is very common."

"No," says the thin one, laughing and shaking his finger at me, "Indian women are better. I'm telling you, Indian women are better!"

I smile and say I like Indian women, too. "In fact . . ." and here I go. I tell them the whole story. I even include details Gagan has not heard. Shira arrives a few minutes into the conversation and translates occasionally when they need it. They think my story is high comedy!

"So, were any of the girls nice ones? Light skinned ones with big tits?" asks the skinny one.

"Yes, yes," I reply, "a lot of very cute girls. But I am going to be honest. I didn't want to marry a girl that young. I think that is what got me into so much trouble."

"No!" says the fat one, "Not to marry! Just to fuck!"

"Hey! What's the difference between a Nepalese wife and a tsunami? They both moan like hell when they come, and then try to take the house from you when they leave!" says the skinny one, and he laughs.

And that's how the conversation goes for more than an hour. I take every opportunity to let them know mine is a minor legal trouble that has turned into a year-long ordeal. I stress that all I want is to get home to my aging mother and father to care for them. I assure them nobody is ever going to hear about my case. Regardless, they just keep on joking and horsing around. I have learned by now not to mention bribes outright. I will just let them bring up the amount of "tip" they expect for their services.

"This is a good man!" says the skinny one.

"Yes," says the fat one, "he is so good, he should come to a party with us!"

"Yes!" replies the skinny one, "We must have a party, with plenty of whiskey!"

"We will invite all the border guards. An international party. A festival!"

"I think ten thousand rupees should pay for it," says the skinny one.

"We want good whiskey, though. Better whiskey. Make it twenty thousand," replies the fat one.

"Wait a minute! What about girls? What's a party without girls? Make it thirty thousand!"

"Good Nepalese girls!"

"No," exclaims the skinny one, "I tell you Indian girls are better! But more expensive!"

In the end, they want fifty thousand rupees, almost 700 U.S. dollars. I give them the money and my passport and they stroll out the door. They are still laughing when they leave, but I am exhausted and disgusted by all the sexual bullshitting, and I am angry. I seriously suspect I have just thrown away my passport to this couple of whoring idiots. I slam down the money for the check and storm off.

I cannot sleep all night, thinking of those fools drinking whiskey and fucking whores with my money.

In the morning, I wake Shira. "Do you think my passport is ready yet?"

"Guru *Sant* Singh, the sun is barely up," he moans. "Go back to bed."

"How can you sleep? My God, what have I done! What have I done!"

"Guru *Sant* Singh, my friend, I think you should do your meditations now."

So I do. I meditate for hours, sort of. It is impossible to go very deep, but at least this gives me something to do. Shira goes to Gagan Prashant's office as soon as he gets up, but he comes back saying it is closed. He checks back in the afternoon, but it does not appear to have been opened all day. My stomach is in knots.

I imagine Gagan and these two guards running off with my money. How long can three men live on fifty thousand rupees in Nepal? Six months? Perhaps they only used the money for a trip to the Punjab so they could turn me in to the police and get an even bigger reward. Maybe they are buying little Nepalese girls as sex slaves right now, starting their own operation, going underground. The limits of my paranoid imagination know no bounds.

Night falls and Shira and I head up to the roof of the guesthouse, where he collapses in a lawn chair and I pace frenetically. We try to talk about anything but my passport. Finally, a silence falls, and Shira eventually says, without conviction, "We must wait until tomorrow. Gagan Prashant will show up in the end."

"Like hell!" I bellow and storm downstairs, past the surprised desk clerk, and out the door. Shira follows as I weave through construction sites, hop over holes in the ground, and evade feral dogs all along the unlit streets. I finally arrive at the travel agency. There is a dim light on inside! I pound on the door until finally it creaks open a little. The face of death appears in the crack. It is Gagan Prashant with a hangover like nothing I have ever seen.

"Guru *Sant* Singh," he croaks in a tone that makes it clear he had forgotten about my existence entirely. "Do come in."

Inside, his two guard friends are sprawled on the floor, looking a lot like Gagan. One clutches an empty whiskey bottle; the other, his head. Gagan shuffles to his desk and riffles through the drawer. He pulls out fistfuls of forms and schedules, scatters them on the desk in disarray. Finally, he exclaims, "Ah ha!" then flinches from the sound of his own voice. His friends groan in protest.

Gagan holds out his hand. In it is a small blue book. My passport. I reach for it tentatively, wondering when the catch-22 is going to hit. I expect him to snatch it back and demand another bribe, but he is in no mood for further shenanigans. I take the passport and look inside. There they are: two glorious stamps.

In dull black ink, unadorned and perfectly ordinary-looking, they indicate my exit from India and subsequent entry into Nepal. I cannot believe what I am holding in my hand. It is perfectly legit. And it means I'm going home.

chapter 65

Trash is strewn around in front of the check-in counter at the Kathmandu airport—chai cups and candy wrappers mostly. I haul my bags up the escalator and into a vast waiting room. There, I spend my last Nepalese rupees on some breath mints. I left Shira behind in Sonauli, with enough money for a nice vacation in Pokhara before he heads home. I wanted to do this last leg of the journey alone.

The room is broad but low-ceilinged—a low-investment imitation of the collection of shops Americans have devised for taking your money while you wait and wait and wait. Two monks in orange robes scratch their heads in unison. A gaggle of women wear matching saris and those plastic shoes that click-clack across the floor. They might be stewardesses. Families sit around on the plastic seats. A sleeping baby's brown limbs flop around as it sleeps in its father's arms. I try to imagine myself in that role—a little kid or two flopping around in my arms. At this point, it is pretty impossible.

My group is ushered through a checkpoint where a man frisks me as a matter of routine. The next man is an immigration officer and he stamps my Nepalese Visa inside my passport with the necessary exit stamp and checks my boarding pass. I am nervous but actually, for once, have nothing to hide. I head into another public waiting room, and the routine continues. After waiting a while, I get frisked again and my briefcase is searched. I have to remind myself not to worry. I head into a third waiting room.

I love that I am in an airport, that I have the proper documents, that I am waiting endlessly just like everyone else. I love that police are walking right by me, not paying me any mind. I love that families with innocent sleeping children are clustered around me.

The airport officials next put my group on a bus that takes us across the tarmac to the airplane. There is another line to get frisked before getting on the plane.

The funny thing about all this frisking is that they take it so seriously, yet do it so badly. The friskers barely touch you each time. I could have drugs in my underwear, my shoes, pretty much anywhere except my pockets. With each frisk I sense my anxiety rising, as if they are going to find something on me. But I am innocent.

As the airplane takes off, I go into a meditation, thanking God for all my blessings, and for this second chance at life. I can hardly believe it as we soar over the clouds.

Before I know it, the plane is ending the first leg of my journey to New Mexico. We have landed in Qatar, on the Persian Gulf. Before leaving Kathmandu, I arranged online for a hotel here. No sense taking any more chances. The only one I could pre-book was pretty ritzy, so here, as I descend the ramp, is my limo driver, with my name on a sign!

He drives me past the high-rises and clover-leaf highways of this ultra-modern, proudly independent, oil-rich nation. Everything here gleams. Everything here is solid, bright, enormous, and valuable. It takes my breath away. At the hotel, a young man takes my bags and lets me into my room. A palace. The sheer amount of private space I have seems somehow immoral. The richness of the velvet draperies is like something from a dream. Oh, and the bed! A real mattress, with springs inside and a box spring under it.

I am horrified to realize I do not have the right type of money to tip the porter, but he simply smiles and retreats.

I recline on my bed, the softest mattress on which I have lain since I left the USA, more than two years ago. Knowing I am now safely out of South Asia and the reach of the corrupt Indian legal system, I take time to reflect on my journey. What was it all about?

A line from *Gurbani*—the Guru's message, written by Guru Nanak springs into my mind:

Dukh daroo sukh rog bhaiyaa …

Pleasure is the disease and pain is the medicine,

Where there is pleasure, there is no desire for God.

***

Salok Mahala Pehla (Guru Nanak)

***

There it is: my answer.

Had I continued my comfortable life in New Mexico, I would never have experienced the profound lessons Guru Sahib gave me in India. Fear, uncertainty, doubt, frustration, betrayal, sadness, depression… all these were medicine to cure my disease. My malady was a life of easy money, dubious business dealings and a cult-like certainty that I was in the right because I blindly followed whatever Yogi Bhajan told me. I had forgotten that I had not only the choice, but the responsibility to decide between right and wrong.

***

I came close to being stranded, penniless in a third-world country; perhaps having to spend the rest of my life in jail. I might even have been "disappeared." Yet I never lost faith in my Guru, "Guru Sahib" as we Sikhs call that ever-loving, ever-powerful presence that guides and protects us.

Guru Sahib daily gave spiritual inspiration to my troubled mind. He brought so many people to me who selflessly offered me help. In spite of many difficulties, I never went hungry and always had a roof over my head. Even those people who, for their own selfish reasons, tried to harm me were a blessing. They forced me to dig deep and find resources within myself that I never knew I had.

I now have an unshakable faith in Sikhi. I believe that the light of Guru Nanak guides me and watches over me as long as I keep my end of the bargain by conscientiously following the path of Guru Nanak.

Maybe when I arrived in India I was too full of myself; too much under the sway of my own ego and my own sense of self importance. Maybe I had to suffer through these heavy lessons to learn to live in humility—which is truly how a Sikh should live. Maybe I had to experience the untruths of Yogi Bhajan so that—when I found the true path of Sikhi—I could fully appreciate its radiant power. After all, Guru Nanak said:

The Truth is High; but Higher Still is Truthful Living

One thing of which I am very sure: I can't do it alone. No matter how much I think about things, no matter how much I try to plan, things never seem to work out as I want them to. When I surrender and give my life up to Guru Sahib, things have a way of working out.

***

If you were to ask me "what has been your main lesson from this adventure?"

I would probably say: It is only through the Grace of God and Guru that we find happiness.

***

Tomorrow I will get my plane home and have to face Sat Siri Kaur, Hari Jiwan Singh, a Motel 6 for a home, and the backlash from a newspaper article where the chief of the Punjabi Police declared me "a little bit guilty." Worst of all, I will have to face my memories of Yogi Bhajan. Every sagebrush bush, every tumbleweed, every coyote fence, and especially the golden-domed Gurdwara that stands amid this landscape—it will all remind me of him.

I do not know if I can ever stop loving him, but I have stopped believing in him. After thirty years, it leaves a hole in my heart, it really does. But I am letting God and my love for Guru Nanak fill that hole, gradually.

I lie back on the saffron-silk coverlet in my luxury suite, pick up the phone, and order room service. I will indulge myself while I can; knowing this moment is nothing but a beautiful illusion. And like every illusion, it too will fade.

Epilogue

Gursant Singh eventually found the Gursikh Punjabi bride of his dreams. He and his wife now happily live in Yuba City California.

Glossary of Punjabi, Hindi, and 3HO Words

Adi Granth Sahib

Adi means first, Adi Granth is the first edition of the Guru Granth Sahib, the compilation of Sikh Holy Writings compiled by Guru Arjun in 1604.

Akali

Literally immortal and a term often used to describe the Nihung warriors of the Punjab who live according to the ancient ways of Guru Gobind Singh's army. Also used for the Akali Dal, the political party of the Sikhs.

Akal Purakh

Timeless One, a common Sikh description of the Supreme Being.

Akal Takht

Literally Throne of God. A building close to the Golden Temple considered to be the highest seat of authority for all Sikhs.

Amrit

Literally nectar. A name for the specially-prepared water given to drink during the Khalsa initiation ceremony.

Anand Karaj

Literally: blissful work. Sikh wedding ceremony.

Ashram

Secluded dwelling of a Hindu sage and his disciples. In 3HO usage, ashram means a building where students of Yogi Bhajan live and practice his teachings.

Baba Bakala

A small town in the Punjab where the ninth Sikh Guru, Guru Tegh Bahadur, meditated for twenty years.

Bani

An abbreviation of Gurbani, applied to any of the writings which appear in the Guru Granth Sahib.

Banis

When used with English plural, it means the prayers that a devout Sikh should read or recite every day (see Nitnem)

Bhagavad Gita

700–verse Hindu scripture that is part of the ancient Sanskrit epic Mahabharata. This scripture contains a conversation between Pandava prince Arjuna and his guide Krishna on a variety of philosophical issues.

Bandi Chhorh Divas

A holy day celebrating the release from prison of the Sixth Guru, Guru Hargobind who affected the release of 52 captive Hindu princes along with his own in October 1619. Following their release, Guru Hargobind arrived in Amritsar in the midst of the Diwali festival, and the day was henceforth associated with his liberation.

Bhindranwale

Born Jarnail Singh (12 February 1947 – 6 June 1984) he was 14th Chief of the Damdami Taksal, a Sikh religious group based in India. He and a group of followers sought refuge in the Golden Temple complex in 1982. On June 6th 1984, Indira Gandhi sent in the Indian army to remove Bhindranwale and his men in Operation Bluestar. Bhindranwale and most of his men were martyred.

Brahmin

A Priest and member of the highest caste of Hindu Dharma

Chai

Beverage from the Indian Subcontinent made by brewing tea with a mixture of aromatic Indian spices and herbs.

Chai Wallah

One who sells or serves tea to others for a living.

Challan

Formal criminal charge in Indian law.

Cheera

Brutal practice of Punjabi police in stretching victim's legs to 180-degree angles.

Darshan

Sanskrit term meaning "sight" in the sense of an instance of seeing or beholding, vision, apparition, or glimpse. It is most commonly used for "visions of the divine" by the sight of a very holy person. One could "receive" darshan or blessing from a saintly person, such as a great saint.

Dharma

Religion, teaching or lifestyle, as in Sikh Dharma.

Dhoti

Rectangular piece of unstitched cloth, worn by Hindus, usually around 4.5 metres long, wrapped around the waist and the legs and knotted at the waist.

Diwali

Popularly known as the "Festival of Lights", it is a festival celebrated between mid-October and mid-December. For Hindus, Diwali is one of the most important festivals of the year and is celebrated in families by performing traditional activities together in their homes.

Diwan

Congregational worship where Guru Granth Sahib is present.

Ek Ong Kar

These are the very first, few words in Siri Guru Granth Sahib and form part of the Mool Mantra, the beginning of Guru Nanak's sacred prayer of Japji Sahib. It means: One God.

Ghat

Series of steps leading down to a body of water, usually a holy river. In Benaras (Varanasi) this set of stairs is used for the cremation of dead bodies according to Hindu rites.

Gora

Indian adjective or noun for a yellow-skinned or light-brown person. The term is often used by English-speaking Indians to refer to Caucasians, especially Caucasian Sikhs. In this form, it has taken on racial connotations and so has acquired the status of a slur, though it is not inherently pejorative.

Gurbani

The writings of the Gurus.

Gurbani Kirtan

Singing musical praise of the Divine, specifically from the writings of the Sikh Gurus or other writings from Siri Guru Granth Sahib.

Gurdwara

Name given to a Sikh temple. It means 'Gateway to the Guru'

Gurmukhi

Name given to both the script and the language used in Siri Guru Granth Sahib.

Guru

Term for a spiritual guide, teacher and en-lightener; a person who leads us away from the darkness of spiritual ignorance and towards enlightenment of reality - a vision of God; a roadmap of nature or the laws of the Universe. The one generally accepted in Sikhi is that derived from the syllable 'gu' standing for darkness and 'ru' (light) for the removal of darkness. Thus guru is he who banishes the darkness of ignorance. According to Sikh belief, guidance of the guru is essential for one's spiritual enlightenment.

Guru Granth Sahib

Siri Guru Granth Sahib is more than just a scripture of the Sikhs, for the Sikhs treat this Granth (holy book) as their living Guru. The holy text spans 1430 pages and contains the actual words spoken by the founders of the Sikh religion (the Ten Sikh Gurus) and the words of various other Saints from other religions including Hinduism and Islam. The Adi Granth Sahib was given the Guruship by the last of the living Sikh Masters, Guru Gobind Singh in 1708.

Gutka

Small prayer book containing chosen hymns or Banis from Sikh Scriptures.

Harimandir

Correct name for the Golden Temple.

Haumay

Pride and self-centeredness.

Izzat

Concept of honor prevalent in the culture of North India, Afghanistan and Pakistan. It applies universally across religions (Hindu, Moslem and Sikh), communities and genders. Maintaining the reputation of oneself and one's family (especially women) is part of the concept of izzat, as is the obligatory taking of revenge when one's izzat has been violated.

Japji Sahib

First sacred composition found in Siri Guru Granth Sahib. A concise summary of Sikh Philosophy, compiled by the founder of Sikhi and its first spiritual guide, Guru Nanak.

Ji

Suffix or postposition used in India with a name or title to show respect.

Karma

Action or deed. That which causes the entire cycle of cause and effect.

Kaur

Middle or last name of a Sikh female. Mandatory last name for a Khalsa Sikh female.

Khalistan

Literally the Land of the Pure. The ideal of a political secessionist movement which seeks to create a separate Sikh state in the Punjab Region of South Asia.

Khalsa

Literally The Pure. The Khalsa is the nation of the Sikhs. Yogi Bhajan instructed his followers to all use Khalsa as a last name.

Khanda

Double edged sword used in preparation of the baptismal amrit (nectar) for the Khalsa

Kirtan

Poetic verses of Gurbani sung in adoration of the Divine. (See Gurbani Kirtan)

Kundalini Yoga

A form of yoga specifically designed to raise Kundalini Shakti energy, an energy believed to reside in potential within the human body. The teaching of Kundalini Yoga was unknown in the West before Yogi Bhajan began teaching. In spite of considerable research, scholars have found little of Yogi Bhajan's form of yoga to have any relationship to other known forms of yoga and have surmised that most of his Kundalini yoga was his own creation.

Kurta

A traditional item of clothing worn in Afghanistan, Pakistan, Nepal, India, Bangla Desh and Sri Lanka. It is a loose shirt falling either just above or somewhere below the knees of the wearer, and is worn by both men and women

Lakh

Unit in the South Asian numbering system equal to one hundred thousand.

Langar

Term used amongst the Sikhs or in Punjab in general for a common kitchen/canteen in a Gurdwara, where food is served to all (without distinction of background) for free. Only vegetarian food is served, to ensure that all people, regardless of their dietary restrictions, can eat as equals. Langar is open to Sikhs and non-Sikhs alike.

Lohri

An extremely popular festival celebrated by Punjabis, commemorating the passing of Winter Solstice and the growth of the winter crop.

Long Ek Ongkar

Combination of English and Gurmukhi words referring to the original mantra and technique for chanting that was given by Yogi Bhajan when he first came to the USA in 1969.

Mahan Tantric

A title supposedly given to the highest authority of Tantrism in the world. According to Yogi Bhajan there could only be one Mahan tantric in the world at any given time – which was him. Scholars have researched extensively and have failed to find a reference to this term and concept in any known tantric system in the world today.

Mandir

Hindu temple

Maya

"Illusion" of the material world that separates us from God. Also called "mammon", not the true reality.

Maryada

Code of rules and regulations. See Sikh Rehit Maryada

Miri (and Piri)

The concept of worldly and spiritual matters both being important. Sikhs are expected to maintain the balance between the two. This idea was introduced by Guru Hargobind, the sixth Guru, and represented by two swords.

Mughal

The imperial family directly descended from two of the world's greatest conquerors, Genghis Khan and the Amir, Taimurlong, also known as Tamerlane the Great. Hailing from Persia they ruled over North India in varying degrees from 1526 to 1757.

Namaste

A common spoken greeting used in India. As it is most commonly used, Namaste is roughly equivalent to "greetings" or "good day," in English, implicitly with the connotation "to be well."

Nigura

One who has no guru.

Nitnem

The daily prayers that devout Sikhs are expected to read.

Nivas

Place of residence. In Amritsar a rest house for pilgrims.

Parantha

One of the most popular flat-breads in Indian cuisine. It is made by pan frying whole-wheat dough, usually with copious amounts of butter or ghee (clarified butter)—on a cast iron type of skillet called a tava.

Parikarma

The marble causeway surrounding the sarovar in Amritsar.

Piri

See Miri.

Puri

Round fried bread.

Ragi

A musician who sings the shabads (hymns) of the Guru Granth Sahib in Gurdwaras.

Rehit

Living in a manner of moral conduct, observing particular principles, and employing ethics habitually as a way of life. In Sikhism, rehat is used in conjunction with the word maryada and refers to a specific code of conduct known as Sikh Rehat Maryada.

Sadhana

Spiritual practice. In 3HO, Sadhana refers to the group spiritual practice performed between 4am and 7am in most 3HO ashrams. It is considered to be mandatory for everyone.

Sahib

Term of respect used for the Sikh Holy Book as well as historical Gurdwaras.

Sant

A holy person or saint.

Sarovar

Nectar pool for spiritual ablution.

Sat Nam

Literally God is Truth. Used by 3HO people as a greeting.

Sat Sri Akal

A Sikh greeting meaning 'God is the ultimate truth, Generally Yogi Bhajan's students eschew this greeting and use Sat Nam.

Sanyasi

Religious ascetic who has renounced the world by performing his or her own funeral and abandoning all claims to social or family standing. A renunciate.

Seva

Service to ones fellow beings, a cornerstone of Sikhism.

Sevadar

One who performs Seva.

Siddhi

A mystical power acquired by spiritual or psychic means.

Sikh

One who follows the path of Sikhi as laid down by Guru Nanak and his successors.

Sikh Rehat Maryada

A document created in 1950 as a modern, standard code of conduct for all Sikhs.

Sikhi

The path to be followed by a Sikh.

Sipahi

Soldier. Originally a mounted soldier (similar to cavalry).

Siri Guru Granth Sahib

The living Guru for all Sikhs in the form of a sacred book (granth). See Guru Granth Sahib.

Swami

Yogi or ascetic who has been initiated into the order of Swamis. In Siri Guru Granth Sahib, it is used in its original sense, meaning Lord, and is a synonym for God.

Tuk-tuk

A three-wheeled cabin cycle for hire. Ubiquitous in Indian cities and also other parts of South Asia, it is a motorized version of the traditional cycle rickshaw. Cheap, noisy and uncomfortable.

Vanaprastha

The third of four phases of a man's life in the Hindu tradition, this stage denotes a transition phase from material to spiritual life. A Vanaprastha is 50 to 75 years old and requires the disciple to gradually detach from the material world while still providing for one's wife, ostensibly giving over duties to one's sons and daughters, spending more time in contemplation of the truth, and making holy pilgrimages.

Waheguru

The highest and most popular name for the Divine in Sikhi.

White Tantric Yoga

A form of yoga brought to the West by Yogi Bhajan. Generally done with people sitting in long lines facing each other, men on one side, women on the other. The participants then hold their arms and hands in various positions or mudras for long periods of time while chanting. Yogic scholars have been unable to find any reference to this type of yoga in any known tantric system and have concluded it to be a creation of Yogi Bhajan.

Yatra

A journey with a spiritual purpose. Sikhs do not generally use this term; 3HO people do.

21385488R00247

Made in the USA
Lexington, KY
09 March 2013